Well-Worn
Paths

ISBN: 979-8-218-49565-7

Melanie Chitwood, Editor

Nelly Murariu, Cover and Interior Designer

Rachel Hill, Illustrations

Well-Worn Paths

Treading Paths of Joy Through a Study of Philippians

CATHERINE L HILL

Table of Contents

A Note From Catherine

Welcome! I am glad you have chosen to tread paths of joy through Philippians with me! I look forward to discovering fresh insights and sharing delightful moments as we take this journey together.

Before we begin, let's visit a minute about well-worn paths. The picture of well-worn paths on the cover was taken in the pasture of my parents' ranch. That path was not formed by accident. It is a two-track road formed by years of my dad—and my granddad before him—intentionally undertaking the task of driving their trucks along the same path day in and day out. As I grew up, some of my most treasured memories were made bouncing over the pasture's rutted paths. Those paths paved the way for meaningful conversations while riding with my parents or grandparents to feed cattle or check water, as well as for learning to drive well before age sixteen. Traversing those paths led to picnics in the pasture with friends and our church's Easter sunrise services as the early morning rays beamed over a hill with a cross. Admittedly, the initial forging of those paths was not easy, but the joyful vision of "what could be" motivated action more than the challenges deterred it. And every time we cross the pasture now, we certainly appreciate the investment in creating those paths.

The forging of our well-worn paths of joy in this study will be similar. Their development will be neither accidental nor easy, but our efforts will still be joyful. Somehow, joy exists in the present when there is anticipation of something better coming...oh, and there is something better coming! So join me, ladies. Join me in the task of removing the rocks of doubt and fear that are in our way. Join me in trampling down the tall grasses of worry and pain. Join me in developing the delightful habit of joy as we tread the paths Paul gives in Philippians.

Then, seven weeks from now, *let's keep treading*. Long after this study is over, you and I get to continue our steps on the paths of joy we establish. And that continued treading is necessary! Neglected paths become lost as grass regrows and rocks roll. Attended paths keep the grass and rocks on the sideline while pointing us in the direction we envisioned.

Finally, although you may be a part of a group of path-treaders cheering and praying for each other during this study (and I hope you are), you must form your own paths. You will need to establish the vision in your mind and perform the task to bring the path to fruition in your life. Still, even in forming your own path, you do not do so alone. As you are treading, your Savior walks beside you. And together, you form a two-track road...well-worn paths that lead toward heaven on the horizon while producing a joyful, stronger, deeper relationship with Christ now.

And every time you travel through pain or difficulty, you will be glad you took the time to establish those well-worn paths.

You make known to me the path of life; in your presence there is fullness of joy; at your right hand are pleasures forevermore. (Psalm 16:11)

GROUP

SESSION 1

The Path Ahead

Introductory Activity for Week 1

Welcome to the first group session. Your leader has a couple of fun games planned (nothing embarrassing and nothing requiring physical exertion), so enjoy getting to know each other or getting to know each other a little better!

PART 1
A Survey of Joy

I am excited for us to begin our study today! Although most of this journey will focus on the book of Philippians, the lessons these first couple of weeks will help us lay the groundwork necessary for the rest of the study.

In the introductory note, I shared a little about my parents' ranch. Long before my parents or grand-parents owned the land, someone rode through the pasture on horseback to develop a vision of what it could be. Before that person tackled the immense task of forming a ranch and bringing in cattle, he needed the answers to a few basic questions, such as: *Why might this be a favorable location for a ranch? What characteristics qualify this property as "good" ranch land? How can this land help me fulfill my goals as a rancher?* With questions like these in his mind, the rancher would have been intentional in his observation and discerning in his evaluation of the land. In the process, he would have gained critical insight that laid the groundwork for wise, long-range decision-making. And I'm sure he would have been excited about his prospects.

Throughout this week, we will be asking questions about joy and surveying Scripture to find answers. I encourage you to approach each day with intention, discernment, and prayer. In the process, I'm confident you will gain critical insights that lay the groundwork for wise and joyful long-range decision-making. Hopefully, you also feel a little excited about cooper-ating with God in this life-impacting endeavor!

So, let's pray and pull on our boots and stride into Day 1 because, in this study, our boots are gonna do some joyful treading!

WEEK 1
Why Tread Paths of Joy

WEEK 1, DAY 1

What is joy?

You make known to me the path of life; in your presence there is fullness of joy; at your right hand are pleasures forevermore. (Ps. 16:11)

Question: Why do cows have bells?

Answer: Because their horns don't work!

(Question: Are you rolling your eyes at me? Maybe with a hint of a smile?)

When I was growing up, my dad was known for telling jokes like this. He told "dad jokes" long before that was a thing. He still tells them. And we still lovingly roll our eyes at him. Somehow, it's rather endearing.

Have you ever wondered why so many jokes start with a question? Okay, maybe not...but it makes sense because questions pique your interest and set your mind on a search for a possible answer. Think how different your reaction would have been if the first line above was...

Cows wear bells because their horns don't work.

Without a question to prompt curiosity and "clue you in" this was a joke, the statement would have seemed like nonsense. In O.S. Hawkins' book *The Jesus Code: 52 Scripture Questions Every Believer Should Answer*, he made the following statement: "Those who continue to grow in spirit and in wisdom ask a lot of questions."[1] So let's ask some questions! Let yourself wonder about what you will examine and what you want to learn in this study of joy. As you do, jot down two or three questions below.

❋ ....

❋ ....

❋ ....

Some of the questions that came to my mind are ones we will answer this week:

* ✻ What is joy?

* ✻ Why frame the learning process as "treading paths" of joy?

* ✻ Why tread paths of joy?

* ✻ With all the references to joy in the Bible, why focus on Philippians?

In your own words, answer the first question, *What is joy?*

....

....

....

....

Our goal this week is to develop a greater understanding of joy and its bearing on our lives. When my son used to tell me his room was clean, I would ask, "Clean according to whose definition—yours or mine?" (Can any mamas out there relate?) I needed to make sure "clean" had the same meaning to both of us. For our study, we want to have the same perspective of *joy*. We need a common definition, so let's answer that first question together:

What is joy?

We will start by looking in the dictionary. *Merriam Webster* defines joy as "the emotion evoked by well-being, success, or good fortune or by the prospect of possessing what one desires; the expression or exhibition of such emotion."[2] Let's read a few verses and see if that definition aligns with Scripture.

In the following verses, circle what aligns with the definition and underline what does not.

❋ **James 1:2-3.** "Count it all joy, my brothers, when you meet trials of various kinds, for you know that the testing of your faith produces steadfastness."

❋ **Hebrews 10:34.** "For you had compassion on those in prison, and you joyfully accepted the plundering of your property, since you knew that you yourselves had a better possession and an abiding one."

❋ **2 Corinthians 7:4.** "I am acting with great boldness toward you; I have great pride in you; I am filled with comfort. In all our affliction, I am overflowing with joy."

❋ **Galatians 5:22-23.** "But the fruit of the Spirit is love, joy, peace, patience, kindness, goodness, faithfulness, gentleness, self-control; against such things there is no law."

From a Christian perspective, would you agree with the dictionary definition? Why or why not?

....

....

....

Goal for this week

❋ To develop a greater understanding of joy and its bearing on our lives

Guiding Questions

❋ What is joy?

❋ Why frame the learning process as "treading paths" of joy?

❋ Why tread paths of joy?

❋ With all the references to joy in the Bible, why focus on Philippians?

The definition from *Merriam Webster* hints at a measure of self-gratification in joy, whereas the first three verses plainly demonstrate self-sacrifice. Also, I don't observe in any of the verses, particularly the last one, a clear indication that joy is simply an emotion; instead, I see intent and purpose. This makes sense because, as a characteristic of the fruit of the Spirit, joy is a quality that abides in all Christians. It may require nurturing to develop and gain strength, but it ought to be consistent, not ebbing and flowing with circumstances. Considering this, I do not believe the definition by *Merriam Webster* is accurate with respect to the joy we experience *as Christians*.

Let's consider a different perspective of joy from a pair of researchers at Fuller Theological Seminary. They believe joy is better understood as a virtue than an emotion.[3] When viewed as a virtue, joy becomes a purposefully developed habit[4] that "directs our thoughts, feelings, and actions toward what God intends."[5] The primary researcher, Dr. Pamela Ebstyne King, summarizes the research in an interview by defining joy as "an enduring, deep delight in what holds the most significance."[6]

Use the paragraph above to complete the table. List words that highlight the contrast between the two perspectives found in the dictionary and the research.

Earthly joy (Dictionary definition)	Christian joy (Research-based definition)
Emotion	
Evoked	
Well-being, success, good fortune	
Prospect of possessing what one desires	

These differences lead to the following observations for us as Christians:

* Defining joy as a virtue elevates it beyond emotion. It implies an "enduring" nature contrary to the temporary "evoking" of emotion. Will brief moments still occur when a feeling wells up in us and we reach heights of joy? Absolutely, but regarding joy as a *habit* awakens us to the breadth and depth of joy—joy as a consistent, intentional practice of finding delight in what God desires.

* In Matthew 22:35-40, Jesus clarified the greatest commandments as loving God first, then loving others. Accordingly, the motivation for our thoughts, feelings, and actions needs to come from the desire to benefit those relationships, not our own well-being, success, or good fortune.

* Joy is not a response to external circumstances. Instead, joy is an internal virtue, developed over time, that moves us to demonstrate outwardly our deep delight in matters of eternal significance.

Now, scan the verses on p. 6 one more time with these questions in mind:

* Is there evidence of the internal presence of abiding joy?

* Is there evidence of a deep delight in matters of eternal significance rather than self-satisfaction?

When I compare the verses with the perspective of joy from Dr. King's research, I see an alignment that tells me Christian joy is broader and richer than what is expressed in the definition from *Merriam Webster*. I want to study and understand and live with this broader, richer joy! So, join me in studying this joy as we use the following definition to guide us:

> *Joy is an enduring, deep delight in what holds the most significance.*

To help us begin to understand this perspective of joy, let's consider an example of unexpected joy.

Read Acts 11:1-18 and answer the questions in the table below.

Unexpected joy	
What ultimately held the most significance for the men in Jerusalem?	What thoughts, feelings, or actions testified to the Jewish believers' enduring, deep delight in that most significant thing?

Did you see the challenge to and change in the men's understanding? They did not anticipate finding joy in Peter eating with uncircumcised men; but, when they silently focused on what was most significant, they responded by glorifying God.

Anytime we face a challenge that requires change, there is a process of recognizing the challenge, struggling with it, then accepting or rejecting the required change. As we go through this study, we will be challenged, we will wrestle with our understanding of circumstances and difficulties and joy, and we will make a choice. I pray we all choose joy. I pray we find unexpected joy as we seek to habitually focus on what really matters.

> As you reflect on today's lesson, *What is joy?*, what resonated strongly with you? What do you still need to think about?
>
> ....
>
> ....

Here's to the start of our joyful path-treading!

WEEK 1, DAY 2

Why tread paths of joy? (Part 1)

You make known to me the path of life; in your presence there is fullness of joy; at your right hand are pleasures forevermore. (Ps. 16:11)

Goal for this week

* To develop a greater understanding of joy and its bearing on our lives

Guiding Questions

* What is joy?

* Why frame the learning process as "treading paths" of joy?

* Why tread paths of joy?

* With all the references to joy in the Bible, why focus on Philippians?

Psalm 1:1-2.

"Blessed is the man
   who walks not in the counsel of the wicked,
nor stands in the way of sinners,
   nor sits in the seat of scoffers;
but his delight is in the law of the LORD,
   and on his law he meditates day and night."

Psalm 40:8. "I delight to do your will, O my God; your law is within my heart."

Psalm 112:1. "Praise the LORD! Blessed is the man who fears the LORD, who greatly delights in his commandments!"

Psalm 119:16. "I will delight in your statutes; I will not forget your word."

Jeremiah 15:16. "Your words were found, and I ate them, and your words became to me a joy and the delight of my heart, for I am called by your name, O LORD, God of hosts"

Romans 7:22. "For I delight in the law of God, in my inner being,"

What a way to start the day—reading God's amazing, inspired Word! No introduction. No instructions. Just Scripture. Did you notice a common theme in the verses? I'm sure you did! Take a moment to underline those similar words or phrases.

✳ Now write below our definition of joy from yesterday.

....

....

....

....

✳ What connection do you see between the verses and the definition?

....

....

....

✳ Both the verses and the definition use the word *delight*. If the definition speaks to delighting in what has the most significance and the verses express delight in God's Word, what can we infer?

....

....

....

(Note: It may help to clarify that the phrase "what holds the most significance" refers to a *category* of supremely significant matters, not a single matter ranked above all others. Therefore, God's Word is part of a group of matters holding the highest level of significance. In yesterday's look at Peter's encounter, the truth that "God had granted salvation to the Gentiles" was a matter of supreme significance in that situation. Later this week, we will see that "sharing the gospel" also belongs in this group.)

So, we can have joy by delighting in God's Word. This delight goes beyond simply finding pleasure in our daily devotional reading, however. James 1:22 reminds us to be "doers of the word, and not hearers only" or we deceive ourselves, and Jesus said in Luke 11:28 that we are "blessed" when we "hear the word of God and keep it." In other words, delighting in God's Word implies obedience.

But how does this move us toward answering today's question:

Why tread paths of joy?

The following scriptures help us draw the connections we need. Each verse contains the verb *rejoice* rather than the noun *joy*, so we will adapt our definition accordingly: *to rejoice is to express enduring, deep delight in what holds the most significance.* As we begin, determine a special marking or highlight for the words rejoice, joy, and joyful that you can use throughout this study. My marking is the same for all three words, something of a mini-explosion or starburst pattern like this,

rejoice

but you choose what is meaningful to you.

Mark *rejoice* in the following verses.

* **1 Thessalonians 5:16-18.** "Rejoice always, pray without ceasing, give thanks in all circumstances; for this is the will of God in Christ Jesus for you."

* **1 Peter 4:12-13.** "Beloved, do not be surprised at the fiery trial when it comes upon you to test you, as though something strange were happening to you. But rejoice insofar as you share Christ's sufferings, that you may also rejoice and be glad when his glory is revealed."

✳ **Matthew 5:11-12.** "Blessed are you when others revile you and persecute you and utter all kinds of evil against you falsely on my account. Rejoice and be glad, for your reward is great in heaven, for so they persecuted the prophets who were before you."

✳ **Luke 10:17-18, 20.** "The seventy-two returned with joy, saying, 'Lord, even the demons are subject to us in your name!' And he said to them, 'I saw Satan fall like lightning from heaven...Nevertheless, do not rejoice in this, that the spirits are subject to you, but rejoice that your names are written in heaven.'"

Now, review these verses and determine whether "rejoice" is used to make a statement (declarative) or as a command (imperative). Finally, identify the reason for rejoicing.

Verse	Type of Sentence	Why rejoice?
1 Thessalonians 5:16-18	☐ Statement ☐ Command	
1 Peter 4:12-13 (Consider both uses of "rejoice.")	☐ Statement ☐ Command	
	☐ Statement ☐ Command	
Matthew 5:11-12	☐ Statement ☐ Command	
Luke 10:17-18, 20 (Consider only the 2nd use of "rejoice.")	☐ Statement ☐ Command	

Would you place all the answers you wrote in the last column into the category "what holds the most significance"? ....
If so, then those matters are worthy of our efforts to develop deep, enduring delight in them. Which of those challenges you the most from that perspective? ....
Which easily fills you with joy as you read it? ....

Based on most of the boxes you checked in the third column, why should we tread paths of joy?

....

....

....

Think about how you felt when you wrote something to the effect of "It's a commandment." Did you write it easily or did a hint of rebellion want to rise in you? Is it odd to think about being commanded to rejoice? Let's see if we can better understand by looking at one more set of verses from Jesus:

John 15:10-11. "'If you keep my commandments, you will abide in my love, just as I have kept my Father's commandments and abide in his love. These things I have spoken to you, that my joy may be in you, and that your joy may be full.'"

Wait. Don't move on just yet. Breathe in those words again that God breathed out (2 Tim. 3:16). Marvel that the Savior of the world wants you and me

...to abide in His love

...to have a relationship with Him

...to have a relationship with Him *like what He has with the Father.*

You and me! So throw that rock of rebellion out of your path right now and intentionally choose to obey! Why? Because this is joy! His joy in you and your joy to the full!

Back to our question: Why tread paths of joy? It is the right thing to do. It is an act of obedience motivated by love for our Savior. And, because our obedience impacts our relationship with God our Father and our Lord Jesus Christ, it is a matter of supreme significance. When we develop an enduring, deep delight in obedience, we experience greater joy. And, when we experience greater joy, we delight even more in pleasing our Father and our Savior. It's a beautiful cycle that spirals us ever closer to our Savior...and ever closer to living out joy as a virtue.

I mentioned yesterday that our goal this week is to develop a greater understanding of joy and its bearing on our lives. I think we are well on our way with a view of Christian joy, recognizing the blessings of abiding in Jesus' love and experiencing the fullness of His joy in us when we delight in obedience. The words of the old hymn "Trust and Obey" capture this idea well. Let the lyrics of the first verse and refrain echo in your mind as we close today.

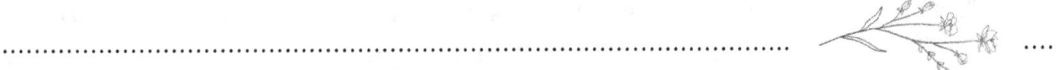

Trust and Obey
by John H. Sammis

When we walk with the Lord in the light of His Word,
What a glory He sheds on our way!
While we do His good will, He abides with us still,
And with all who will trust and obey.

Refrain:
Trust and obey, for there's no other way
To be happy in Jesus, but to trust and obey.[7]

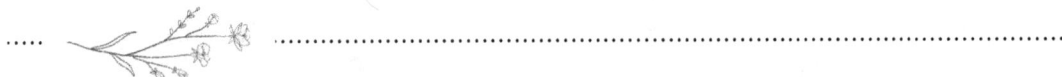

WEEK 1, DAY 3

Why tread paths of joy? (Part 2)

You make known to me the path of life; in your presence there is fullness of joy; at your right hand are pleasures forevermore. (Ps. 16:11)

Goal for this week

* To develop a greater understanding of joy and its bearing on our lives

Guiding Questions

* What is joy?

* Why frame the learning process as "treading paths" of joy?

* Why tread paths of joy?

* With all the references to joy in the Bible, why focus on Philippians?

But what if it's dark?

What if my pain is overwhelming?

What if my life feels like it is falling apart?

Do any of these questions echo your thoughts right now? If so, I want you to know I do not emphasize rejoicing or choosing joy without really grappling with how that may sound to you—without giving careful thought to the suffering or sorrow you may be experiencing. In fact, I've written and rewritten and stared without knowing what to write in the paragraphs before you: words in black and white...as if the choice is that easy; words with perfect margins...as if we ought to have everything together; words that flow together coherently (hopefully)...as if life should make sense. I do not want the words you read to seem like glib advice or insensitive text. I do not want the concept of joy to come across like a cheer at a football game. (Chooooooose joy! Toe touch. Go team!) And so, I have prayed over this, and I have prayed over you...because your pain is real and because purposefully rejoicing is a lot harder than it sounds at times. Which leads me to ask again:

Why tread paths of joy?

Specifically, why should *you* tread paths of joy? If you are a single mom struggling to meet the emotional needs of your children while still working enough to pay the bills, why should you tread paths of joy? If you are or a loved one is suffering from a disability or illness that exacts daily demands mentally and/or physically, why should you tread paths of joy? For you who feel alone—whether still single or again single or currently in a difficult marriage—why joy? For you who have suffered the loss of a loved one and grief hangs so heavy on your heart and threatens to consume you, why joy? For others who feel isolated or rejected or misunderstood or unloved or overwhelmed or inadequate or discouraged or just plain hurt, why should you tread paths of joy?

Oh, please join me in our walk through these pages today as we seek a response to this question. In our pursuit of an answer yesterday, we discovered that Jesus Himself commanded us to rejoice and promised us a closer, more joy-filled relationship with Him. But let us not limit our understanding of *why joy* to obedience only. Our God is bigger than this one dimension!

Look up Philippians 3:1 and write it below. You will find another, rather unexpected, dimension of joy.

....

....

....

....

As you ponder Paul's choice of words, keep in mind he had been either in prison or under house arrest for almost four years at the time he wrote Philippians, not to mention all the previous threats to his life during his ministry. Paul's words were not empty encouragement; they were a message proven true through the fire of trials. The message had been true for him. It would be true for the Philippians. It is true for us.

Before moving on, go back to the verse you wrote and mark *rejoice* in the way you determined yesterday; then, underline the object of your rejoicing. Finally, draw a box around the words expressing Paul's purpose for joy—the phrase with *safe* or *safeguard* or *protection* in it. Think of that box as a symbol of God's protection, hemming us in when we express enduring, deep delight in Him.

But can I really write that God "hems us in"? Don't Christians still suffer physical, mental, emotional, and even spiritual trauma—sometimes *because* of their faith?

Yes, we know from Paul's life, from the lives of other Christians, and even from our own lives that the safety guaranteed by rejoicing in the Lord is not a "protective bubble" blocking pain from our lives. This safety is not protection *from* difficulty; rather, protection *in* difficulty. This safety provides both temporal and eternal hope. Paul gives a powerful example of this in his second letter to the Corinthian church. Don't read it too quickly. Pause and recognize the hurt and the hope he is communicating:

> **2 Corinthians 1:8-10.** "For we do not want you to be unaware, brothers, of the affliction we experienced in Asia. For we were so utterly burdened beyond our strength that we despaired of life itself. Indeed, we felt that we had received the sentence of death. But that was to make us rely not on ourselves but on God who raises the dead. He delivered us from such a deadly peril, and he will deliver us. On him we have set our hope that he will deliver us again."

Use the verse to fill in the chart below.

How did Paul feel during his affliction?	Why was the affliction permitted?	What did he learn about God as a result of the affliction?

I wanted you to write this in a chart so you could see it as a whole. As Paul was feeling *utterly burdened, beyond strength, despairing of life itself,* and *under the sentence of death,* he was compelled to rely on God who holds the power of life in His hands. And because Paul chose to rely on God, he came to know Him as "safe"—the One in whom his hope for deliverance was not limited to this one instance but was *set* for all future deliverances in all future afflictions. The implication is stability even when the present and future are desperately unstable.

The ideas of safety and stability remind me of a song from my childhood that illustrates the concept well: "The Wise Man Built His House upon the Rock." The song is based on a parable Jesus told in Matthew 7 and Luke 6. As you read Luke's account below, allow Jesus' storytelling to draw a picture in your mind—an experience similar to those who hung on His words so many years ago.

Luke 6:47-49. "'Everyone who comes to me and hears my words and does them, I will show you what he is like: he is like a man building a house, who dug deep and laid the foundation on the rock. And when a flood arose, the stream broke against that house and could not shake it, because it had been well built. But the one who hears and does not do them is like a man who built a house on the ground without a foundation. When the stream broke against it, immediately it fell, and the ruin of that house was great.'"

Below are two sketches of the houses described above. Beside each picture, write the phrases Jesus used to describe the house and its reaction to the storm.

First house   **Second house**

The Wise Man and the Foolish Man
by Ann Omley

The wise man built his house upon the Rock,
The wise man built his house upon the Rock,
The wise man built his house upon the Rock,
And the rains came tumbling down.

The rains came down and the floods came up,
The rains came down and the floods came up,
The rains came down and the floods came up,
But the house on the Rock stood firm.

The foolish man built his house upon the sand,
The foolish man built his house upon the sand,
The foolish man built his house upon the sand,
And the rains came tumbling down.

The rains came down and the floods came up,
The rains came down and the floods came up,
The rains came down and the floods came up,
And the house on the sand fell flat.

So build your life on the Lord Jesus Christ,
So build your life on the Lord Jesus Christ,
So build your life on the Lord Jesus Christ,
And the blessings will come down.

The blessings come down as your prayers go up,
The blessings come down as your prayers go up,
The blessings come down as your prayers go up,
So build your life on the Lord.[8]

Now, go back and underline the word *when* in the verses from Luke 6. Why didn't Jesus say *if*?

....

....

....

As I'm sure you noted, Jesus' use of *when* reveals we *will* have trouble; it is a certainty. Whether we build our lives on the solid foundation of Christ our Rock or on our own unsteady strength, we will face adversity. And yet, if we look more deeply, we can perceive a detail easily overlooked: The effects of the storm on the houses are not described as if viewing the *aftermath* of the storm; no, they occur *while the storm is raging*. Jesus' words lead us to see vividly in our minds that during a massive downpour, amid rising flood waters, as the stream is breaking against walls, one house stands. The house on the rock is unshakeable *in* the storm!

Often in this life, we yearn for the peace and rest we associate with traditional safety—with freedom from sorrow and difficulties. But we live in a fallen world, so storms rage on. Satan longs for us to feel unstable as he tries to divert our gaze from our Savior to our struggles, disrupt our faith with fear, and shift us from God-reliance to self-reliance. His desire is to make us feel unsafe in God's care. In addition, we have seen how Paul despaired of life in 2 Corinthians and how, in Luke 6 the person who heard God's words and did them was caught in a hurricane.

But still, somehow, in the middle of those storms—in the middle of our storms—a truth begins to emerge. Let's allow it to fully come to light:

* *While* despairing of life, Paul found joy in relying on God.

* *While* under attack, the person in Luke 6 was obedient; thus, drawing from yesterday, this obedient person was filled with joy.

* *While* you mourn a situation, you can also rejoice in God's presence (Ps. 9:9-10).

What an amazing truth: *Joy and sorrow can be experienced simultaneously!* You don't need to be free *from* sorrow to experience joy; you can experience joy *in* your sorrow. Every trial you face is an opportunity to rely on Christ and set your hope in Him. Times of sorrow are moments when you can find endur- ing, deep delight in what holds the most significance. Thus, expressing both joy and sorrow at the same time allows you to stand safely through the storm.

Don't feel guilty over lingering sadness. The house could not control the length or ferocity of the storm. But don't waste this time, either. Use your "storm" to reinforce that your focus and reliance are on Christ, your Rock, even when you hurt...especially when you hurt.

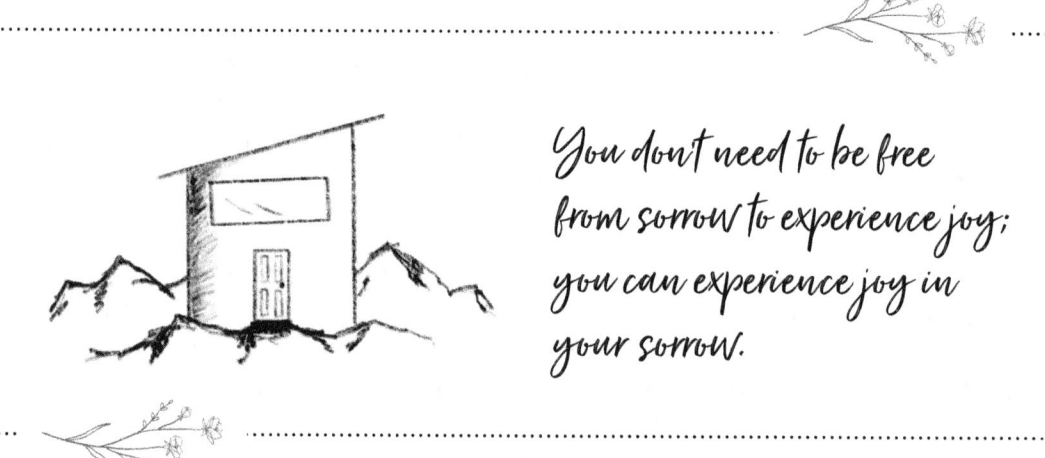

You don't need to be free from sorrow to experience joy; you can experience joy in your sorrow.

I cannot let you leave today without stating another truth. We have alluded to it all day, but it needs to be stated clearly. The struggles we face are filtered through God's loving hand (Job 1:12; 2:6) so that we may know Him better (Job 42:5). We may feel threatened or embattled physically, mentally, emotionally, and spiritually. And yet, we can focus on the spiritual safety God provides as what matters most. We can develop a habit of finding shelter under His wings (Ps. 91:4), protection in the strong tower of His name (Prov. 18:10), and ultimately, eternal security in heaven with our Savior (John 3:16).

If you do not know you have placed your faith in Jesus Christ as your Lord and Savior, you do not have access to this safety. But you can!

* Option 1: Contact a Christian friend or your Bible study leader or a pastor to pray with you and help you secure your eternal future today.

* Option 2: Call out to God on your own. Turn to p. 102 and read about placing your faith in Christ. Follow the steps; then, pray the prayer at the bottom of the page. Once you are done, please contact a Christian friend and let them know so they can rejoice with you.

Whether you choose Option 1 or 2, your decision will start a party in heaven! Luke 15:7 says: "Just so, I tell you, there will be more joy in heaven over one sinner who repents than over ninety-nine righteous persons who need no repentance." (I think I "see" a little heavenly confetti being tossed on the streets of gold in your honor!)

If you know that you have placed your faith in Jesus as your Savior, but you have experienced trauma that you can't seem to move past, please seek professional Christian counseling. Currently, many counselors meet with their clients virtually, so access is available to you. A Christian counselor can help you focus your thoughts, feelings, and actions on what matters most, not what has hurt the most, and move you toward the safety of joy.

Tomorrow we will ask the same question one more time—*Why tread paths of joy?*—and explore it from another perspective. See you then!

WEEK 1, DAY 4

Why tread paths of joy? (Part 3)

You make known to me the path of life; in your presence there is fullness of joy; at your right hand are pleasures forevermore. (Ps. 16:11)

Goal for this week

✳ To develop a greater understanding of joy and its bearing on our lives

Guiding Questions

✳ What is joy?

✳ Why frame the learning process as "treading paths" of joy?

✳ Why tread paths of joy?

✳ With all the references to joy in the Bible, why focus on Philippians?

We now have two answers to our question, *Why tread paths of joy?* (1) Rejoicing is the right thing to do. Obedience leads us to abide in His love and experience His joy to the full. (2) Rejoicing in the Lord is the safe thing to do for it drives us to rely on God regardless of circumstances. Let's return to our *Wondering Why* game you played with the group to see if there might be another good reason.

Why should I tread paths of joy?	Because it is the obedient thing and the safe thing to do.
Why is rejoicing obedient and safe?	Because God says it is.
Why does God say it's obedient and safe to rejoice?	Because He knows what's best for us.
Why does He know what's best for us?	Because He made us.
Why did He make—wait! (Lightbulb moment!) Since He *made* us, is there something in our *design as humans* that provides a reason to tread paths of joy?	

Approaching joy from a human design perspective may be a bit unusual for a Bible study. However, because God formed us as a potter forms a vessel (Is. 64:8) and He breathed His breath into us (Gen. 2:7), it is not a stretch to consider this perspective when supported with Scripture. Let's take another command from Philippians to launch today's study.

Write Philippians 2:14 below.

....

....

Ouch! That may hit us pretty hard. I mean, don't we all complain a little? Isn't it okay to vent sometimes? Not according to this verse. And, although the results of academic research give us a little more leeway (it is from humans and not God-inspired, after all), many findings reveal there are consequences to our murmurings. Let's use these findings to gain insight into God's masterful design of humans.

Think for a moment about the last complaining statement you made and the event that prompted it. (Don't let yourself get upset again. Just recognize the complaint so we can analyze it.)

What was the purpose of complaining about that event?

....

Were you trying to calmly process the situation to seek a satisfying resolution of the problem?

....

The event that prompted the statement was probably at least mildly stressful and elicited an emotional response even if you hid it at the time. Although your retelling *may* have been an effort at satisfactory resolution of the incident, more often a disgruntled reiteration is for justification or validation of feelings.[9] However, this "reliving" of the situation is a problem. The brain and body experience the initial emotional stress again. If a person tells the tale to two or three more people? Well, you get the picture.

You see, God designed our bodies to respond to stress with the release of stress hormones. Throughout the ages, that burst of hormones has helped people physically and mentally as they sought to escape threatening situations.[10] So, whatever the event you thought of in the preceding paragraph, you likely experienced a burst of hormones to help you deal with it. However, when you complained—when you brought the event back to your mind as if going through it again—your body responded to the relived situation by releasing the same stress hormones.[11]

In particular, the hormone cortisol has a potentially damaging effect on your brain. When you dwell on stressful situations, you increase the likelihood of chronically elevated cortisol levels,[12] and excess cortisol literally shrinks the hippocampus of your brain—the place where critical memory-making occurs.[13] One psychologist went so far as to say chronic stress resulted in cortisol acting as an "acid bath" on the hippocampus![14] Another doctor commented that "stress and cortisol are erasing your memory, dashing your emotions, causing you anxiety, and killing your brain cells."[15] Ugh! All this information makes me think there could be more to Philippians 2:14 than we see on the surface. Let's continue our discovery.

For many years, scientists believed our brains reached their full development during childhood or adolescence.[16] However, recent findings disprove this. The phrase "neurons that fire together wire together" has become prevalent in brain research. It means physical changes occur in the brain throughout our lifetime as a result of repeated focus of attention. Over time, the connections (synapses) formed from that repeated focus become stronger, and the likelihood of our brains following those connections increases.[17] In other words, every time we complain, our neurons are firing and wiring a path that makes negativity an easier choice. A path of least resistance. A rutted road that leads to a negative outlook.[18]

Now, based on what we have learned, let's look at the following verse:

* **Proverbs 17:22.** "A joyful heart is good medicine, but a crushed spirit dries up the bones."

a. What two elements are being compared in this verse (including their adjectives)? ....

b. What are the contrasting effects of these two elements?

....

c. Why might the second phrase be a fitting description of someone with a negative outlook?

....

....

d. Based on what you have read so far today, why should you tread paths of joy?

....

....

e. Take a moment to write a brief prayer telling God why you want to tread these paths and asking Him for His help in doing so. Don't feel compelled to use today's *why.* Just be real in what you write.

....

....

....

In part d above, you may have said something along the lines of *It's the healthy/rational/logical thing to do.* And it is! Don't worry if you know you already have some pretty good paths established for complaining. It will take some focused effort, but those paths can be abandoned.

Let's tie a few things together before we consider another human design element.

❋   What is our definition of joy?

....

....

....

❋   Do you think we can achieve "enduring, deep delight" through "repeated focus of attention"? If so, what does the phrase "neurons that fire together wire together" have to do with treading paths of joy?

....

....

....

❋   The following paragraph appeared earlier when discussing complaining and negativity. Fill in the blanks now with either *rejoice* or *joy* or *joyful*.

In other words, every time we .... , our neurons are firing

and wiring a path that makes .... an easier choice. A path of

least resistance. A rutted road that leads to a .... outlook.

Now do you see why we are "treading paths of joy" in this Bible study?! We want to have a good start on creating well-worn paths of joy—paths that will define us as ladies who live with deep, enduring delight in what has the most significance.

We need a little more information if we are going to get this path-treading started on the right foot. First, though, let's review our approach: We are viewing joy as a virtue—an intentionally developed habit—that directs our thoughts, feelings, and action toward what God intends. That "intentionally developed" phrase is particularly important when considering our design as humans.

Now let's begin to gather more information...

Did you know our brains and our minds are not the same thing? When God created us, He created our brains so they would take in, process, and store information—somewhat like a computer. Our minds, however, were created to allow us to reason and focus our attention and make decisions. The brain and mind are different, but God created them to work together.[19]

As you read the following verses, underline what is common in each:

* **Romans 12:2a.** "Do not be conformed to this world, but be transformed by the renewal of your mind,"

* **Matthew 22:37.** "And he said to him, 'You shall love the Lord your God with all your heart and with all your soul and with all your mind.'"

* **1 Chronicles 22:19a.** "Now set your mind and heart to seek the LORD your God."

Do you see how Scripture addresses the mind? These are all active processes that require reasoning and focused attention and decision-making. If you seek to create rejoicing pathways and abandon "complaining" pathways, you must use your mind to make choices that help your brain fire and wire the right things. You have to focus on what matters most to intentionally develop the habit of joy.

Guess what? There's a verse for that! Look up Philippians 4:8 and fill in the blanks according to your favorite version. As you go through this study, these words should characterize the matters that fill your "what matters most" category.

* **Philippians 4:8.** "Finally, brothers, whatever is ...., whatever is ...., whatever is ...., whatever is ...., whatever is ...., whatever is ...., if there is ...., if there is ...., think about these things."

One final thought as we reflect on God's amazing design displayed in us: As Christians, we have a distinct advantage in the work of treading paths of joy because we have the Holy Spirit as our Helper. God did not leave us to our own resources in this endeavor. Furthermore, treading paths of joy is worthy work for it means setting our minds on things of the Spirit (Rom. 8:5) while purposefully trampling things of the flesh.

We have three of our questions answered now, and the fourth is our focus tomorrow. However, at this point, I'm more interested in the goal for the week. Do you have a greater understanding of joy and its bearing on your life? Glance back through your notes from these four days. Write below three or four statements about what has been meaningful to you.

....

....

....

....

....

....

....

....

WEEK 1, DAY 5

Why study joy in Philippians?

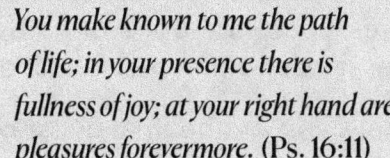

You make known to me the path of life; in your presence there is fullness of joy; at your right hand are pleasures forevermore. (Ps. 16:11)

My initial thought today is...Wow! We have learned a lot this week! Our goal has been to develop a greater understanding of joy and its bearing on our lives through seeking answers to some guiding questions. We still lack one question, but for now, write a brief answer to the following based on what you have studied.

Goal for this week

❉ To develop a greater understanding of joy and its bearing on our lives

Guiding Questions

❉ What is joy?

❉ Why frame the learning process as "treading paths" of joy?

❉ Why tread paths of joy?

❉ With all the references to joy in the Bible, why focus on Philippians?

❉ What is joy?

....

....

❉ Why frame the learning process as "treading paths" of joy?

....

....

❉ Why tread paths of joy? (3 reasons)

....

....

....

We will continue to ask questions throughout this study. They will lead us to discover truths from Scripture and develop awareness of their relevance to our lives. Soon, the book of Philippians will be as personal and meaningful to us as it was to that first Christian church in Europe around 61 or 62 AD.

Now, let's answer the final question:

> ### *With all the references to joy in the Bible, why focus on Philippians?*

The following references are all from Philippians. As you read the verses, match each reference with its expression of joy. (One more quick reminder: I am using the ESV.)

.... Phil. 1:4	1.	"complete my joy"
.... Phil. 1:18	2.	"I rejoiced in the Lord greatly"
.... Phil. 1:25	3.	"always...making my prayer with joy"
.... Phil. 2:2	4.	"rejoice at seeing him again"
.... Phil. 2:17	5.	"Finally...rejoice in the Lord"
.... Phil. 2:18	6.	"I am glad and rejoice with you all"
.... Phil. 2:28	7.	"in that I rejoice...and I will rejoice"
.... Phil. 2:29	8.	"Rejoice in the Lord always...again...rejoice"
.... Phil. 3:1	9.	"be glad and rejoice with me"
.... Phil. 4:1	10.	"my joy and crown"
.... Phil. 4:4	11.	"I will remain...for your progress and joy in the faith"
.... Phil. 4:10	12.	"receive him in the Lord with all joy"

As you read these verses purposefully placed throughout Philippians, *joy* emerges as a conspicuous feature of the landscape of this letter. In fact, joy is the theme of Philippians and a virtue of Paul's life. He delighted in God's desires, so he directed his thoughts, feelings, and actions to those matters.

So, what *did* matter most to Paul as he sat...waiting...still under house arrest... after almost four years? A passage from the first chapter of Philippians helps us see the situation from Paul's perspective.

Read Philippians 1:12-18.

Let's read between the lines a bit. The Philippian church was justifiably worried about the transmission of the gospel message during Paul's lengthy incarceration. Furthermore, it troubled them that some people were preaching with wrong motives, taking advantage of Paul's time in prison. This thoughtful church sent one of their own, Epaphroditus, to care for Paul, and he had probably conveyed the church's distress. Hence, Paul took this opportunity to reassure the Philippians. He acknowledged their concerns while also helping them realize that, with God, things are not always what they appear.

As we look at the passage again, I have provided a few markings to help us notice a pattern.

> I want you to know, brothers, that <u>what has happened to me</u> has really <u>served to advance the gospel,</u> so that it has become <u>known throughout</u> the whole imperial guard and to all the rest that <u>my imprisonment is for Christ</u>. And **most of the brothers**, having **become confident in the Lord** by my imprisonment, are **much more bold to speak the word without fear**. *Some* indeed *preach Christ from envy and rivalry,* but **others** from **good will**. The **latter** do it **out of love, knowing that I am put here for the defense of the gospel**. The *former proclaim Christ out of selfish ambition, not sincerely* but *thinking to afflict me* in my imprisonment. WHAT THEN? ONLY THAT IN EVERY WAY, WHETHER IN PRETENSE OR IN TRUTH, CHRIST IS PROCLAIMED, AND IN THAT I REJOICE. YES, AND I WILL REJOICE. (Philippians 1:12-18)

Take a minute to write down what you notice about the markings above. What do you think Paul is trying to convey to the Philippians?

✳ <u>Underlined portion</u>

....

....

....

✳ **Bold portion**

....

....

....

✳ *Italicized portion*

....

....

....

✳ CAPITALIZED PORTION

....

....

....

The following observations are given using the markings from above:

First, Paul reassured them that the gospel message was still spreading. Then, he alternated his message with **good news**, *bad news*, **good news**, *bad news*. He didn't deny or downplay the situation; but he did ensure that the Philippians knew **most** of the preaching came from pure motives and love for Christ.

THEN, HE MADE HIS "WHAT MATTERS MOST" STATEMENT. What mattered most to Paul in this situation?

....

....

....

Now stop and think a minute: Was this an easy thing for Paul to say? No! Paul loved sharing the gospel. Following his conversion, his life's work had been proclaiming Christ. Although the two years of house arrest were more lenient than the previous two years in prison, I'm sure Paul's heart ached to be on another missionary journey. As news came in of speakers with false motives, it was likely very difficult for him to hear. At some point, though, he had simply trusted God for the results. He did not have control over the situation, so he released control to the One who did—the One who could make truth known regardless of the motive of the speaker.

> Consider your own life from the perspective of that last sentence: Is your joy being hindered because you are trying to control a situation that is out of your control? If so, take a moment and prayerfully submit that situation to the Lord.
>
> ....
>
> ....
>
> ....

We need to take special notice of one more statement Paul made.

Write the last five words from the passage we've been examining.

....

Long before there were "choose joy" signs for people to hang on their walls or set on their desks, Paul stated that he chose joy. It was intentional. It was purposeful. It was continual. He has chosen joy; he is choosing joy; he will choose joy. He will have joy despite circumstances, not wait on circumstances to produce joy. He *will* rejoice. Paul's neurons had had plenty of practice firing and wiring together. For Paul, joy was a well-worn path.

When we classify joy as a virtue—an intentionally developed habit that directs our thoughts, feelings, and actions toward what God intends—we begin to see how to develop in our own lives the joy Paul had in his. When we further define joy as enduring, deep delight in what holds the most significance, we have a framework for examining Scripture and making it applicable to our lives through questions about significance, endurance, and delight. With these concepts in place, as well as a clear understanding of why treading paths of joy is important (*i.e.*, choosing joy is obedient, safe, and healthy), I believe we have laid valuable groundwork that will benefit our study. Next week we will get a little better *lay of the land* of the book of Philippians by getting to know Paul and the Philippian church, so keep your treading boots handy.

As we prepare to move forward, keep in mind that God wants us to be joyful. Our endeavor to develop this virtue is God-honoring, so don't miss hearing His cheering from the sidelines!

Notes from this week

....

....

....

....

....

....

....

....

....

Part 1 Summary - A Survey of Joy

Goal for the week: To develop a greater understanding of joy and its bearing on our lives

Adopted definition of joy: *Joy is enduring, deep delight in what holds the most significance.*

Why frame the learning process as "treading paths of joy"?

* The learning process requires intentional, repeated efforts for a specific purpose—much like establishing a path through the pasture that makes travel efficient. Specifically, we are learning the delightful habit of willingly choosing to do or think or feel what is right in order to glorify Christ.

* As we repeatedly choose joy (or complaining), our neurons "fire and wire" together, building literal paths in our brains that become the way our brains are more likely to go. Although the choosing process initially requires the decision-making power of our minds, in cooperation with and strengthened by the Holy Spirit, if made often enough, that path becomes well-worn. It is not necessarily an automatic response, but it is less often a conscious choice. We have a habit of being joyful.

Why tread paths of joy? These reasons reveal the power of *joy* in and on our lives.

* Rejoicing is obedient. It leads us to abide in Christ's love and experience His joy to the full.

* Rejoicing in the Lord is safe. It drives us to rely on God regardless of circumstances.

* Rejoicing is healthy. It promotes our mental (and spiritual) health, protecting us from negativity as we set our minds on things of the Spirit.

With all the references to *joy* in the Bible, why focus on Philippians?

* The theme of Philippians is *joy.*

* Joy characterizes the life of Paul, the author of Philippians, and the relationship he has with the Philippian church.

Remember, this is
God-honoring work.
As you take steps to
establish paths of joy,
your Lord is cheering
you on from
the sidelines!

Exploring Paths

Below are pictures of my parents' pasture. These pictures and captions are here to help you have a visual of some of the concepts you learned this week. Feel free to reference them anytime you need a little reminder!

This picture represents the open "land" in your brain—ready for your mind to cooperate with the Holy Spirit and make intentional path building decisions.

These are the well-worn paths you have seen before and now know are formed by repeated firing and wiring. They are habits now—more brain than mind—but you want to make sure they are paths of joy, not complaining.

This is an abandoned road that grass is beginning to reclaim. It represents two possible outcomes:

1. You have focused on building joyful paths, so complaining pathways are becoming less usable. Pat yourself on the back!

2. At some point in the future, you have not continued to tread the paths of joy you worked so hard to establish in this study. They are becoming overgrown. Remember that joy is a habit. Keep treading paths of joy with intention!

The Path Behind

Group Discussion of Week 1

....

....

....

....

....

....

....

....

SESSION 2

The Path Ahead

Introductory Activity for Week 2

Part I - The Story

Watch and listen for the next few minutes.

GROUP

Part II - Your Thoughts

As you reflect on this adaptation of the account from Acts 5:14-42, take a couple of minutes to write down what you noticed that was either new or renewed in your mind, as well as any questions you had. These can be related to the events, the culture, or the people.

Observations	Questions
....	....
....	....
....	....
....	....
....	....
....	....
....	....
....	....

SESSION 2

Part III - Group Discussion

Now, share your thoughts with the other group members. What stood out to you about Saul (Paul)? I encourage you to jot down what other group members noticed, as well.

....

....

....

....

....

....

Hopefully, we will address some of your thoughts or questions as we go through this week. If not, be sure to bring them up when you meet again with your group. One question you may have had was about the role Saul played in this event. Scripture does not record him as having been a part of the debate, but Saul was a rising star among the Pharisees (Gal. 1:14). As such, his attendance as an observer with a vested interest in the outcome was quite possible. While this possibility is only speculation, there is no need to speculate about his actions soon after. We know Paul was "ravaging the church" and imprisoning Christians (Acts 8:3).

PART 2
Getting the Lay of the Land

Welcome to week 2! Last week we laid some valuable groundwork for our study. (See pp. 37 and 39 for a quick review.) This week we begin to get the *lay of the land* of the book of Philippians.

Let's place that possibly unfamiliar term back in the context of a ranch. A rancher who wants to find the lay of his land will need to identify characteristics of the land, such as high and low places, points where water is available, and locations of rocky or sandy soil. He will use that information to determine where and why different grasses are growing; where he should construct fences to separate cattle or to rotate them and prevent overgrazing; and how to make the available water accessible for his cattle. The wise rancher started with a guiding groundwork of knowledge, and through a process, he develops a deeper understanding of his land. This understanding is critical before he undertakes the task of establishing efficient, effective paths that allow him to care for his cattle well.

For us, *finding the lay of the land* means we will do a bit of background exploration to determine the context of our study. This will give us the opportunity to become better acquainted with Paul, the writer of this letter, and with the church at Philippi, the letter's beloved recipients. Equipped with a better understanding of characteristics and culture, we will have greater insight into Paul's communication with the Philippians in about 61 or 62 AD. We will also establish a strong foundation for discovering its relevance to our lives today.

We may observe the landscape from a bit of a different perspective in the next few days, but I hope it brings a fresh understanding of familiar events.

WEEK 2

Getting to know Paul and the Philippians

WEEK 2, DAY 1

Knowing Saul (Part 1)

Rejoice in the Lord always; again I will say, rejoice. (Phil. 4:4)

Almost anyone can discover details about a ranch—how many acres it covers, how many head of cattle are on it, and so on. However, a good rancher who truly knows the lay of his land can tell you more. For example, he can look at the weather and know how it will affect specific areas of his property much like you know how different looks or tones of voice impact a loved one. In other words, a good rancher *knows* the land; he doesn't just know *about* the land.

The first part of this week, I want us to get to *know* Saul/Paul, not just know facts *about* him. The aim is to develop a connection to him by considering his motivations and characteristics. Let's begin to get the lay of his life by briefly putting ourselves in his shoes.

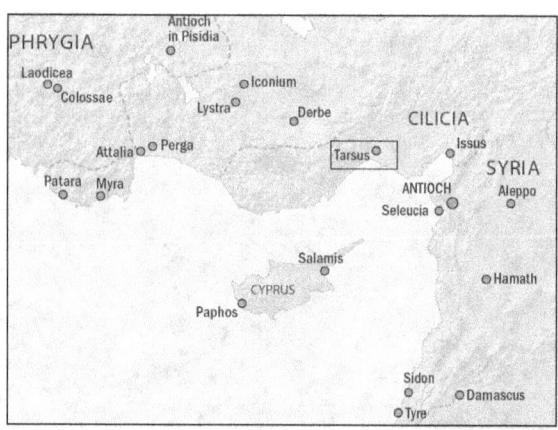

Tarsus, capital of Cilicia and Paul's hometown[1]

Early life: *As Saul, you begin your life in Tarsus (Acts 22:3). It is the capital city of Cilicia, which is a Roman province in Asia Minor (modern day Turkey). As you grow up, you learn to be proud of your hometown, for Tarsus is known for more than its role as the capital city. It is a place of commerce, textile production, and renowned schools of rhetoric.[2] You are aware that others recognize the importance of this location as well, for you will later claim, "I am a Jew, from Tarsus in Cilicia, a citizen of no obscure city" (Acts 21:39).*

The circumstances of your life seem to destine you for leadership. Your birth in Tarsus provides you with the favored status of being a Roman citizen by birth—a highly-prized designation in the first century AD. One benefit of this citizenship is that you have a Roman name, Paul. However, you rarely use this name until later in your life because your family values their Israelite heritage.

Your esteemed heritage as an Israelite plays a role in your leadership development, as well. As the son of Jewish parents of the tribe of Benjamin (Phil. 3:5), you are sent to Jerusalem to attend school in the synagogue at about thirteen years of age. There, you have the incredible privilege of learning from the great teacher Gamaliel.[3] What more could any young person want?

Getting to know Saul: Reading between the lines a bit, what do you see in this information that helps you *know* Saul a little better?

....

....

....

....

Check what skills or motivations or personality traits you think young Saul developed from these early influences. Feel free to add your own at the end.

☐ Confidence   ☐ Knowledge of the Old Testament Law

☐ Humility   ☐ Concern for people

☐ Sense of authority   ☐ Loyalty to family and faith

☐ Sense of self-importance   ☐ Intelligence

☐ Understanding of others' viewpoints   ☐ Independence

☐ Ability to reason and argue   ☐ Tact

☐ Hometown pride   ☐ Ability to make tents

☐ Personal pride   ☐ Other ....

☐ Pride as a Roman citizen   ☐ Other ....

Ponder the possibility: Based on the history above and on his own testimony in Acts 22:3, Saul would have been in Jerusalem for several years before his first mention in Scripture. If so, what would have been happening there and in the surrounding area during his mid-twenties?

....

....

....

Yes, it is likely that Saul was in Jerusalem during Jesus' ministry. He would have overheard conversations among the rabbis and Pharisees. He would have seen the intense reactions of the religious leaders. We can only wonder if he was a part of the crowd at the crucifixion; but we can be certain the incident would have impacted him deeply. And what followed—the nonsense about a resurrection and the disciples' incessant promotion of that lie (Paul's perspective)—sent him into a fury.

Saul's résumé: The following verses contain information Saul could have used as a young adult to create a convincing résumé; they tell you details *about* him.

As you read each verse, underline the words or phrases that give his achievements.

❋   **Philippians 3:5-6.** "...circumcised on the eighth day, of the people of Israel, of the tribe of Benjamin, a Hebrew of Hebrews; as to the law, a Pharisee; as to zeal, a persecutor of the church; as to righteousness under the law, blameless."

Goal for this week

❋ To *know* Paul and the Philippian church, not just know *about* them

Guiding Questions

❋ What do I know *about* Saul/Paul?

❋ In what ways do I *know* Saul/Paul?

❋ What do I learn from Paul's life that I can apply to my own?

❋ What do I know about the Philippian church and what can I learn from them?

❋ Why was there such a special relationship between Paul and the church at Philippi?

❊ **Acts 22:3-4.** "'I am a Jew, born in Tarsus in Cilicia, but brought up in [Jerusalem], educated at the feet of Gamaliel according to the strict manner of the law of our fathers, being zealous for God as all of you are this day.'"

❊ **Galatians 1:14.** "And I was advancing in Judaism beyond many of my own age among my people, so extremely zealous was I for the traditions of my fathers."

❊ **Acts 7:56-58; 8:1, 3.** "And [Stephen] said, 'Behold, I see the heavens opened, and the Son of Man standing at the right hand of God.' But [the elders, the scribes, and the members of the council] cried out with a loud voice and stopped their ears and rushed together at him. Then they cast him out of the city and stoned him. And the witnesses laid down their garments at the feet of a young man named Saul... And Saul approved of his execution. And there arose on that day a great persecution against the church in Jerusalem, and they were all scattered throughout the regions of Judea and Samaria, except the apostles...But Saul was ravaging the church, and entering house after house, he dragged off men and women and committed them to prison."

Now re-read the verses and think about what they tell you regarding Saul's character and motivation. Although you may infer some traits from previously underlined words, you will also see obvious descriptors of Paul's character and motivation. This time, circle these words or phrases. When you feel like you have gained a little more insight into who Saul was, move to the next section.

A letter of recommendation: Above, we thought about the achievements Saul would have put on a résumé. Now let's change perspectives. Suppose Saul has asked you to write a (positive) letter of recommendation for him. As you plan, you ask yourself: What adjectives characterize him? What personality traits does he exhibit? Record your thoughts on the next page.

Write down five or six words or phrases you would use to accurately describe Saul.

....

....

....

It's just a guess, but I bet *joyful* did not make the list! To finish today, reread what you have written and add below any insights you don't want to forget—anything that helps you *know* Saul better.

....

....

....

I hope Saul has become a little more real to you today. We've only looked at the first "half" of his life, though. We will continue our discovery tomorrow.

WEEK 2, DAY 2

Knowing Saul (Part 2)

Rejoice in the Lord always; again I will say, rejoice. (Phil. 4:4)

Yesterday, we left Saul steaming! Remember?

✱ **Acts 8:3.** "But Saul was ravaging the church, and entering house after house, he dragged off men and women and committed them to prison."

But we were only beginning our survey of the lay of Saul's life. We were just getting to *know* him.

As we start today, let's again place ourselves in Saul's shoes for a moment. Think about how...

...you are "still breathing threats and murder against the disciples of the Lord" (Acts 9:1) as you make an impassioned journey beyond the walls of Jerusalem to bring back some of those scoundrel Christians who think they are beyond the reach of your righteous judgment! (Wait. Read that again a little faster and as if you are breathing threats!)

Can you feel the furious pace and nature of Saul's trip? He has letters from the high priest. He can bind followers of the Way and bring them back to Jerusalem. He has a mission! Maybe the clip of his driven steps is matched by the pace of his racing thoughts, "They won't get away from me! I'll show them they can't escape. I am willing to travel and to do whatever it takes to defend my God and to stamp out this blasphemous teaching! Why I'll even—" And then...

Goal for this week

✱ To *know* Paul and the Philippian church, not just know *about* them

Guiding Questions

✱ What do I know *about* Saul/Paul?

✱ In what ways do I *know* Saul/Paul?

✱ What do I learn from Paul's life that I can apply to my own?

✱ What do I know about the Philippian church and what can I learn from them?

✱ Why was there such a special relationship between Paul and the church at Philippi?

...his world is turned upside down...

Read Acts 9:3-9 for an account of Paul's "upside down" experience.

Getting to know Saul: Now back up to Acts 9:1-2 and contrast it with 9:8-9. Fill in the chart with the contrasts you see regarding Saul.

Saul in Acts 9:1-2	Saul in Acts 9:8-9
Based on your analysis, describe Saul in one word:	Based on your analysis, describe Saul in one word:

In between these two passages, Saul has a unique encounter—a crossroads experience—with...

...the One he thinks had lied and deceived people

...the One he thinks is dead

...the One who knows his name

...the One whom he calls Lord even before he is sure who He is.

✳ And how does Jesus respond? (v. 5)

....

✳ How should these words encourage us when we are experiencing difficulties?

....

....

....

Imagine again the thoughts in Saul's mind, thoughts that now tumble over each other in confusion: "Why am I persecuting *You*? I thought I was afflicting followers of the Way. I thought my targets were men and women, flesh and bone. I don't understand! And why can't I see?!"

But then we see Saul's first acts of obedience, acts that lead to a life marked by obedience.

What two things did he do? (Read Acts 9:6 and 9:8)

....

....

....

Continue reading in Acts 9:10-20 as you answer the following questions:

✳ What is Saul doing in Judas' house? (v. 11) ....

✳ How did the Lord describe Saul to Ananias? (v. 15) ....

✳ What would be Saul's calling or purpose? (v. 15) ....

✳ What would the Lord show Saul about his life? (v. 16) ....

....

✳ Before we continue, speculate on what your reaction would be to such news if you were in Paul's shoes. Write your thoughts below.

....

....

❋   In vv. 18-20, we see Saul's sequenced steps in response to the news. Number the following according to the order in which the action occurred in the passage.

...... He was strengthened.   ...... He immediately proclaimed Jesus in the synagogues.

...... He rose.   ...... He ate.

...... He regained his sight.   ...... He was baptized.

❋   How does this help you *know* Saul a little better?

....

....

....

....

Does your heart go out to Saul now as you visualize his three days in that room? Kneeling. Praying. Wondering. Waiting. Can you feel his yearning to understand who Jesus is and what He accomplished while on earth? Can you sense his wrestling with the personal implications of that understanding—striving to pivot from the clarity of the familiar to the haze of the unknown, struggling to give up his identity based on résumé-worthy achievements, and dealing with remorse over who he had been and what he had done?

Then came Ananias with God's unexpected message. So, Saul had to also process the knowledge he had been chosen to do something amazing, though few would understand. And, in addition to all of this, frequent suffering would accompany his calling. It was a lot to take in!

Examine your own life for a minute. Can you relate in some way? Have you had an eye-opening encounter that changed your perspective on something? A discovery that "rocked your world" to a degree? Or perhaps you have wrangled with releasing an esteemed identity. Not necessarily a title with power or fame, but a meaningful role distinguished by your personal investment in it. Or maybe you are dealing with remorse over choices made before you were saved...or choices made since. You *know* you are forgiven, but that knot in your stomach or the heaviness in your spirit?—well, they testify that *knowing* you're forgiven and *accepting* it are two different things. Or what about the possibility you have felt called to do something that does not make sense from an earthly perspective? Wrapping your mind around the calling is challenging, but the lack of understanding from others can make it even harder.

Near the end of Week 1, Day 1, we mentioned briefly the process of change. What a challenge to sit in the tension of what the change asks of you, then agree (or disagree) to make the change, then prepare for it, and finally, to do it! Let's look back to your questions and ordered list covering Acts 9:10-20 and notice what Saul did in his strenuous situation.

First, Saul prayed as he sat in that place of tension and wrestled with the issues of new perspectives, identity, remorse, and calling; he did not try to figure it out on his own. When Saul was ready, God sent a messenger, and Saul listened. Then, he took simple, basic steps to prepare himself (#1-5 on your ordered list). He did not get "all his ducks in a row" because that style of preparation hinders action. Instead, he did the bare minimum and "immediately" began his ministry (Acts 9:20). I'm sure it wasn't easy, but with God's help and the assurance of godly counsel, Saul let go of the past and embraced the future.

I think we can discern a few things from Saul's process that make the challenges of change a little more bearable:

1. Pray through the time of tension, don't just sit in it. Rely on God's grace to help you release the past and accept the future. (P.S. Don't expect this step to be easy. Remember Paul's three days.)

2. Make simple preparations, not burdensome ones. Get ready for the immediate future and trust God for the additional equipping you will need.

3. Do what God asks when He asks. Remember, "one who is faithful in a very little is also faithful in much" (Luke 16:10).

And whenever God brings His messenger(s) alongside you in this process, recognize the value of wise counsel and godly support. You and I may not complete the change process as quickly as Saul, but I think we will tread paths of joy through the process more easily when we learn his steps.

In closing today, we will look at just a few verses to learn about Saul in his new role. These scriptures help us *know* Saul better by answering two questions.

1. How was Saul different after the encounter on the road to Damascus?

    a) 2 Corinthians 4:8-10

    b) 1 Corinthians 15:9

    c) Galatians 1:10

2. How was he the same after the encounter on the road to Damascus?

    a) 1 Corinthians 15:10

    b) Galatians 2:12-14

    c) Acts 13:4 (Hint: In Acts 26:11, Paul says he "persecuted them *even to foreign cities.*" [italics, mine])

What a testimony to our Sovereign, Creator God! Long before He called Saul, God equipped him with the desire to work harder than his peers, the courage to stand for what he believed, and the willingness to travel for his mission. God used Saul's strengths, but He changed his desires. No longer would Saul persecute Christians; instead, he would be persecuted for Christ. No longer would he act in pride; in contrast, he would serve in humility. And no longer would he seek to please men; rather, to please God.

I don't know about you, but I feel more at peace working through these last exercises than I did at the beginning. I think that's a reflection of the peace Jesus brought to Saul's life. May each of us faithfully fix our mind on Jesus and find rest in Him today (Is. 26:3).

WEEK 2, DAY 3

Knowing ~~Saul~~ ~~(Part 3)~~ Paul

Rejoice in the Lord always; again I will say, rejoice. (Phil. 4:4)

As I prepare to write this lesson today, I cannot help but think of the Pixar movie *Up* and a young Ellie exclaiming with her snaggle-toothed grin, "Adventure is out there!"[4] It makes me wonder if Saul knew just how much "adventure" would be "out there" when he prepared himself and began preaching the gospel immediately in Damascus. Maybe he adapted that mantra just a bit to better fit his calling: "Gentiles are out there!" As you imagine him saying it, can you hear the passion in his voice? Do you see the smile on his face? Don't miss the gleam in his eyes! Those things would have been evident, for he lived the rest of his life joyfully fulfilling his mission to share Christ with the Gentile people.

But I'm getting a little ahead. At this point, we need to know a few things *about* Saul so we can *know* him better. Let's take a short trip with him to see how he became such an adventurer...and when he came to be known as Paul. (Hence, the unusual title for today's lesson.)

Goal for this week

❋ To *know* Paul and the Philippian church, not just know *about* them

Guiding Questions

❋ What do I know *about* Saul/Paul?

❋ In what ways do I *know* Saul/Paul?

❋ What do I learn from Paul's life that I can apply to my own?

❋ What do I know about the Philippian church and what can I learn from them?

❋ Why was there such a special relationship between Paul and the church at Philippi?

Read Galatians 1:11-24 and use the passage to fill in the blanks.

From Damascus, Saul went to .... Then, he went back to

.... It was .... years before he went to Jerusalem.

When he did, he only saw .... and ....,

and he only stayed for .... days. Then he went to ....

and ....

Remember that Saul, though a scholar, was a new believer at this time. If he didn't learn about Jesus from the apostles in Jerusalem, how did he develop the understanding that allowed him to know truths deeply and communicate them effectively?

Reread Galatians 1:11-12, then flip back and read Acts 22:12-15 to clarify.

....

....

We learn as the Holy Spirit teaches us. But Saul? *He* learned from Jesus Christ Himself![5] Imagine the time he spent thinking deeply about what Jesus revealed to him. With freshly opened eyes, he could see connections between Old Testament prophecies and their fulfillment in Christ. With deeper understanding, he probably pondered justifications he would use to prove Jesus is the Messiah. Oh, and with reverent humility, he wholeheartedly submitted himself to the One who had shone in his heart "the light of the knowledge of the glory of God in the face of Jesus Christ" (2 Cor. 4:6). Truly, Saul did not waste his privilege of learning from the Master Teacher.

Although Saul's experience is beyond our comprehension, it was followed by a period of years about which we have very little detail in Scripture. Think for a moment about Saul's enthusiasm; it was a characteristic trait of his life. You may have used *enthusiastic* to describe Saul in your letter of recommendation on Day 1 of this week. Although Paul had changed in many respects, he was still driven. Through Ananias, God told Saul what He wanted him to do—and Saul did what he could—but his lived experience wasn't quite aligning with all Ananias had said.

Why do you think God waited about a dozen years after Saul's conversion before calling him to go on his first missionary journey?

....

....

Does this situation apply to your life? Do you know you have a calling and a purpose, but you seem unable to fully live it? How does looking at the delay in Saul's life reassure you?

....

....

....

Now let's take a few minutes to examine that first missionary journey. Read Acts 13:1-3 and answer the following questions.

✳ Where is the church? (v. 1)

....

✳ Who was supposed to be set apart? (v. 2)

....

✳ Who set them apart? (v. 2)

....

✳ You are getting to know Saul now. How do you think he is feeling?

....

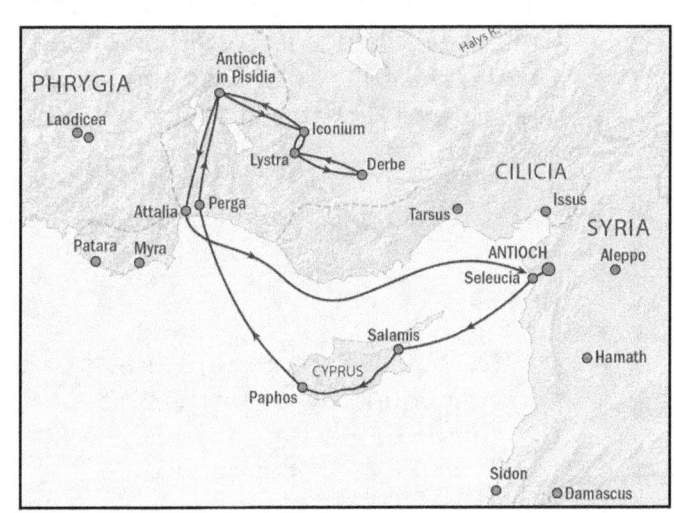

Paul's first missionary journey as chronicled in Acts 13 – 14[6]

Before we read the next set of verses, think through what you have learned about Saul. Reflect on how you *know* him, as well as what you know *about* him.

> Now, read the rest of Acts 13 with that in mind. Jot down things you notice about Saul as you go.
>
> ....
>
> ....
>
> ....

What a change—from "breathing threats and murder" to proclaiming the gospel! I hope your spirit soared a little with Paul as he laid out the whole story, and the Gentiles believed. Did you notice that even though the result was persecution and being driven from the city, Paul and Barnabas "were filled with joy and with the Holy Spirit" (Acts 13:52)? I want to be like that.

Oh, and one more thing: Did you notice Saul began going by Paul in v. 9? On Day 1 this week, we learned that Saul, by virtue of being born in a Roman colony, had a Roman name, Paul; yet he did not use it until this time. From this point on, though, Paul would be traveling extensively in the Gentile world. His Roman citizenship would be of benefit to him in his missionary endeavors. God knew Paul would need that all along, for He knew that "Gentiles are out there!"—and He wanted Paul to help bring them in.

As we close our focus on "getting the lay of Paul's life," think about what you have learned and the "relationship" you have developed with him.

> Do you have common interests or characteristics? How can you apply what you know or learned about Paul to your life? Write your observations below.
>
> ....
>
> ....

WEEK 2, DAY 4

Who is Phil?

*Rejoice in the Lord always;
again I will say, rejoice.* (Phil. 4:4)

As my daughter was growing up, Jesus and softball were her passions. So, it seemed logical that she would order a cross-shaped patch with an embroidered scripture reference when she received her varsity letter jacket. When the patch came in, she was pleased with its appearance and the *Phil. 4:13* reference. We had the patch sewn on the sleeve, and Rachel proudly wore her jacket to school...and someone asked her who "Phil" was.

So, in the interest of clarity, we will discover more about "Phil" as we continue to get a lay of the land of the book of Philippians.

Philippi was a Roman colony rich with history in a region abounding with natural resources. Located just a few miles inland from the port city of Neapolis, it lay on the major trade route that connected Rome to the East.

Philippi was constructed in 356 BC by Philip II of Macedon, father of Alexander the Great. A fortified city in a fertile area, it was known for its natural springs and its mines producing gold and silver. Although later destroyed in battle, Philippi rose to prominence again when Roman Emperor Octavian rebuilt it and encouraged his veteran soldiers to live there.[7] Thus, in the first century AD, the city's approximately 10,000 residents consisted primarily of Romans and Macedonians, then Greeks, along with a few other nationalities.[8] Girded by their history, resources, location, and

Goal for this week

❋ To *know* Paul and the Philippian church, not just know *about* them

Guiding Questions

❋ What do I know *about* Saul/Paul?

❋ In what ways do I *know* Saul/Paul?

❋ What do I learn from Paul's life that I can apply to my own?

❋ What do I know about the Philippian church and what can I learn from them?

❋ Why was there such a special relationship between Paul and the church at Philippi?

Roman citizenship, the people of this town had many reasons to take pride in being known as *Philippians*.

The renowned city was home to a church that held prominence, as well. The Philippian church was the first Christian church established in Europe.[9] Let's discover the story behind this distinction.

In 49 AD, two years after Paul and Barnabas returned from the first missionary journey, they thought it time to revisit the churches (Acts 15:36). However, "a sharp disagreement" (Acts 15:39) arose between the two over the question of John Mark accompanying them, and Silas became Paul's traveling partner for his second missionary journey (Acts 15:40). Let's keep our Bibles open to Acts 15-16 as we join them on their travels step by step.

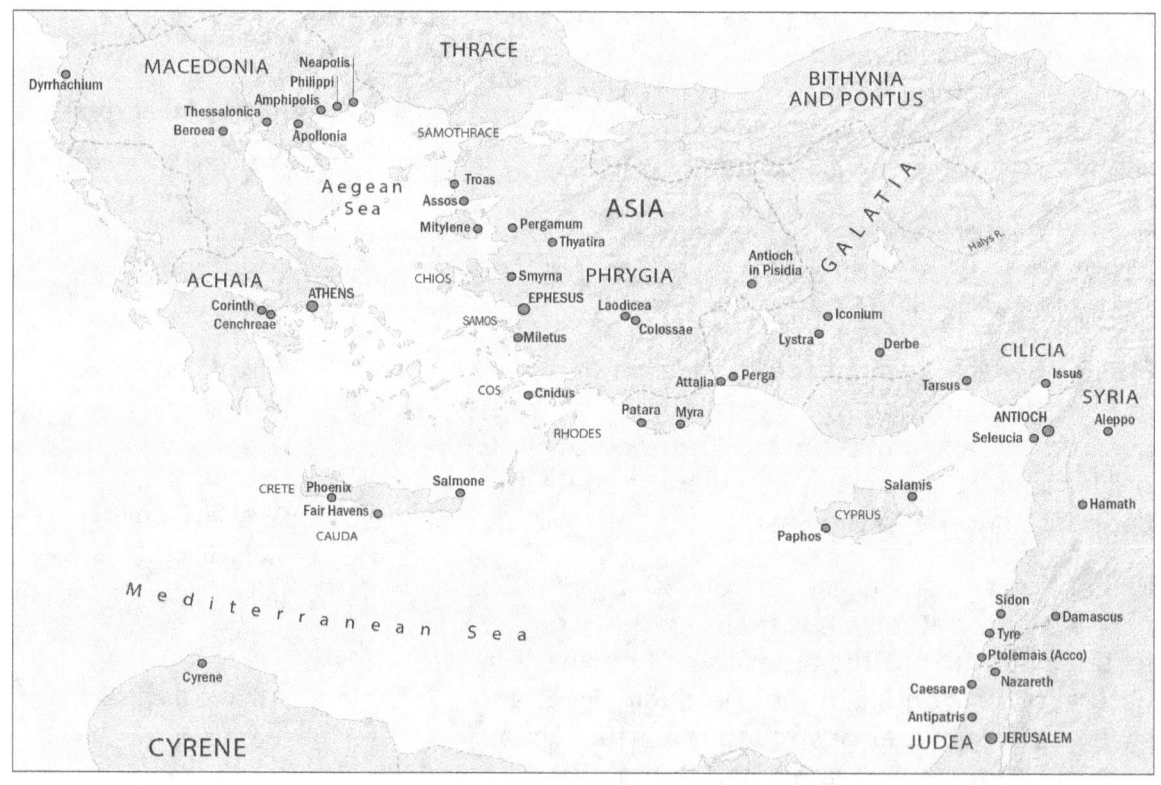

The lands of Paul's second missionary journey[10]

Step 1: Identifying a new protégé

As you read Acts 15:40-16:5, mark the path on the map. Also, write below the name of the young man who joined Paul and Silas, and note his family background.

....

Step 2: Playing red light, green light

As you read Acts 16:6-8, note the "go/don't go" nature of their travels. On your map, mark an **X** where the Holy Spirit stopped them from going; then, continue your previous path through the areas they visited.

Remember Paul's calling and his "get-it-done" nature. Do you think he might have wondered why he wasn't supposed to share the gospel in those places?

Although he may have wondered briefly, I think Paul trusted that God had a plan. He was obedient even if it didn't make sense to him.

Have you ever been in a similar situation? Note below a specific time when you thought you were doing something God wanted, but He closed the door.

....

....

Reflect on your levels of trust and obedience in response to God's direction. How would you respond to the same situation today?

....

....

....

Step 3: Getting a clear vision

We're going to see God's bigger plan come into focus in Acts 16:9-15—literally.

Use the information from these verses to determine if the statements below are true or false. If false, mark out what is incorrect and write what is needed to make it a true statement.

T   F   1. The vision appeared to Paul when he was staying in Macedonia. (vv. 8-9)

T   F   2. Paul concluded he was supposed to leave immediately to preach in Macedonia. (v. 10)

T   F   3. Luke joined Paul, Silas, and Timothy in Troas. (v. 10-11) (Hint: Luke wrote Acts.)

T   F   4. On the Sabbath, Paul went to the synagogue, as was his custom. (v. 13)

T   F   5. Paul spoke to the men and women who were gathered there. (v. 13)

T   F   6. Lydia, a seller of purple cloth, was the first Philippian believer. (vv. 14-15)

The whole story intrigues me when I see God's plan executed because Paul chose to obey and to do so with urgency. So Paul, Silas, Timothy, and Luke arrived in Philippi and spent a few days getting the lay of the city. Usually, when in a new city, Paul went to the synagogue; but here he did not. To have a synagogue, a city must have had ten Jewish men, so we assume the requirement was not met in Philippi.[11] Therefore, when the Sabbath rolled around, Paul and his team reasoned there was probably a place of prayer by the river. There is no record of Philippian men in the group at the river, but Paul and his crew did not let that deter their mission. Contrary to first-century custom, these men sat down and shared the gospel with the women. Ladies, do you see God's hand divinely orchestrating a way to show us how valuable we are in His sight? If you are feeling unloved or unworthy, please read this passage again! God turned Paul away from Asia and Bithynia to make sure the Philippian women heard—and to make sure we hear today. God loves us!

Step 4: Establishing the first church in Europe

Paul was on his way to establishing the first Christian church in Europe. He had baptized its first few members: Lydia and her household. However, the establishment of this church would not go unchallenged. The worship of multiple gods was another characteristic of the lay of the land of Philippi. Due to the Greek and Roman influences, as well as the trade route, the practice was both prevalent and profitable.[12] As a result, Paul and his companions ran into a problem during their stay. But God was at work, and the problem unexpectedly led to another "charter family" for the Philippian church.

> Read Acts 16:16-34 with this context in mind. As you read, you will notice problems and responses. In the table below, a "problem" from the passage is given in the left column. Write the "response" to the problem in the right column. I have provided the first one as an example.

Problem	Response
A slave girl with a spirit of divination kept following and yelling.	(v. 18) *Paul became annoyed and cast out the spirit.*
The girl's owners dragged Paul and Silas before the rulers in the marketplace and accused them.	(vv. 22-23)
Paul and Silas were in the inner prison with their feet in stocks.	(v. 25)

There was an earthquake. All the prison doors were opened, and the prisoners' stocks unfastened.	(v. 27)
Paul yelled that all the prisoners were still in there.	(vv. 29-30)
Paul and Silas spoke the word of the Lord to the jailer and his household.	(vv. 33-34)

Did you notice the last sentence in v. 34? My version says, "And [the jailer] rejoiced along with his entire household that he had believed in God" (Acts 16:34). Take a moment right now and rejoice that you have believed in God.

> Express in writing your enduring, deep delight in knowing that you have believed in Him—another most significant thing!
>
> ....
>
> ....
>
> ....

P.S. If you wonder what happened to John Mark, Barnabas (the encourager) took him on a trip to Cyprus near the same time Paul left with Silas. Although John Mark's life is not detailed in Scripture, we know he continued in ministry, writing the gospel of Mark and becoming "very useful" to Paul (2 Tim. 4:11).

WEEK 2, DAY 5

A special relationship

Rejoice in the Lord always; again I will say, rejoice. (Phil. 4:4)

Do you feel you have a good understanding of the lay of the land of Philippians? I hope so. We will supply additional context today, but let's take a minute to reconnect with our characters first. You do not have to write answers to the following questions, simply make sure you can answer them mentally.

❋ What circumstances in Saul's early life prepared him for leadership?

❋ What characteristics did Saul possess that made him effective in his calling to the Gentiles?

❋ When and why did Saul begin going by his Roman name, Paul?

❋ Why might first-century Philippi be called a prosperous city?

❋ Why did the people of Philippi feel a sense of pride in their city and themselves?

❋ What was it in Paul's background that might have made him feel like he had common ground with the Philippians and could relate well to them?

❋ What about the Philippians' culture made it difficult both to believe in one true God and to live out that faith?

Goal for this week

❋ To *know* Paul and the Philippian church, not just know *about* them

Guiding Questions

❋ What do I know *about* Saul/Paul?

❋ In what ways do I *know* Saul/Paul?

❋ What do I learn from Paul's life that I can apply to my own?

❋ What do I know about the Philippian church and what can I learn from them?

❋ Why was there such a special relationship between Paul and the church at Philippi?

✳ Remember the converts we read about yesterday—a businesswoman, a jailer, and their families. What makes this an unlikely combination of people to start a successful church?

As you answered the last question, contrasts in class, gender, confidence, culture, etc. may have come to your mind. Still, despite the differences, the church worked! This almost entirely Gentile church became somewhat of a hub of early Christianity[13] that Paul would visit twice more on his third missionary journey in 52-56 AD (Acts 20:1-6).

Now look about five years beyond that third journey, at least ten years after the church was founded. Peek into the house in Rome where Paul sits under house arrest. He is dictating a letter to his beloved Philippians and preparing to send it back to them by the hand of Epaphroditus.

Epaphroditus was an emissary of the Philippian church, sent to deliver their sacrificial offering and to aid Paul while in prison (Phil. 2:25-26). In the process of fulfilling this mission, Epaphroditus had become Paul's "brother and fellow worker and fellow soldier" (Phil. 2:25). However, his home church was worried about him because he had also been quite ill during this time. Therefore, Paul felt it best to send him back so the Philippian church could rejoice at his homecoming and Paul could be a little more at ease (Phil. 2:28). Epaphroditus was coming home with Paul's treasured words in hand.

Think about the day Epaphroditus arrives. Can you feel the emotions of a warm reception tinged with excitement? The Philippians fill the church as Epaphroditus opens the letter and begins to share,

> "Paul and Timothy, servants of Christ Jesus, to all the saints in Christ Jesus who are at Philippi, with the overseers and deacons:" (Phil. 1:1).

Rarely does Paul begin a letter without stating his apostleship, but not here. Here, Paul simply refers to himself and Timothy as "servants of Christ Jesus." Perhaps he feels no need to prove himself to the members of the church at Philippi? In addition, he includes Timothy in this greeting, though the rest of the letter is obviously from Paul only. Could it be he is reassuring the church that it is okay to send back Epaphroditus; he is not alone? Whatever the reason for these two alterations to his normal greeting, it is the rest of this address that we should take some time to examine.

> Read Philippians 1:1 again and underline the three recipients of this letter. What does this address tell you about the church in Philippi?

....

....

It had grown! In the years since a businesswoman, a jailer, and their families placed their faith in Christ, this church had increased to the point of requiring organization and roles to oversee the needs of the congregation. How this must have made Paul's heart soar.

Lest you think I exaggerate Paul's affection, take a minute to look at the different ways Paul addressed the Philippian church in this letter. After all, we should always examine Scripture before blindly accepting what someone says. In the book of Philippians, Paul addressed the members of the church using the following terms:

* Saints in Christ Jesus (1:1)

* Partners in the gospel (1:5)

* Partakers with me of grace (1:7)

* Brothers [x 6] (1:12; 3:1, 3:13, 3:17; 4:1, 4:8)

* My beloved [x 2] (2:12; 4:1)

* Citizens of heaven (3:20)

* My joy and crown (4:1)

As you consider Paul's affectionate terms, put an **X** to the right of these three phrases: *partners in the gospel, partakers with me of grace,* and *my joy and crown.* Although some terms appear in Paul's letters to other churches, these three appear only in the book of Philippians. They infer that the Philippian church held a special place in Paul's heart.

Although I have suggested today that Paul's feelings were reciprocated, again we want to verify that through Scripture. What actions do you see in the following verses that testify to the Philippian church's care and concern for Paul?

❋   Philippians 1:19 ....

....

....

❋   Philippians 4:15-16, 18 ....

....

....

Are you getting a feel for the lay of the land with Paul and the Philippians? This was a treasured relationship. More than any other letter Paul wrote, this one emits joy and gratitude. As we study, we will still encounter encouragement and a hint of trouble—similar to other letters—but his focus in Philippians is on joy even though he had been in prison for almost four years when he wrote it.

I want to close today (and this week) with Philippians 1:3-11, then one final thought.

❋   As you read these verses, please do two things: (1) Notice words that Paul uses to communicate his connection to this group of believers, and (2) identify at least one word or phrase that is particularly meaningful to you. Write these in the table provided.

Words of connection	**Meaningful to you**

Did you get a feel for how much Paul loved these people? This was truly a special relationship!

And to an extent, I get it. I treasure these verses for their relevance to my life. I taught high school students for more than twenty years, and I developed some amazing relationships during that time. In addition, my husband and I worked with many of my students at church on Wednesday nights. We prayed for those kids. We took them snow skiing. We planned movies and meals and game nights for them. We had them in our home for weekend retreats. Today, those students have moved on, as have we; yet we still feel a connection to them. I can look at these verses and echo Paul's gratitude to God when I think of or pray for those young people because of the meaningful connections we made as we discussed faith and the power of Christ in our lives. Those relationships led me to write a graduation song based on these verses. I even worked up the courage to sing it for a few students. (Singing is not one of my gifts!) I humbly share it with you now.

The Graduation Song
©2003 Catherine L Hill

Treasured memories, hope-filled dreams—
God has planted in you all these things.
He has a plan for you He'll reveal in time.
But as you start to seek His heart, I want to share a part of mine...

Chorus:
I thank my God every time I remember you.
In every prayer that I pray, I pray for you all with joy.
For your fellowship in the gospel makes me confident of this thing:
That He who started working in you will work in you always.
God will work in you always.

Smiling faces, tear-filled eyes—
Joy and uncertainty both share this time.
We want to celebrate, yet it means letting go.
But God is there, you're in His care, and I pray you'll always know...

Chorus

Bridge (Spoken)

And this is what I pray for you:

That your love will abound still more and more in knowledge and all discernment,

That you may know the things that are excellent,

That you may be sincere and without offense until the day of Christ's return.

I pray that you will be filled with the fruit of righteousness

Which comes only through the knowledge of Jesus Christ,

And—above all else—I pray that you will live your lives to the glory and praise of God.

Chorus + Tag

Tag

My God will work in you always.

GROUP

The Path Behind

Group Discussion of Week 2

....

....

....

....

....

....

....

....

....

SESSION 3

The Path Ahead

Introductory Activity for Week 3

Part I - Group Activity

Part II - Quote and Related Discussion

....

"A .... without a .... is but a ....

A .... without a .... is ....

A .... and a .... are ...."[1]

....

Charting the paths ahead

For the next four weeks, we will identify a vision and a task in each chapter of Philippians. Each week, we will write the vision in the form "Jesus is my ...." What starts as a vision, we will seek to make into an established path through performance of the task.

Consider Chart 1 below. The dashed arrow shows that the vision informs the task, while the bold arrow represents the path of joy we are treading as we work on the task.

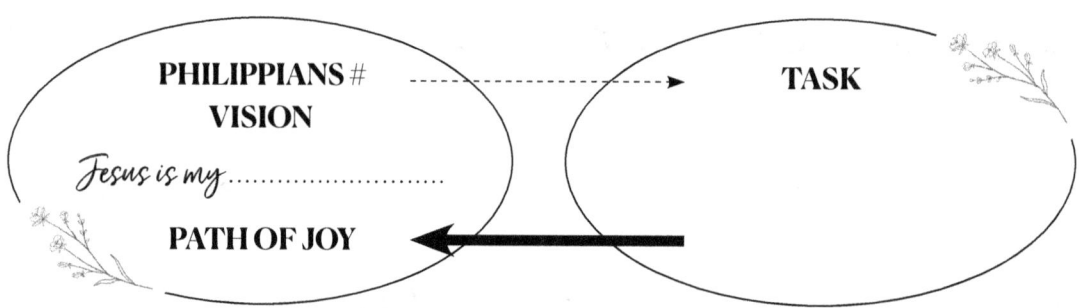

Chart 1: Basic Vision/Path of Joy and Task

As we go through the week, we will use Scripture to develop a greater understanding of what the vision/path means, as well as to determine small actions or mindsets we can use to continuously execute the task. We will gradually build our chart, piece by piece, until it is complete by the end of the week (See Chart 2). This doesn't have to make perfect sense to you now. I just want you to have seen it. The more you see it, the more helpful it will become!

SESSION 3

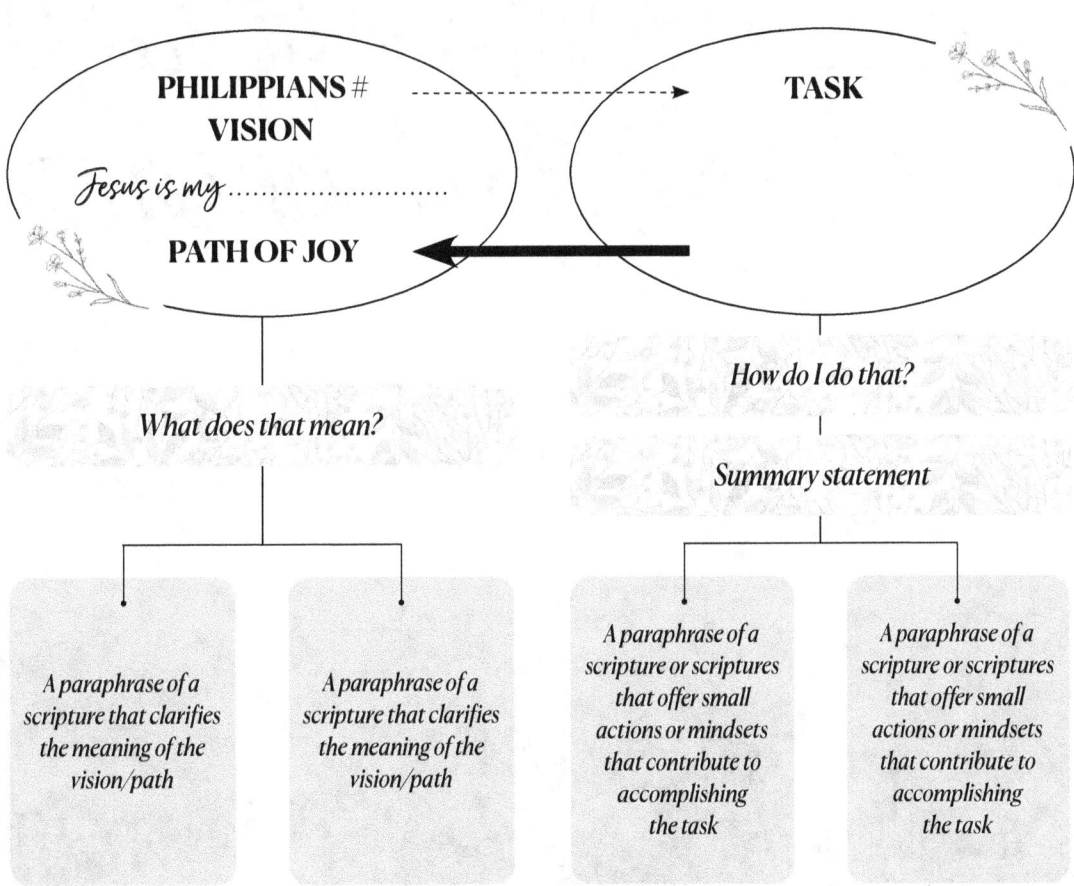

PHILIPPIANS #
VISION

Jesus is my..........................

PATH OF JOY

TASK

What does that mean?

How do I do that?

Summary statement

A paraphrase of a scripture that clarifies the meaning of the vision/path

A paraphrase of a scripture that clarifies the meaning of the vision/path

A paraphrase of a scripture or scriptures that offer small actions or mindsets that contribute to accomplishing the task

A paraphrase of a scripture or scriptures that offer small actions or mindsets that contribute to accomplishing the task

Chart 2: Completed Vision/Path of Joy and Task

Knowing this information will help us start joyfully treading paths now and give us a resource to use in the future as we seek to make our paths of joy "well-worn"!

PART 3
Paths of Joy in Philippians

It's an exciting day! Are you ready to do some path-treading? Me, too! As you do, keep in mind the quote you discussed as a group:

A vision without a task is but a dream.

A task without a vision is drudgery.

A vision and a task are the hope of the world.[1]

Now, to form a two-track road in the pasture as shown in the pictures, the rancher needed a vision of where the path would lead and why. He also required a decisive plan of action for building the path, a way of bringing his vision to reality. He did not cruise randomly across the pasture and hope his paths led somewhere. He intentionally and repeatedly drove paths along fence line and to watering troughs. He forged paths directly impacted by what he learned from his groundwork and his familiarity with the lay of the land. He established paths that purposefully made his care of the cattle an efficient and effective process.

So how do we tread paths of joy? Our discoveries over the next four weeks will lead us to establish each path by identifying a vision and implementing an intentional task to bring the vision to reality. As we tread along, we will build four paths of joy—one from each chapter of Philippians. To get the most benefit from your treading, employ the knowledge gained from your groundwork on joy and call on your familiarity with the lay of the land of Philippians. Make use of all you have learned as you take in the words God has breathed out and allow Him to open your eyes to fresh insights.

One final note: You may be wondering why we need multiple paths of joy. As we go through life, we will have different experiences that lead us to know Jesus more fully. Therefore, a certain path may hold more relevance at a particular time. The truths we study as visions and tasks to build each path will come back into practice throughout our lives, strengthening our connection to our Savior. The steps we take to accomplish the task initially will still be useful in helping us pound down any grass that tries to reclaim our path and roll away any rocks that might trip us in the future.

All right! Let's get started!

WEEK 3

Treading the Path of Joy in Philippians 1

WEEK 3, DAY 1

Finding our Vision/Path in Philippians 1

For to me to live is Christ and to die is gain. (Phil. 1:21)

Imagine the scene. It is early morning, and beams of sunlight are beginning to streak their way through a small window as Paul awakens. He blinks his eyes a few times, looks around the room he has lived in for the past two years, and focuses on the burly Roman guard to whom he is chained. Although he cannot pursue his missionary journeys, Paul acknowledges there are advantages to this house arrest over the two prior years in prison cells. For one, he can have visitors like Timothy and Epaphroditus. They have been so committed in their service to him! He directs thoughts of gratitude to God for this blessing and looks at the guard again. "And, I always have a captive audience for sharing Christ!" He smiles to himself as he enjoys thoughts of how this second advantage has impacted the whole imperial guard (Phil. 1:13)

This morning, Paul has a specific plan in mind for the day. It is an act of loving service, yet also bittersweet. Following his time of prayer, Paul readies pen and parchment for a letter to the church at Philippi. He has been thinking for several days about their generosity in sending Epaphroditus to serve him, along with the thoughtful, sacrificial gifts they sent to meet his needs (Phil. 4:18). What joy Paul feels for these co-recipients of the grace of God (Phil. 1:7). Still, the Philippians' concern regarding Epaphroditus and the illness he has suffered weighs heavily on Paul's heart, and he desires to alleviate their distress (Phil. 2:26-30). Paul takes a deep breath and sighs gently as he acknowledges it is time to send Epaphroditus back to this dear congregation. But not without a special letter written just for them...and, by God's design, for us.*

* This story is a fictional representation of circumstances surrounding the writing of Philippians. Its purpose is to help you better relate to the context and culture. The events should not be taken as factual.

Let's start today as Paul described in this letter. Take a moment and think of a Christian lady you know who brings you joy; someone who lives her life in a way that reminds you to take enduring, deep delight in what holds the most significance. Read Philippians 1:3-5 and pray for that person with gratitude and joy. Below, write the person's name or the prayer as a reminder. If you feel so inclined, jot the prayer on a notecard and send it to the person. I bet it will bring a little joy to her day when she receives it.

....

....

....

....

....

....

For the next four weeks, the purpose of the first lesson is to gain familiarity with the featured chapter. As you read, do so with reflection on what you have learned in this study and with anticipation of what God will show you. Ask Him to reveal the key verse, the vision/path of joy we will tread, and the task establishing that path.

After you pray, read Philippians 1. As you do, write any phrases that have the word *Christ* or a pronoun referring to Christ (*He, Him, His*) along with the verse number. You will also want to write down phrases with the word *gospel* in them. These notes will help you identify the key verse of the chapter, as well as the vision and task for the path.

Goal for this week

❋ To understand and begin actively treading the path of joy in Philippians 1

Guiding Questions

❋ What is the vision/path of joy in Philippians 1?

❋ What does this path mean for me?

❋ What is the task that will help me tread this path?

❋ How do I execute this task effectively?

Phrases with *Christ* - Philippians 1

Example: Servants of Jesus Christ (v. 1)

....

....

....

....

....

....

....

....

....

Phrases with *gospel*

....

....

....

....

....

Now, we want to identify three things. It may be somewhat challenging this first week, but we will do it together. No worries!

❋   First, what key verse seems to summarize the meaning of the chapter? Write the reference below. Hint: It is one of the verses in your list of phrases with *Christ*.

    ....

    ....

❋   Second, use what you gathered from the chapter and the key verse to fill in the following:

                    Jesus is my ....

    This is the first vision/path of joy that we will tread. It is a significant truth in which we hope to develop enduring, deep delight.

❋   Finally, look for a verse that contains a task—something Paul wanted the Philippians to do. This task will also communicate the treading we need to do to establish our path. Write the task below. Hint: The task is in the verses with the phrase *gospel*.

    ....

Now double-check yourself:

❋   The key verse is Philippians 1:21, "For to me to live is Christ and to die is gain."

❋   Vision/Path #1 of Joy is *Jesus is my life*.

❋   The task that helps us tread that path is *Live worthy of the gospel*.

Let's complete our chart below. Tomorrow we will take a closer look at our path and what it means to say *Jesus is my life*.

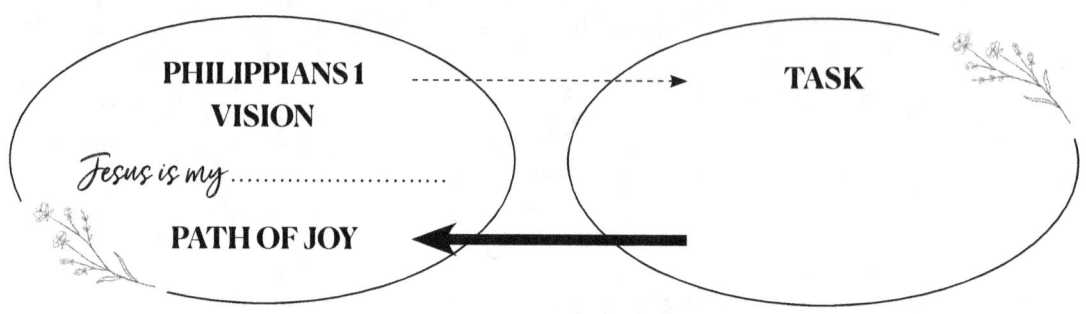

KEY VERSE: For to me to live is Christ and to die is gain.
(Phil. 1:21)

WEEK 3, DAY 2

Vision/Path #1: Jesus is my life.

For to me to live is Christ and to die is gain. (Phil. 1:21)

It was a week after Betsie [my sister] had died in Ravensbruck [a German concentration camp for women during World War II] that I took my place in the ranks of women prisoners standing together in the icy cold of the early morning.

"66730!"

"That is my number," I said weakly as we took our places for roll call...

"Stand on Number 1 on the roll call."

I went to the place to the far right, where I could overlook the entire square of the bleak camp. Standing in the crowd I could not feel the draft, but now, standing in the bitter cold, the wind whipped through my ragged prison dress. Another girl, young and frightened, was sent to stand beside me...

"Why must I stand here?" I asked through chattering teeth.

Her answer was barely audible as it came from her blue lips. "Death sentence."

I turned back to the Lord. "Perhaps I'll see you soon face-to-face, like Betsie does now, Lord. Let it not be too cruel a killing. Not gas, Lord, nor hanging. I prefer shooting. It is so quick. You see something, you hear something, and it is finished."

Goal for this week

✳ To understand and begin actively treading the path of joy in Philippians 1

Guiding Questions

✳ What is the vision/path of joy in Philippians 1?

✳ What does this path mean for me?

✳ What is the task that will help me tread this path?

✳ How do I execute this task effectively?

I looked back at the young girl beside me. "Lord, this is perhaps the last chance I will have to bring someone to You before I arrive in heaven. Use me, Lord. Give me all the love and wisdom I need...

"Do you believe God exists?"

"I do. I wish I knew more about Him. Do you know Him?"...

...For almost three hours we talked while the guards completed the roll call. It was a miracle, for I had a chance to explain many things about Jesus. The prisoners behind us listened, too. I felt happy. Perhaps this was my last chance in life, but what joy![2] [inserts, mine]

The writings of Corrie ten Boom have had a profound influence on my faith. The story recounted above, from her book *Tramp for the Lord,* was not her last chance to bring someone to Christ. She traveled the globe twice after her "inadvertent"* release from the concentration camp and the end of World War II, boldly sharing about her Lord and Savior.[3] Repeatedly, I have turned to her example of complete and total surrender to God as she has described the events of her life, always expressing joy for and awe in her Lord's providential hand. We determined yesterday that *Jesus is my life* would be the vision for our first path of joy. However, for Corrie ten Boom, *Jesus is my life* was no longer a vision but an established path, well-worn from years of treading.

Let's take a few minutes to build our understanding of that phrase using what we know of Paul's life and his words in Philippians 1. Turn back to yesterday's lesson and read the phrases you wrote that had *Christ* in them. On the scale below, place an **X** where would you mark Paul's life.

Uninterested in Jesus; does not make Jesus a priority in life at all	Believes in Jesus, but gets caught up in the things of the world; struggles with a wholehearted commitment to and a complete trust in Christ in everything	Sold out for Jesus; lives with a wholehearted commitment to and full trust in Christ

*The release of Corrie ten Boom was later determined to have been a clerical error, but Corrie called it "a miracle of God."[4]

In Paul's words, we see that he pointed to, surrendered to, and lived for Christ in every area of his life. Christ was his purpose for existence. And in that Christ-focused existence, Paul found joy. Now, think about where you would mark yourself on that scale. We may not be where Paul is, but we do want to move in that direction.

　❋　Let's start by writing below our key verse from chapter one, Philippians 1:21. If Paul lived by this truth and his life was marked by joy, we want to spend a bit of time here.

....

....

....

　❋　We will come back to the first phrase. For now, consider the second phrase in combination with v. 23. What does Paul mean when he says, "to die is gain" (Phil. 1:21)?

....

....

....

I'm sure we can all agree living eternally in the presence of Jesus would be far better than living through the challenges we face on earth. We can understand "to die is gain." The process of getting to that point, though? The thought of what the last few years, months, days, or hours of our lives might entail? That gives us pause.

Come to think of it, the thought of what the *next* few years, months, days, or hours of our lives might entail may give us pause, too. And that's okay. We just need to sit with the thought and process for a moment, then refocus on what holds the most significance: *To live is Christ*...the first phrase...the one that shapes our first path of joy, *Jesus is my life*...the truth worthy of enduring, deep delight.

We can see evidence of thoughtful processing in today's opening story. The thought of how she might die gave Corrie pause as she prayed for something specific, but it didn't spark panic. She *responded* to the situation, rather than *reacting* to it.[5] If you remember from Week 1 Day 1, we learned that joy, when defined as a virtue, directs our thoughts, feelings, and actions toward what God intends. In the "pause" space, that is what Corrie did—she directed her thoughts and feelings to God's purpose, and then acted in *response* to that purpose. After the brief prayer, she shifted her attention to the person beside her and to that person's eternal salvation. When Corrie shared Jesus in that moment, she set aside her own desires and honored Christ. She abandoned the temporal to embrace the eternal. Corrie stepped expectantly and courageously onto a path of enduring, deep delight: *Jesus is my life.* As she did, she showed the young girl how to tread that path, too, and Corrie felt joy.

Can we see a similar pattern with Paul? In Philippians 1:19-20, there are phrases that reveal Paul has made a habit of processing in the "pause" spaces when facing challenges throughout his ministry. In fact, for these verses Paul was responding by simply restating truths learned previously as he guided his thoughts, feelings, and actions to what God desired. Afterward, he made a purposeful statement that shed light on what it meant for Jesus to be his life. Let's write those *truths learned in the pause* and *purposeful* phrases below:

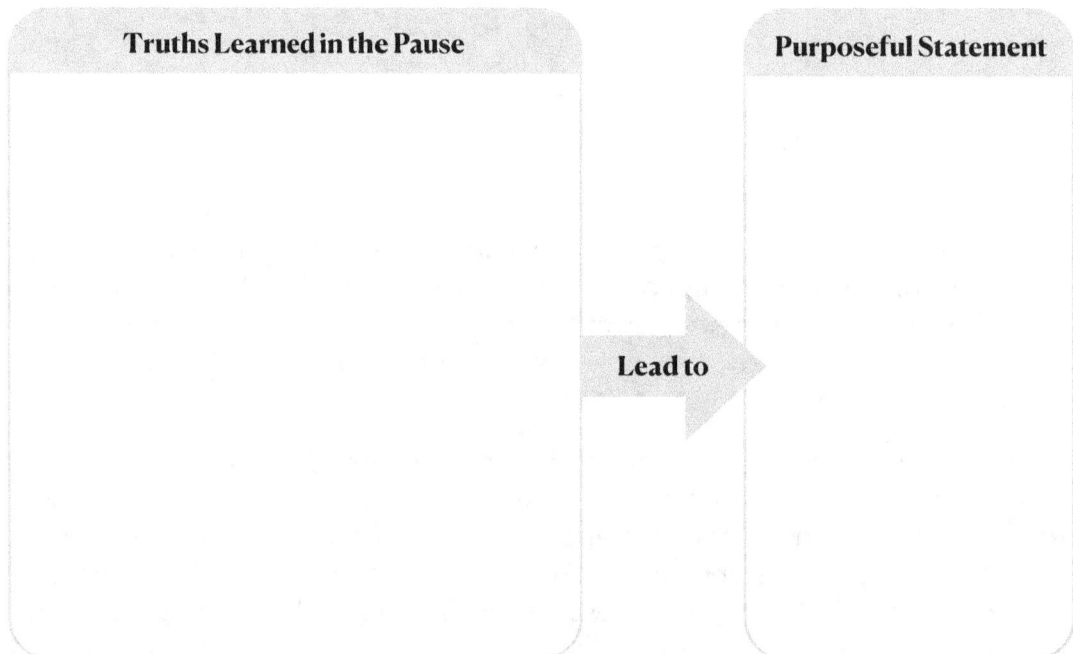

Truths Learned in the Pause

Purposeful Statement

Lead to

Now, let's look at Philippians 1:22-26 and repeat the process. Here, though, we see a little more processing, not simply restating, as Paul considered what might be in store for his life.

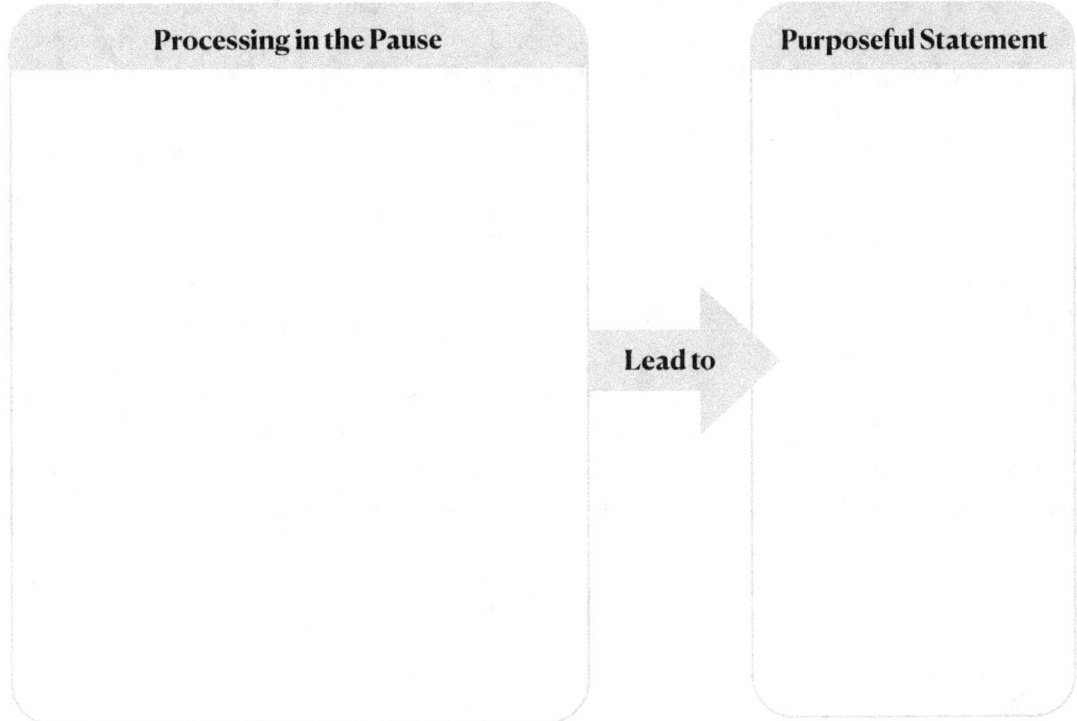

These two passages should lead to a better understanding of what it means to say *Jesus is my life*. In vv. 19-20, Paul stood on established truths. He relied on the prayers of the Philippians and the support of the Spirit of Christ for deliverance, whether by life or death. With his face tilted up and his head leaned forward[6] in hope, he confidently anticipated his life would be so full of Christ-honoring courage that shame could find no crack or crevice in which to poke its ugly head. These truths kept fear at bay and allowed Paul to purposefully state, "I will honor Christ in life or in death." Then, in vv. 22-26, Paul went through a bit of an internal tug-of-war. He loved serving Christ, but—oh!—the thought of *being* with Him! Nevertheless, for the continued growth and joy of the Philippians, Paul believed he would remain and carry on his earthly ministry. He boldly declared he would sacrifice his own desires to glorify Christ. Sandwiched between these two purposeful statements of honoring Christ and living sacrificially for Christ is that key verse: "For to me to live is Christ, and to die is gain."

Think about a difficult situation you faced recently. Now, think about pausing to respond in a way that reflects Jesus is my life. What truths do you find in these verses that you could begin storing in your mind? Identify truths the Holy Spirit could prompt you to recall in the "pause" that would direct your thoughts, feelings, and actions toward God's intentions. (Note: We must have the help of the Holy Spirit; we can't do this alone.)

....

....

Paul's purposeful responses on the previous pages clarify the vision that will become our path. Let's state them explicitly: The vision/path of joy from Philippians 1 is *Jesus is my life*. That statement means (1) I honor Christ in my life and in my death (v. 20), and (2) I sacrifice my desires to glorify Christ (vv. 23-26). We will look at the task that helps us move this from vision to path over the next three days. For now, use this to fill in the chart below.

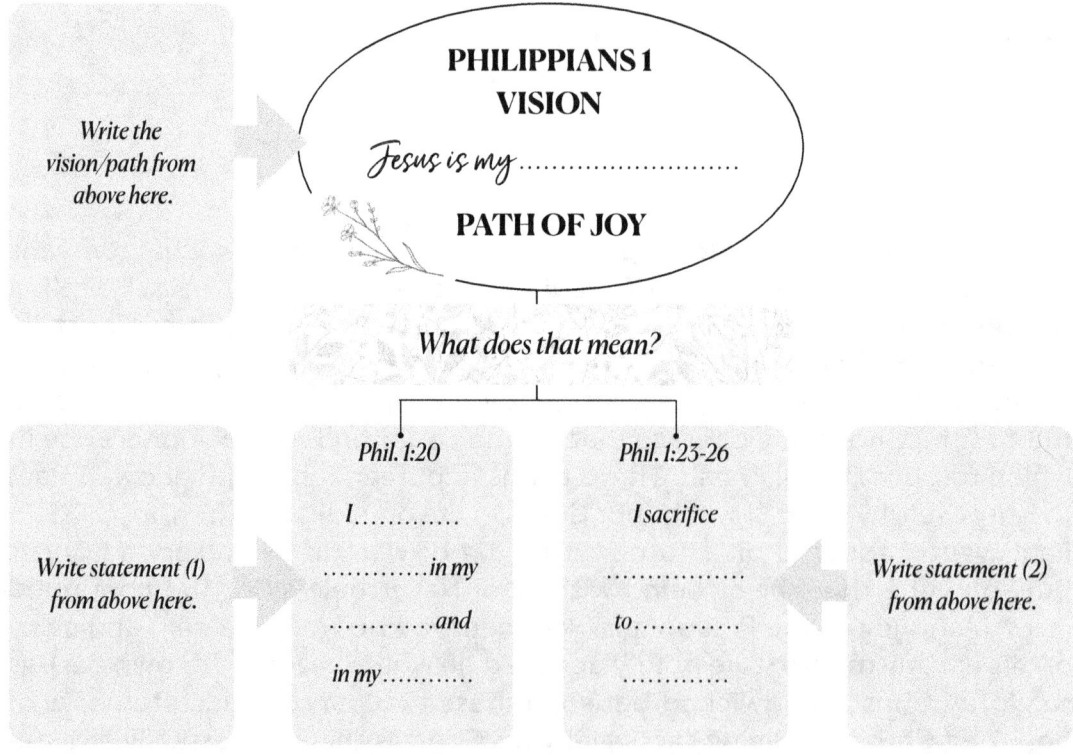

Write the vision/path from above here.

PHILIPPIANS 1 VISION

Jesus is my ....

PATH OF JOY

What does that mean?

Phil. 1:20

I.............
.............*in my*
.............*and*
in my...........

Phil. 1:23-26

I sacrifice
....
to.............
....

Write statement (1) from above here.

Write statement (2) from above here.

KEY VERSE: For to me to live is Christ and to die is gain. (Phil. 1:21)

In closing today, a word of clarification may be necessary. You and I *have* life in Jesus when we place our faith in Him for our eternal salvation but saying "He *is* my life" is different. That statement moves us to a place characterized by deeper relationship and stronger dependency.

In difficult times, *Jesus is my life* calls us individually to pause, rise above circumstances, and focus on living for Him. In the mundane trappings of everyday life, *Jesus is my life* raises our eyes from laundry and cooking and cleaning and work and commitments that want to drive our days...to...take...a...deep...breath...and fix our attention on Christ and His will for that day. In moments of quiet, *Jesus is my life* beckons us to sit with Him in gratitude and intimacy rather than filling the quiet with the noise of the world. Basically, *Jesus is my life* provides us with a godly perspective of living. It is a path marked by complete trust that allows us to respond in accordance with God's purposes rather than react. It is a path that leads us to honor Him in life or death and to willingly sacrifice our desires that He may be glorified. It is a path of joy.

The statement Jesus is my life moves us to a place characterized by deeper relationship and stronger dependency.

WEEK 3, DAY 3

The Gospel

For to me to live is Christ and to die is gain. (Phil. 1:21)

Goal for this week

✳ To understand and begin actively treading the path of joy in Philippians 1

Guiding Questions

✳ What is the vision/path of joy in Philippians 1?

✳ What does this path mean for me?

✳ What is the task that will help me tread this path?

✳ How do I execute this task effectively?

Familiarity is a funny thing. Although the old maxim says *familiarity breeds contempt*—and it might if you ate hamburgers every meal for a couple of months—more often it seems to breed disregard. We begin to take things for granted, using them without acknowledgment. We rarely stop and intentionally appreciate washing machines or cars or running water or even consistently good health. We tend to accept them as part of life... until they're not.

Yesterday, we established a vision for our first path of joy, *Jesus is my life,* and we studied the meaning of that statement. (Glance back at yesterday's chart if you can't remember what it means.) The first day of this week, we also found a task in Philippians 1 to help us tread that path.

Write below the task we identified and the scripture reference for it.

....

....

....

....

If we practice living worthy of the gospel of Christ daily, that practice will become a habit that influences our behavior. The truths of the gospel will continually grow stronger in our minds until they exert a greater power in the "pause" than our old reactive thoughts. We will be more likely to obediently, safely, and healthfully choose the path *Jesus is my life* because we have found enduring, deep delight in the significance of that truth.

At least we can if we know what the *gospel* is.

But we do know, don't we? It's summed up pretty well in 1 Corinthians 15, right?

* **1 Corinthians 15:1, 3-4.** "Now I would remind you, brothers, of the gospel I preached to you, which you received, in which you stand...For I delivered to you as of first importance what I also received: that Christ died for our sins in accordance with the Scriptures, that he was buried, that he was raised on the third day in accordance with the Scriptures."

Perhaps the issue at times is not a lack of knowledge of the gospel, but an over-familiarity with it. Perhaps, as we go to work each day and attend church each week, we settle into a routine and the gospel that should inspire joy and awe in us...doesn't. It's not that we aren't grateful, but the gospel may be such a part of our lives that it doesn't garner much regard, while the pressures of the world clamor for attention.

So, let's take a day to step out of those pressures. Set them aside for a while. As we go through various scriptures, slow down and let awe take over. Anticipate the delight of joy. Even though the passages will probably be quite familiar, allow yourself to discover them anew and to stand amazed at God your Father and Jesus your Savior. Then, let's do it again tomorrow...and tomorrow...and tomorrow...until *wonder* is our natural reaction to the truths of the gospel. Until there is no chance of us taking the gospel for granted. Before you begin, pause, and breathe a prayer asking God to bless today with wonder and awe and joy.

Read the following verses. Below each reference, write the words used to characterize God:

Revelation 1:8	Psalm 50:6	Isaiah 57:15

Our God, who is self-existent and exalted above all, has a nature that does not change: He is and always has been and always will be righteous and holy. Yet He took the time to form man in His image, to breathe into man the breath of life; in part, for the purpose of relationship with Him. As we know, though, the first man (and woman) listened to the deceitful words of the serpent and disobeyed God's command to not eat of the tree of the knowledge of good and evil.

Underline the results in the verse below.

❋ **Romans 5:12.** "Therefore, just as sin came into the world through one man, and death through sin, and so death spread to all men because all sinned."

Because God dwells "in the high and holy place" and sees all of eternity at once (Is. 57:15), God could see in an instant that one black spot of sin and the consequence of death spread like spilled ink from a giant inkwell...

...flowing beyond the Garden of Eden

...streaming down through all of time

...flooding your soul

...engulfing mine

...staining all mankind.

Adam's sin made us sinners—enemies of God. His sin left all of us eternally separated from God and sentenced to death. His sin marked us as unworthy and unable to be in the presence of the One who is holy and righteous because of the blackness of our sin-stained souls.

Unless, somehow, our God could remain just (righteous[7]) while also acting as Justifier (the One who "declares sinners righteous in His sight"[8]) (Rom. 3:26). He could not simply overlook our sin for that would be contrary to His nature. No, someone would have to stand in our place and willingly take the punishment of God's wrath against all sin. That "someone" would have to be perfect to qualify as worthy of making us righteous in God's sight. No human could ever meet that standard. For that reason, despite the condition of humanity and the great personal cost, "God so loved the world, that he gave his only Son, that whoever believes in him should not perish but have eternal life" (John 3:16).

"For God so loved the world..." (John 3:16)

Use the word bank at the top of the opposite page and the references beside each blank to sketch a portion of the awe-inspiring gospel. (Note: I used the English Standard Version (ESV) for the following.)

At just the right .... (Gal. 4:4), God sent Jesus. Jesus willingly took on .... (Heb. 2:14) to be made in the likeness of men. While He lived on the earth, He was .... (Heb. 4:15) in every way we are, yet He remained .... (Heb. 4:15). Although He was fully God, He was .... (Phil. 2:8) to His Father even when it meant .... (Phil. 2:8). It wasn't easy. In the Garden of Gethsemane before He was crucified, Jesus asked His Father three times to .... (Matt. 26:39, 42, 44). He sweat great .... (Luke 22:44), and He prayed with .... (Heb. 5:7). But, in everything, He still submitted and obeyed, yielding .... (Matt. 26:39, 42, 44) to that of His Father. So, for our sake, God made Him .... (2 Cor. 5:21) even though He had never sinned, so that when we place our faith in Him, we might become the .... (2 Cor. 5:21). Because we were .... (Col. 2:13) in our trespasses, He was delivered up for our .... (Rom. 4:25). Because He was raised to life for our .... (Rom. 4:25) (raised so that God could declare us righteous in His sight) we have been made .... (Col. 2:13). Our debt has been .... (Col. 2:14) and we have been .... (2 Cor. 5:18) to God through Christ. Christ has been .... (Acts 2:33) and He now appears in the presence of God .... (Heb. 9:24)! Therefore, even though sin reigned in .... (Rom. 5:21), grace reigns through .... (Rom. 5:21) leading to .... (Rom. 5:21) through Jesus Christ our Lord!

WORD BANK

Trespasses	Without sin	Obedient
Flesh and blood	Loud cries and tears	His will
Drops of blood	Death on a cross	On our behalf
Exalted	Dead	Alive together with Him
Death	Let the cup pass from Him	Time
Canceled	Justification	Righteousness of God
To be sin	Tempted	Reconciled
Righteousness	Eternal life	

Read that through one more time, allowing awe and wonder and joy to flow over you. Jot below any key phrases or scripture references that God has used to prompt these thoughts.

....

....

....

....

....

....

God's plan allowed Him to be both just and Justifier. God's provision made a way for all who place their faith in Christ and believe in His saving work to say with conviction, "God has declared me righteous in His sight." It was a plan that existed before time (Eph. 1:4; Titus 1:2), was implemented at just the right time (Gal. 4:4), and extends beyond time (John 3:16).

How I pray that the gospel never becomes too familiar for you or me. How I pray that it *does* become a significant matter in which we can always find enduring, deep delight!

Joy in Justification

"I have been saved."

"For God so loved the world, that he gave his only Son, that whoever believes in him should not perish but have eternal life." (John 3:16)

"If you do the crime, you gotta do the time." I'm sure I heard that on some TV show. Basically, we believe a penalty should be paid for wrongdoing. We expect it. It violates our sense of justice when a person does something wrong, and he or she doesn't suffer any consequences. We feel that way, and we're not perfect. Imagine how God feels, in His complete righteousness and perfection, when we sin, committing a crime of rebellion against His authority.

And yet, according to Scripture, in *justification* God declares us righteous in His sight. In this courtroom drama, the Righteous Judge offers an unexpected, exceedingly gracious sentencing option, "Although the wages of sin is death (Rom. 6:23), I have made a way for you to be righteous by grace through faith (Eph. 2:8) because I love you! I sent My only Son whom I love dearly to pay the penalty for your sins by dying in your place (1 Cor. 6:20; 1 Peter 2:24). You can't do anything to remove the penalty yourself (Eph. 2:9). My salvation and the forgiveness of your sins is a gift (Rom. 3:24). You can receive this gift and the promise of eternal life through faith in My Son, Jesus. Will you be saved?"

The steps to place your faith in Christ or to share with someone else how they can do the same are given below, along with a prayer to receive God's gracious gift.

1. **Repent.** Repentance is a change of mind that leads to a change in behavior.[9] Admit you are a sinner, and you cannot make yourself good enough to stand before a holy God. Cease self-reliance for righteousness and fully rely on God's provision through Christ.

2. **Believe.** Believe that Jesus is the Son of God, He lived a life without sin on earth, He died for our sins, and He was resurrected from the dead. Trust that Jesus' death on the cross and His resurrection was enough for God to declare you righteous in His sight. Believe Jesus Christ alone is your source of salvation.

3. **Confess.** Confess that Jesus Christ is Lord (Master[10]) of your life. Relinquish your control to the authority of Christ. Acknowledge His sovereignty and live in the confidence that He will always act in your best interest.

Prayer

Dear God, I confess that I am a sinner, and I acknowledge I cannot save myself. I believe that Jesus Christ, Your Son, died on the cross for my sins, was buried, and rose again for my justification. I trust that His death was enough to pay the penalty for my sins. Therefore, I confess Jesus Christ as my Lord and Master. I yield control of my life to Him. In Jesus' name, Amen.

When someone repents, believes, and confesses as described above, then prays the prayer of faith, that person has been saved. A lifelong walk with Christ begins. There is assurance of righteousness in God's sight now and forever. The person receives the Holy Spirit as a guarantee of eternal life, and the Holy Spirit produces...(wait for iiiitttt)...JOY (Gal. 5:22)!

WEEK 3, DAY 4

The Task: Live Worthy of the Gospel (Part 1)

For to me to live is Christ and to die is gain. (Phil. 1:21)

Goal for this week

* To understand and begin actively treading the path of joy in Philippians 1

Guiding Questions

* What is the vision/path of joy in Philippians 1?

* What does this path mean for me?

* What is the task that will help me tread this path?

* How do I execute this task effectively?

Random thoughts as I start the day: I think I will cook meatloaf for dinner tonight (my husband's favorite). I wonder if I will need to go to the grocery store first. We may be low on ketchup...

* Did you catch the vision? Meatloaf for dinner. (I can actually "see" my husband's happy dance!) It will be a reality, but it's not yet.

* Do you know the task? Make the meatloaf: Dig your hands into a bowl of hamburger meat, eggs, breadcrumbs, and seasonings to mix them together; then, form a loaf and bake.

* Anything else? Yes, there are a few preliminary things (like gathering ingredients) that make the task doable.

That's where we are today—those preliminary steps that make possible the task of treading the path *Jesus is my life*. Really, we started yesterday. To *live worthy of the gospel*—to make that task doable—we needed to find wonder in the gospel. There is not much motivation to live worthy of something if it doesn't inspire awe and joy, so take a minute now to go back and read p. 100. We don't want to find wonder once; we want it to be our natural reaction to the truths of the gospel.

Let's take a couple more preliminary steps we will glean from Philippians 1:27.

Read Philippians 1:27 and write below two key words that are each repeated twice.

....

....

....

The first repeated word is *gospel*...again? Yes. It is the same gospel, but Paul spoke of it in specific ways in this letter to the Philippian church. You wrote them down on Day 1 of this week. The first mention (v. 5) recognized that the Philippians partnered with Paul in the gospel. In other words, there was a common interest for a common purpose. Check the boxes for the actions related to the gospel occurring in verses 7 and 12. (v. 16 is similar to v. 7.)

☐ Pray for the spread of the gospel   ☐ Approve the gospel

☐ Defend the gospel   ☐ Advance the gospel

☐ Confirm the gospel   ☐ Preach the gospel

Read Philippians 1:27 again, and let's focus for a moment on the actions of the last two phrases.

Which phrase from v. 27 seems to align more with the action in v. 7 and which with v. 12?

.... 1. standing firm   A. Philippians 1:12

.... 2. striving   B. Philippians 1:7

Do you see that the first action conveys the same message as v. 7? "You stand firm" is the Greek word *stēkete*, and it means "to be stationary," as in "to persevere."[11] If someone is challenging you, you are going to stand your ground, confirming and defending your beliefs. The second phrase in v. 27 emphasizes the action of v. 12. The Greek word for "striving" is *synathlountes*, and it means "to wrestle in company with, i.e. to seek jointly."[12] When placed back in the second phrase, "the thought may be that we are unitedly to fight for [the gospel's] growing power in our own hearts and in the hearts of others."[13] This is an offensive advancing of the gospel.

Now turn your attention to the second repeated word: *one*. Look at these words that appear throughout this chapter.

* To all the saints (v. 1)

* You all (vv. 4, 7, 8, 25)

* Partnership (v. 5)

* Partakers with me (v. 7)

* Brothers (v. 12)

* One spirit, one mind (v. 27)

* Side by side (v. 27)

Check the box that you think best represents Paul's use of the word *one* in v. 27.

☐ Individuality   ☐ Unity   ☐ Cannot be determined

With respect to the gospel, neither offense nor defense is a solo performance. Paul emphasized united efforts for the gospel throughout this chapter.

What are the benefits of unity in efforts for the gospel? Is joy one of those benefits? You might reflect on Bible study groups, church ministries (for members and for outreach), or mission trips to help answer this question.

....

....

....

....

....

We need one more piece of information to integrate the ideas of unity with advancing and defending the gospel in the first part of Philippians 1:27. In Ephesians 4:1, Colossians 1:10, and 1 Thessalonians 2:12, Paul says to *walk* worthy. Here, however—in the letter to the church in Philippi—he emphasizes worthiness of their "manner of life" (1:27). That phrase, *let your manner of life*, means "behave as a citizen."[14]

Recall the lay of the land of Philippi we studied in Week 2, Days 4 and 5. Philippi was a Roman colony, and veteran soldiers had been encouraged to settle there.

> Based on this background, why might Paul have emphasized citizenry, unity, advancing, and defense?

....

....

....

....

....

....

The Philippians knew what it was like to be part of a distant empire. They didn't live in Rome, but they lived by Roman laws and held all the rights and privileges of Roman citizenship. Distance did not diminish the fact they were united with all Romans in all territories as proud, loyal citizens. In addition, because many of the people of Philippi were veteran soldiers, the citizens knew what it was like to be expected to defend and confirm their territory, as well as to advance the boundaries of Rome. They knew they belonged to the greatest empire of its time, and it was a privilege to live worthy of the Roman way of life.[15]

Look at the mastery of Paul's choice of words in this verse! When Paul encouraged the church at Philippi to have a manner of life worthy of the gospel, he drew on their *cultural* understanding to aid in their *Kingdom* understanding.

With that one phrase, he related their citizenship to being citizens of God's Kingdom without actually being in heaven, gave a fresh understanding to unity and loyalty, and shifted their thoughts to living according to Kingdom expectations with Kingdom rights and privileges. With the last couple of phrases, Paul associated the idea of a call to battle—sometimes defending, sometimes advancing, always united in efforts for the faith of the gospel. In this one verse, so well written, Paul reminded them they belonged to a powerful Kingdom, and it was a privilege to live worthy of God's Kingdom way of life!

✳ Read Philippians 1:28. Notice the word that reveals the church at Philippi was truly called to battle for the faith of the gospel:

The Philippian church was to be united, not frightened by its
.... (v. 28).

✳ Does that indicate problems inside or outside the church? ....

So we know this church was battling outside opposition. How does this "battle for the faith of the gospel" apply to us today? In other words, what outside influences threaten the unity of believers currently? (Note: You may want to consider both your country and other countries in your response.)

....

....

....

Now, let's connect this as Paul intended: The Philippians were to live as worthy citizens, united in the defense and advancement of the gospel and unafraid of those who opposed them.

What is your initial reaction to Paul's encouragement to not be frightened of anything in v. 28? Why?

....

....

....

But in 1 Corinthians 2:3, Paul wrote, "And I was with you in weakness and in fear and much trembling."

If Paul admitted his fear in this verse from Corinthians, what might he have meant in Philippians 1:28?

....

....

....

Although Paul spoke in 1 Corinthians 2:3 of his "weakness," "fear," and "trembling," he did not let these apprehensions hinder him in his mission in Corinth or anywhere else! Paul continued to intentionally direct his thoughts, feelings, and actions to God's purposes. He responded to his fears by relying on truths from Scripture rather than reacting with alarm, and that is a key point in Philippians 1:28.

Frightened in this verse conveys the reaction of a startled horse,[16] rearing up, resisting control, seeking escape without rational thought as to how. Remember, though, Paul's language made connections to a military perspective in 1:27-28. When the first century Philippians heard the admonition, they probably envisioned a unit of brave soldiers embroiled in battle who kept their heads and fiercely fought together for a greater purpose. It was a stark contrast to fearful individuals who abandon their calling in a panicked flight to preserve personal safety. Furthermore, the Philippians would have known that, whether standing firm or advancing, an army of courageous, united soldiers sends a foreboding message to the enemy.

In closing today, let's continue developing the chart from Day 2. It's a little bigger than it was, but you can still complete the left side as you did previously, along with the task we began "stepping" into today. Look back if necessary. We will examine it further once you're done.

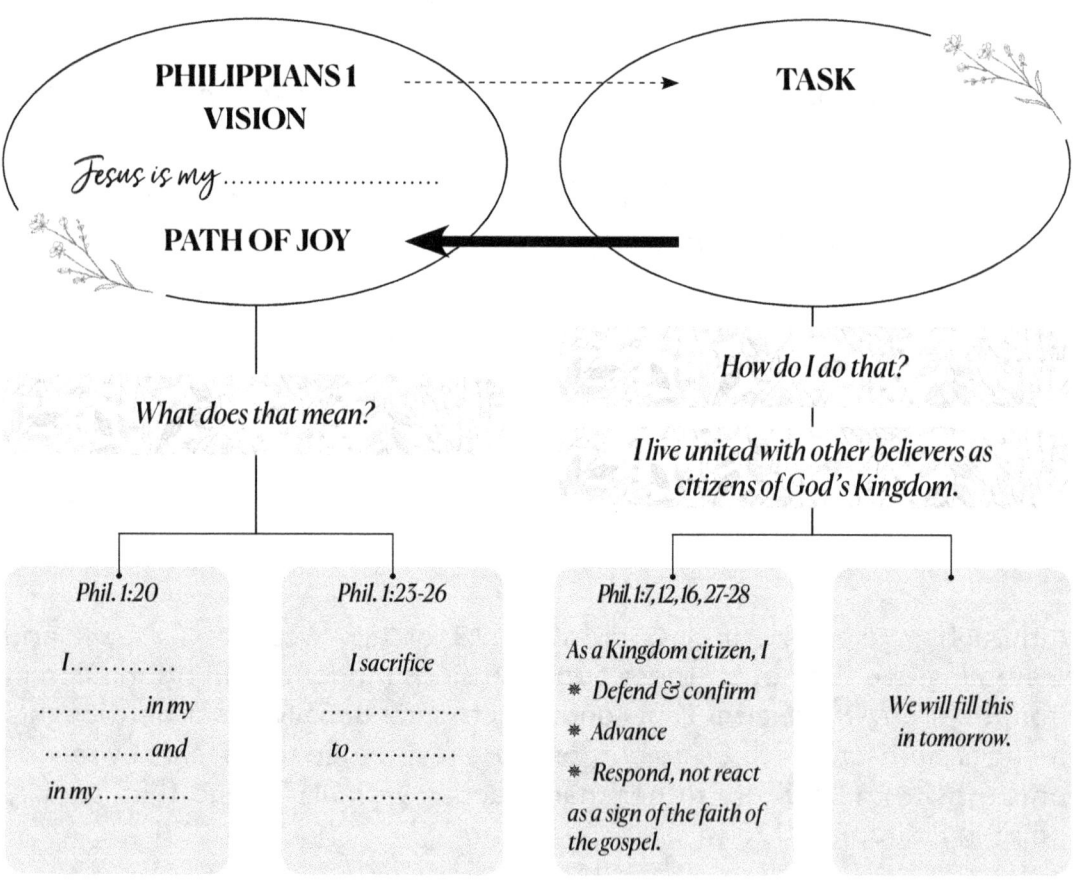

PHILIPPIANS 1 VISION

Jesus is my ....

PATH OF JOY

TASK

What does that mean?

How do I do that?

I live united with other believers as citizens of God's Kingdom.

Phil. 1:20

I.............

.............in my

.............and

in my.............

Phil. 1:23-26

I sacrifice

....

to.............

....

Phil. 1:7, 12, 16, 27-28

As a Kingdom citizen, I
* *Defend & confirm*
* *Advance*
* *Respond, not react*

as a sign of the faith of the gospel.

We will fill this in tomorrow.

KEY VERSE: For to me to live is Christ, and to die is gain. (Phil. 1:21)

We now know the vision for the first path—*Jesus is my life*—and we know it means *I honor Christ in life or death,* and *I sacrifice my desires to glorify Christ.* The dotted arrow represents use of the vision information to help us identify the task: *Live worthy of the gospel.* The thick, dark arrow signifies the start of a well-worn path of joy.

However, between the dotted arrow and the thick arrow, there's a lot of treading to do. To begin the task of treading, we needed to take a few preliminary steps to help us tread rightly. (Not "tread lightly." We are stomping these paths, ladies, and our goal is to be rightly equipped to stomp them well!)

In the chart, I filled in the steps we took today. We spent a lot of time in those details, though, so let's pull back a minute and get some perspective on our path. There is joy in living united with other believers. There is joy in living as privileged citizens of God's Kingdom. There is joy in recognizing who God is and knowing what you believe about Him and the gospel (defend and confirm). There is joy in knowing why you believe the gospel and in seeing others come to believe it as well (advance). There is joy in knowing God's truths so well that they allow you to respond in self-control rather than react. The joy in these steps creates in us a greater desire to *live worthy of the gospel,* which is the worthwhile task of treading a habit of joy that yields the path *Jesus is my life*—a path of enduring, deep delight in what holds the most significance!

WEEK 3, DAY 5

The Task:
Live Worthy of
the Gospel (Part 2)

*For to me to live is Christ and
to die is gain.* (Phil. 1:21)

Goal for this week

❈ To understand and begin
actively treading the path
of joy in Philippians 1

Guiding Questions

❈ What is the vision/path of
joy in Philippians 1?

❈ What does this path mean
for me?

❈ What is the task that will
help me tread this path?

❈ How do I execute this task
effectively?

We should have a pretty good idea now how
to tread our first path of joy: *Jesus is my life.*
Let's start today by finishing a story from Week
2 as we prepare for our last preliminary steps.
Remember the disciples who were beaten and
released on the advice of Gamaliel? If not, you
can review the account in Acts 5:17-42. Do you
think those disciples responded or reacted to
the beating? The questions below will guide you
in answering this.

Read Acts 5:40-42, then answer the following
questions.

a) What did Peter and the apostles do as they left
the presence of the council? (v. 41)

....

b) Of what were the apostles worthy? (v. 41) Does this perspective surprise you?

....

....

c) Not surprisingly, the disciples "responded." Even so, would this have been your response and perspective if you were in their shoes? Why or why not?

....

....

....

d) Referring to v. 42, fill in the blank: "They [the apostles] ....
    teaching and preaching that the Christ is Jesus."

Are these actions amazing to you? Why or why not? Have you ever had
to suffer shame for your faith?

....

....

....

....

Any rule followers out there besides me? That "just-as-easy-to-ask-forgive-ness-as-permission" saying? Nope! I don't buy it. If you're a little like this, too, the idea of rejoicing at being "counted worthy to suffer dishonor" (5:41) is challenging! And then, to continue doing the very thing that resulted in incarceration and beating?! No matter how many times I read these verses, I am awed by these men, their response, and the well-worn path of joy they modeled.

However, the last two verses of Philippians 1 convict me of the need to rede-fine "trouble" or "suffering" from the perspective of Scripture when it is for the sake of Christ.

Read Philippians 1:29-30 and note below the two things granted to you for Christ's sake.

1. ....

2. ....

The first "granting"—belief in Christ—may bring an immediate smile to your face. The concept that belief in Christ is a *gift* reminds us again that God chooses us. He blesses us with the faith to believe in Him. We *get* to believe! The Philippian jailer who accepted Christ on Paul's first trip understood this, for he "rejoiced along with his entire household that he had believed in God" (Acts 16:34).

And then there is the second "granting." How did you react when you read that?

....

....

Whoa, things got heavy in a hurry! Did anybody else kind of stop breathing for a second when reading this part of the verse? Suffering for the sake of Christ is a gift? Almost immediately I became the frightened horse mentioned yesterday that reacts, seeking to escape the terror, except there's not any terror right now. All I did was read the verse.

Then I took a breath. God forewarned Cain in Genesis 4:7 and Peter in the Gospels (Matt. 26:34; Mark 14:30; Luke 22:34; John 13:38) of coming temptations. In these verses in Philippians, He is using both Paul's and the Philippians' current suffering to forewarn us of coming suffering. We shouldn't be surprised when we suffer for Christ's sake. God is giving us time now to prepare for a response rather than a reaction. If we acknowledge the fear or frustration now, we can calmly and purposefully store truth so we can direct thoughts, control feelings, and limit actions to what God intends when suffering hits.

Let's start practicing now. The following table has verses in the left column; on the right is space to write the truths you glean that promote response rather than reaction. Don't restate the verse. Write something brief you can mentally retrieve quickly when needed. I provided an example.

God's Word	Tells me...
"...through many tribulations we must enter the kingdom of God." (Acts 14:22)	*Expect suffering/tribulations.*
"Not only that, but we rejoice in our sufferings, knowing that suffering produces endurance, and endurance produces character, and character produces hope, and hope does not put us to shame, because God's love has been poured into our hearts through the Holy Spirit who has been given to us." (Rom. 5:3-5)	
"for God gave us a spirit not of fear but of power and love and self-control." (2 Tim. 1:7)	
"Beloved, do not be surprised at the fiery trial when it comes upon you to test you, as though something strange were happening to you. But rejoice insofar as you share Christ's sufferings, that you may also rejoice and be glad when his glory is revealed." (1 Pet. 4:12-13)	
"In this you rejoice, though now for a little while, if necessary, you have been grieved by various trials, so that the tested genuineness of your faith—more precious than gold that perishes though it is tested by fire—may be found to result in praise and glory and honor at the revelation of Jesus Christ." (1 Pet. 1:6-7)	
"Rejoice in hope, be patient in tribulation, be constant in prayer." (Rom. 12:12)	
"Our hope for you is unshaken, for we know that as you share in our sufferings, you will also share in our comfort." (2 Cor. 1:7)	
"And after you have suffered a little while, the God of all grace, who has called you to his eternal glory in Christ, will himself restore, confirm, strengthen, and establish you." (1 Pet 5:10)	

Now, read through the right-hand column and preach the truth about suffering to yourself. Then preach it again. *Then preach it again!* As you practice thinking these thoughts, you are redefining suffering. In addition, you are firing and wiring some great pathways in your brain that will make a response of joy more likely than a reaction of fear! (Week 1 Day 4)

Throughout Scripture there are examples of saints who have suffered for their faith. Hebrews 11:35-40 provides examples difficult to read yet ending with hope in God's provision. Following that passage are the first two verses of Hebrews 12—the ultimate encouragement and perfect example of joy in suffering.

These verses also tie in with our use of visions and tasks, as well as our emphasis on the gospel. God's vision was to make a way for us to have eternal life through faith in Jesus. Jesus' task was the cross. To accomplish the task, Jesus focused beyond the suffering to a time of joy with His Father and those He redeemed. The accomplishment of that vision and task truly is the hope of the world. Let's close this portion of today's lesson with these two verses, then do a little path-treading!

* **Hebrews 12:1-2.** "Therefore, since we are surrounded by so great a cloud of witnesses, let us also lay aside every weight, and sin which clings so closely, and let us run with endurance the race that is set before us, looking to Jesus, the founder and perfecter of our faith, who for the joy that was set before him endured the cross, despising the shame, and is seated at the right hand of the throne of God."

Treading the path of joy *Jesus is my life*

Review

Take a few minutes and reacquaint yourself with all we've learned this week. Review the quote about visions and tasks in the introduction. Reread your notes about Christ from Day 1. Ponder again Corrie ten Boom's and Paul's examples of responding rather than reacting in Day 2. Allow the wonder of the gospel to bring joy in Day 3. Remember the joys and privileges of citizenship from Day 4. And preach the truth about suffering to yourself one more time. Find joy in the path *Jesus is my life.*

A full picture

Now, let's complete our chart that displays a full picture of our first path of joy. I have filled in today's steps. Use the completed chart on p. 120 to help with the rest. The goal is not memorization, but familiarization!

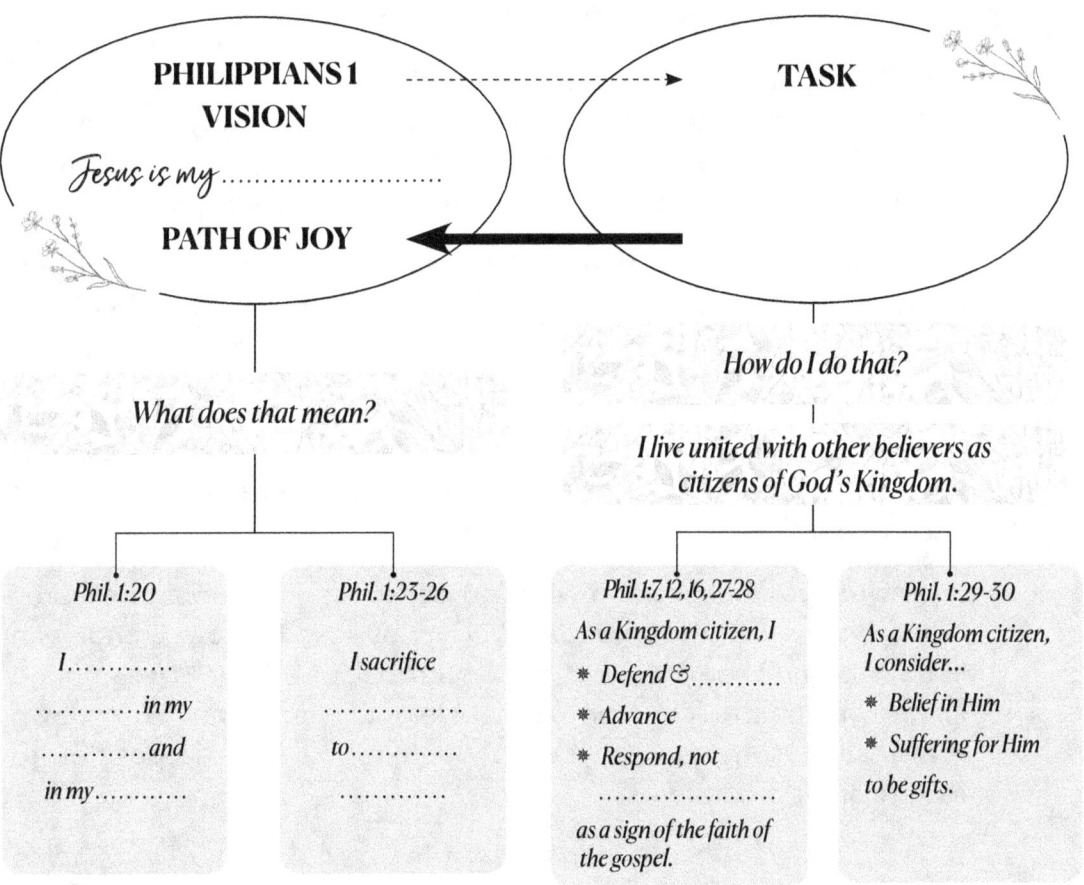

PHILIPPIANS 1 VISION

Jesus is my ....

PATH OF JOY

TASK

What does that mean?

How do I do that?

I live united with other believers as citizens of God's Kingdom.

Phil. 1:20

I.............
.............in my
.............and
in my...........

Phil. 1:23-26

I sacrifice

....
to.............

....

Phil. 1:7, 12, 16, 27-28

As a Kingdom citizen, I
* *Defend &* ....
* *Advance*
* *Respond, not*
....
as a sign of the faith of the gospel.

Phil. 1:29-30

As a Kingdom citizen, I consider...
* *Belief in Him*
* *Suffering for Him*
to be gifts.

KEY VERSE: For to me to live is Christ, and to die is gain. (Phil. 1:21)

Write below any thoughts you want to remember from the review and/or the chart.

....

....

Boots on the ground - Be ready to discuss your thoughts/actions on these with your group!

Finally, sometimes we need practical ideas for how to take the preliminary steps or tread the path. These are a few thoughts I had. Put a check mark beside those you are already doing and an arrow beside those you wish to do. Please add your own thoughts to the list and share them with your group.

* ❋ PRAY! The right-hand side of our "path of joy" chart is a great place to start. Pray that you live worthy. Pray for your community of believers. Pray for the defense and advancement of the gospel. And pray for a sound mind in both soldiering and suffering for the gospel.

* ❋ Live in community with other believers. Find a group of believers if you do not have one. It is difficult to live as a citizen without other citizens. It is difficult to consistently stand for the gospel without support.

* ❋ Be enamored with and awed by the gospel. If your wonder begins to wane, slow down. Let joy overwhelm you as you marvel at His love, His plan to be just and Justifier, and His promise of eternal life through faith in Christ.

* ❋ Know what you believe and why you believe it. Read *Tactics* by Greg Koukl; *Evidence that Demands a Verdict* by Josh McDowell and Sean McDowell; *The Case for Christ* by Lee Strobel; or *I Don't Have Enough Faith to be an Atheist* by Norman Geissler and Frank Turek. Write down what really resonates with you now before you are in a position to need to say it out loud.

    > *...but in your hearts honor Christ the Lord as holy, always being prepared to make a defense to anyone who asks you for a reason for the hope that is in you; yet do it with gentleness and respect.* (1 Peter 3:15)

* ❋ Familiarize yourself with the information on pp. 102-103 so you have a plan to help others place their faith in Christ.

* ❋ Work with Vacation Bible School, go on a mission trip, or sponsor a group of students for a weekend retreat such as DNow. Do something that allows you to advance the gospel and see lives changed.

✳ Memorize verses so you can recall truths that allow you to respond rather than react. There are some great apps to help with this!

✳ Study the lives of those who have lived for Him. Corrie ten Boom, Jim Elliot, Eric Liddell, and others provide great examples of those who considered suffering a gift and truly lived as if *Jesus is my life*.

✳ Compile a list of relevant scriptures as we did today. If you wish, add meaningful quotes from past or present Christian leaders. You can even fix it like a vision board using colors and images. Whatever appeals to you! Keep the list easily accessible for review.

Add your own thoughts below:

....

....

Enjoy time with your group! See you for some joyful path-treading in Philippians 2 soon!

The Path Behind

Group Discussion of Week 3

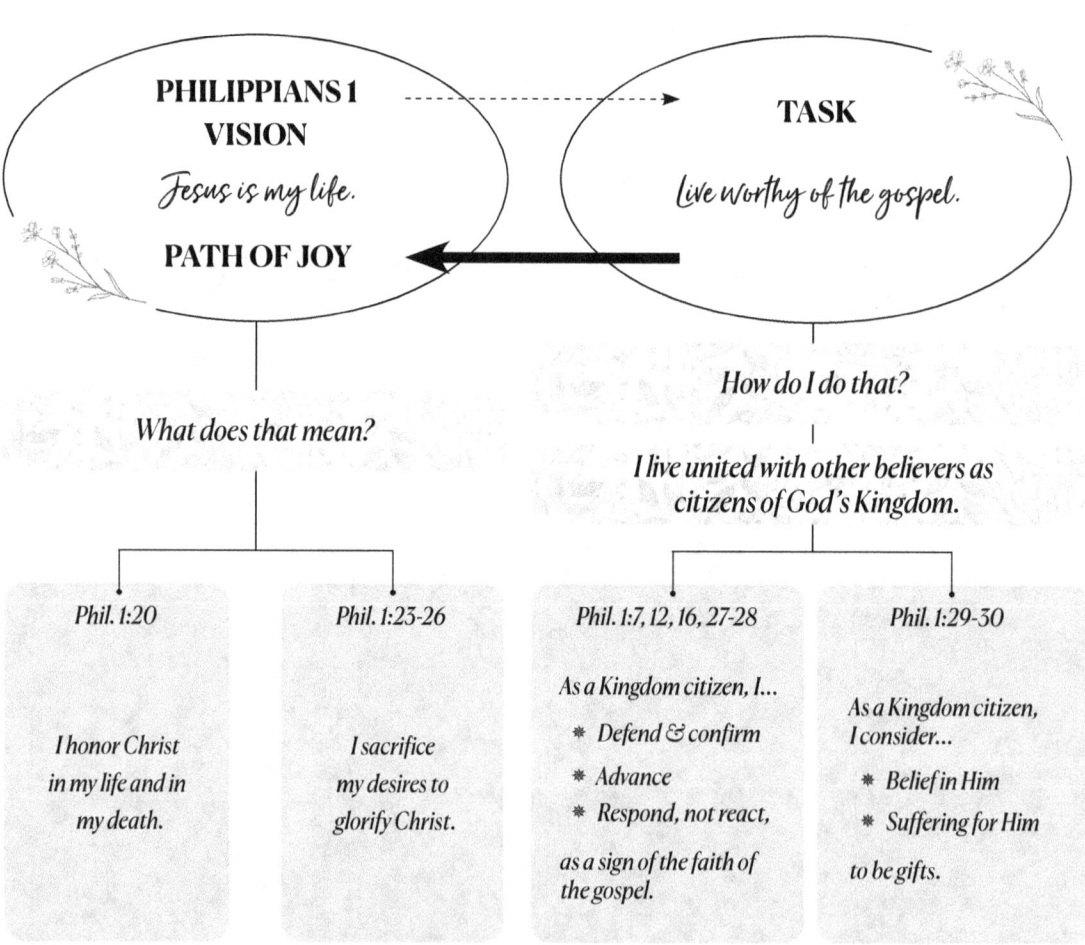

PHILIPPIANS 1 VISION

Jesus is my life.

PATH OF JOY

TASK

Live worthy of the gospel.

What does that mean?

How do I do that?

I live united with other believers as citizens of God's Kingdom.

Phil. 1:20

I honor Christ
in my life and in
my death.

Phil. 1:23-26

I sacrifice
my desires to
glorify Christ.

Phil. 1:7, 12, 16, 27-28

As a Kingdom citizen, I...
* Defend & confirm
* Advance
* Respond, not react,

as a sign of the faith of
the gospel.

Phil. 1:29-30

As a Kingdom citizen,
I consider...
* Belief in Him
* Suffering for Him

to be gifts.

KEY VERSE: For to me to live is Christ, and to die is gain. (Phil. 1:21)

SESSION 4

The Path Ahead

Introductory Activity for Week 4

Part I - Group Activity

Part II - Group Discussion

WEEK 4

Treading the Path of Joy in Philippians 2

WEEK 4, DAY 1

Finding our Vision/Path in Philippians 2

Have this mind among yourselves, which is yours in Christ Jesus. (Phil. 2:5)

Peer inside that small room again where Paul is bound to a burly Roman guard and listen closely. It's just past mid-afternoon, and Paul's chains clank gently as he traces a limited path. The faint scratch of a reed pen on parchment[1] is audible, as well. Timothy is with Paul, attentively capturing each word in script as Paul speaks aloud his letter to the Philippians. Paul sometimes had to dictate his letters because he had trouble with his eyes.[2] Years before, when addressing the Galatians, Paul had closed his letter with "See with what large letters I am writing to you with my own hand" (Gal. 6:11), signaling the use of someone else's script for the earlier part of the letter.

Timothy pauses and rests his hand, patiently waiting as Paul prays before continuing the message he needs to communicate. Together, they have accomplished quite a bit today, but a few more lines are possible before nightfall. The current guard tries to appear uninterested, but secretly waits to hear what more Paul will say. He muses, "With all that is wrong in this prisoner's life, he still speaks of joy? How can that be? What motivates this man to view things from such a different perspective than most people—prisoners or not?"

Paul concludes his prayer. He knows he must address some small issues before they threaten the unity of the church, but he needs to think strategically how to do this. Reflectively, Paul asks Timothy to give him a summary of the letter to this point.

In response, Timothy briefly speaks of Paul's opening lines, his tender expression of love and gratitude for the Philippians, and his communication of the joy they bring him. The young man smiles as he boldly repeats Paul's purposeful statement about choosing to rejoice because the message of

> *Christ trumps the motives of the speakers. Then Timothy, Paul's son in the faith (Phil. 2:22), feels the tug-of-war in his own spirit as he thinks of what might happen to his fatherly mentor. His voice catches slightly as he quotes what Paul considers to be a "win-win" struggle: "to live is Christ, and to die is gain" (Phil. 1:21). He finishes by reading Paul's reminder that, whatever the outcome, the Philippians are citizens in God's Kingdom, and they are called to stand united against opponents of the gospel, even when that means suffering.*
>
> *Timothy's recap seems to settle Paul's thoughts, and he joyfully continues sharing with this beloved church (...and the eavesdropping guard).**

Similarly to last week, this first day's lesson allows time for you to read, reflect, and gain familiarity with the chapter. Before you begin, pause to pray. Ask God to grant insight into the key verse, the vision/path of joy, the task necessary to tread that path, and anything special He wants to say to you specifically. Thank God in advance for all He will show you, for the assurance of finding joy in Him, and for the privilege of bringing Him joy as we seek to glorify Him.

Now, read Philippians 2 as if Paul were trying to inspire the Philippians to do more and be more than they thought possible—a bit like an enthusiastic coach. All coaches know the value of a united team with a common goal and unselfish players. Paul was seeing some areas of concern, so he was addressing them before they impacted the "team" (church) and its effectiveness. Notice his repeated pattern of earnest exhortations supported by compelling examples. (Note: An *exhortation* is "a communication intended to urge or persuade the recipients to take some action."[3] Let's think of it as an *encouraging command*.) Also, pay attention to how Paul occasionally spotlighted the impact of the Philippians' obedience on his own life. You can relate this to how the members of a team take joy in hearing the heartfelt words of their beloved coach, "You make me so proud!" It is a bit of extra motivation.

The following table will allow you to see the pattern of exhortation, example, and impact more easily. The first two verses are somewhat different, so I have completed those. As you read, write a brief, enthusiastic summarization of the exhortation or the name and character trait of the example in the summary column; then, fill in the impact of the action on Paul when that space is open.

---

* This story is a fictional representation of circumstances surrounding the writing of Philippians. Its purpose is to help you better relate to the context and culture. The events should not be taken as factual.

Verses	Summary	Impact on Paul
2:1	Example: *Relationship - What blessings from unity with Christ!*	
2:2	Exhortation: *Same mind! Same love! One in spirit!* *One in purpose!*	*Your unity as believers completes my joy!*
2:3-4	Exhortations (encouraging commands):	
2:5-11	Exhortation (v. 5): Example:	
2:12-16	Exhortations (v. 12, 14, 16):	(v. 16)
2:17-18	Example: Exhortation (v. 18):	(v. 17)
2:19-24	Example:	
2:25-30	Example:	

As you glance over your brief notes above, does Paul inspire you? Are you ready to find joy/more joy in living like Christ? It will benefit both you and others when you do.

Let's finish today by identifying our three key pieces of information.

❋ First, what key verse seems to summarize the meaning of the chapter? Write the reference below. (Hint: It's an early verse with an exhortation.)

❋ Second, fill in what you think our vision/path of joy will be:

Jesus is my ....

You probably wrote the word *example* (or *pattern* or *model*). And those words are perfectly good. However, Jesus is not just *an* example; He is the *ultimate* example. Therefore, I searched for a word that seemed a little more "special"—one that carried more weight in what it conveyed. What I found was the word *paragon,* and you can see why we want to use it as you read its etymology from the *Better Words* website:

"The noun '**paragon**' traces its etymological origins to the Italian word 'paragone,' which means 'touchstone' or 'comparison.' The term 'paragone' was used in the context of testing the quality of precious metals like gold and silver by comparing them to a standard reference, often a black stone known as a touchstone... *Over time, it came to signify a person or thing that is regarded as the embodiment of excellence, perfection, or an ideal standard in a particular category or quality...*"[4] (italics mine)

Jesus is "the embodiment of excellence, perfection, or an ideal standard" in character and conduct. He is the One whom we seek to emulate as we progress in our walk with Him.

Goal for this week

❋ To understand and begin actively treading the path of joy in Philippians 2

Guiding Questions

❋ What is the vision/path of joy in Philippians 2?

❋ What does this path mean for me?

❋ What is the task that will help me tread this path?

❋ How do I execute this task effectively?

Therefore, our vision/path of joy for Philippians 2 will be *Jesus is my paragon*.

❋   Finally, look for a verse containing a task that will help us tread our path of joy, *Jesus is my paragon*. It is an exhortation Paul gave the Philippians. Write the task below. (Hint: The task is in the verses that follow Philippians 2:5-11.)

....

Confirming your thoughts:

❋   The key verse is Philippians 2:5, "Have this mind among yourselves, which is yours in Christ Jesus."

❋   Vision/Path #2 of Joy is *Jesus is my paragon*.

❋   The task that helps us tread that path is from Philippians 2:12: *Work out my salvation*. (Note: Please don't get hung up on the wording here. You are still saved by grace through faith in Christ, not by works. As with each set of lessons, concepts should be much clearer by the end of the fifth day.)

Use this information to complete the portion of our chart that we know. Tomorrow we will gain a clearer vision for our path, *Jesus is my paragon*.

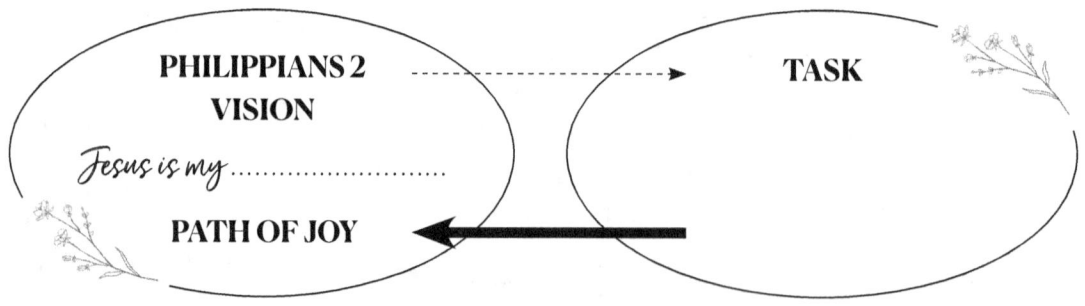

KEY VERSE: Have this mind among yourselves, which is yours in Christ Jesus. (Phil. 2:5)

Also, just in case the guiding quote has slipped your mind, you can review it below. We will use the concepts of visions and tasks each week, and they might not make much sense without the quote.

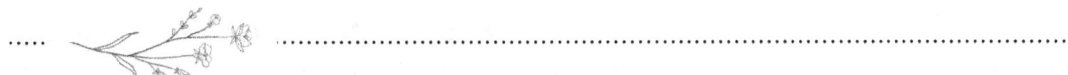

A vision without a task is but a dream.

A task without a vision is drudgery.

A vision and a task are the hope of the world.

Inscription on a church wall in Sussex England c. 1730

WEEK 4, DAY 2

Vision/Path #2: Jesus is my paragon.

Have this mind among yourselves, which is yours in Christ Jesus. (Phil. 2:5)

Goal for this week

❋ To understand and begin actively treading the path of joy in Philippians 2

Guiding Questions

❋ What is the vision/path of joy in Philippians 2?

❋ What does this path mean for me?

❋ What is the task that will help me tread this path?

❋ How do I execute this task effectively?

Charlotte Moon grew up in a wealthy, Southern family who valued faith and education. As she reached her teenage years, though, the faith held dear by her parents failed to garner esteem in her eyes. Oh, but education! That was a different story. She finished high school in 1856 at age fifteen, and soon began attending the Albemarle Female Institute (college) in Charlottesville, Virginia.[5]

Although the girls at Albemarle received strong encouragement to attend weekly church services and have daily devotions, Charlotte adamantly refused these opportunities even at the urging of her closest friends. Imagine their astonishment, then, when she suddenly decided to attend a revival service with them one evening in December 1858. Secretly, Charlotte's plan was to take notes and show her friends the fallacies of their faith; instead, the truth of God's Word spoke to her heart and mind. Later that night, when her friends were in bed, Charlotte crawled from beneath the covers, knelt on the floor, and gave her life to Christ.[6]

For the next two and a half years, Charlotte faithfully led in ministry opportunities while also excelling in her studies. In May 1861, she and four classmates graduated from Albemarle, the first women in the South to earn master's degrees. Although Charlotte had dreamed of being a missionary, it seemed that prospect would remain only a dream. Family demands during the Civil War, meaningful teaching opportunities thereafter, and a policy prohibiting the appointment of single female missionaries by the Southern Baptist Foreign Mission Board appeared to direct her toward a different path.[7]

Then, in 1872, Charlotte's sister delivered surprising news: She had received approval to travel with a couple as a missionary to Chinese women! That revelation was all it took to reignite Charlotte's desire for mission work. A year later, at age 32, Charlotte was on her way to carry the gospel to the people of China.[8]

Although she had long wanted to be a missionary, this was a sacrificial decision for it required declining a marriage proposal, resigning from her job, and leaving her home. It was a sacrificial decision because she experienced rejection and loneliness as she sought to show Christ's love to those hesitant to receive it. And it was a sacrificial decision because she set aside her traditions to adopt the unfamiliar dress, language, and customs of the Chinese people she would serve and love for the rest of her life.[9] Still, when a friend asked her about retiring in 1903, Charlotte replied, "China is my joy and delight. It is my home now."[10] For 39 years, Charlotte, perhaps better known as Lottie Moon, found joy in obedience to God's calling and humble service to the Chinese people.[11]

> Take a minute to reflect on Lottie Moon's life. Then, read Philippians 2:5-11. In what ways do you see Lottie walking the path *Jesus is my paragon*?
>
> ....
>
> ....
>
> ....
>
> ....

This is not an easy path, is it? Yet, Lottie found enduring, deep delight in the humble service and obedience to which God called her! We will, too, when we trust Him. We need to tread with intentional steps of faith. Through His Spirit, God will supply the joy when we are in His will!

The beauty of Philippians 2:5-11 naturally draws our attention. We can easily see Christ as our paragon of love, commitment, obedience, self-sacrifice, and service, but why did Paul place this passage *here*?

> Read Philippians 2:1-4.

In 2:1-2, Paul continued to emphasize unity. Basically, he was saying, *Let the blessings of unity with Christ through the Spirit overflow into your relationships with other believers. Encourage each other to live united in love and purpose. That would fill my cup of joy to the brim!*

> Have you ever observed or been a part of a group of believers who lived out their relationship with Christ in their interactions with each other? Did the experience "fill your cup of joy"? Record the experience below.
>
> ....
>
> ....
>
> ....

As we move into 2:3-4 though, there is a slight shift in Paul's tone.

Last week Paul addressed external threats. What type of threats merited his concern in these verses?

☐ Additional external threats   ☐ Internal threats   ☐ Cannot be determined

Internal unity is vital when facing external threats. However, maintaining internal unity is not easy. Unity with Christ is necessary to overcome the internal threats all relationships face. Therefore, Paul began by promoting that unity in Philippians 2:1-2, then transitioned to address unity disruption.

In the exhortations in 2:3-4, what "unity disruptors" did Paul call out?

....

....

As Christians, consistent monitoring of our motives is critical. We need to prevent these unity disruptors from having a place in our lives—not in church or marriages or family or work. Selfishness and conceit reveal a greater trust in self than in God. They produce blemishes in our character that hinder our unity in and witness for Christ. Not to mention, they stand in the way of joy!

Now let's examine a single word from Paul's exhortations: *humility*. Chuck Swindoll clarifies the term:

> "This is a supernatural kind of selfless humility that has its source
>
> in our identification with and imitation of Christ. It results in love,
>
> fellowship, affection, compassion, unity, service, and joy."[12]

In the explanation above,

* ✳ Circle the adjective that implies we cannot display this humility on our own.

* ✳ Underline the phrase that sounds like our vision/path for this week. (6 words)

* ✳ Draw a box around the result of humility that has been important in our study today. Mark *joy* the way we did in Week 1.

We are beginning to understand the placement of Philippians 2:5-11. Paul was concerned about unity. Humility is necessary for unity but contrary to human nature, so Paul offered Jesus as the paragon of humility. He presented him to remind the Philippians that *unity* with Christ (2:1) provides unlimited access to the supernatural *humility* (2:3) that maintains *unity* among believers (2:2). Do you see how that flows? Don't miss how the process stamps out pride and self-trust to ensure the effectiveness of the church and the message of Christ persist!

Jesus is my paragon. The consequences of our humble steps on this path will impact path-treaders for generations to come. To guide those all-important steps, Paul gave one more exhortation in 2:5 (our key verse) before he began his incomparable example of humility.

Look up Philippians 2:5 in the ESV and write it below.

I confess my curiosity is aroused by "Have this mind...which is yours" (2:5). If "this mind" *is* ours in Christ, why the command to *have* it? Do we have a choice?

Yes, we do. The whole phrase, *have this mind*, comes from the Greek verb *phroneó*. It means "to direct one's mind to a thing, to seek or strive for."[13] (Note: Some translations use "attitude" instead of "mind" in 2:5. The Greek verb and its meaning remain the same regardless of the English translation.) In this study, we have learned that our minds and brains are different; our minds are what we use when reasoning, focusing, and making decisions. Therefore, we *can* shut off the mind of Christ that is ours! We do so by choosing to focus on ourselves and quenching the Holy Spirit (1 Thess. 5:19). However, we can also choose to *have* the mind of Christ by setting our minds on the things of the Spirit (Rom. 8:5-6; 1 Cor. 2:11-13), trusting God, and purposefully directing our thoughts to Christ's perspective.[14]

Technically, the transition from Philippians 2:5 to 2:6 is a shift from exhortation (encouraging commandment) to example. Oh, but this passage is so much more than just an example! These verses are a divine invitation to gain intimate insight into the thoughts, attitudes, and actions of God the Son regarding His incarnation and into the powerful, loving, joyful response of God the Father! "Hear" these God-breathed verses as their honored guest.

1. "Hear" (read) Philippians 2:6-8, then look at the graphic provided.

2. In the tall box, underline or highlight phrases that help you understand Jesus was "in the form of God" (2:6a). Take a minute to pause and soak in those phrases. Envision your Savior seated in power and glory as He inhabits eternity (Is. 57:15).

3. Now, picture Jesus in all His divine fullness literally stepping out of eternity and down into time. Imagine Him willingly emptying Himself of radiant glory for the frailty of human flesh. The words of Philippians 2:6b-8a should continue that picture of descending "steps" in your mind.

4. In Psalm 22:6-8, God inspired David to give insight into the humility required for the last steps. Underline words that reveal the humility of Christ as He lived out Philippians 2:8b, c.

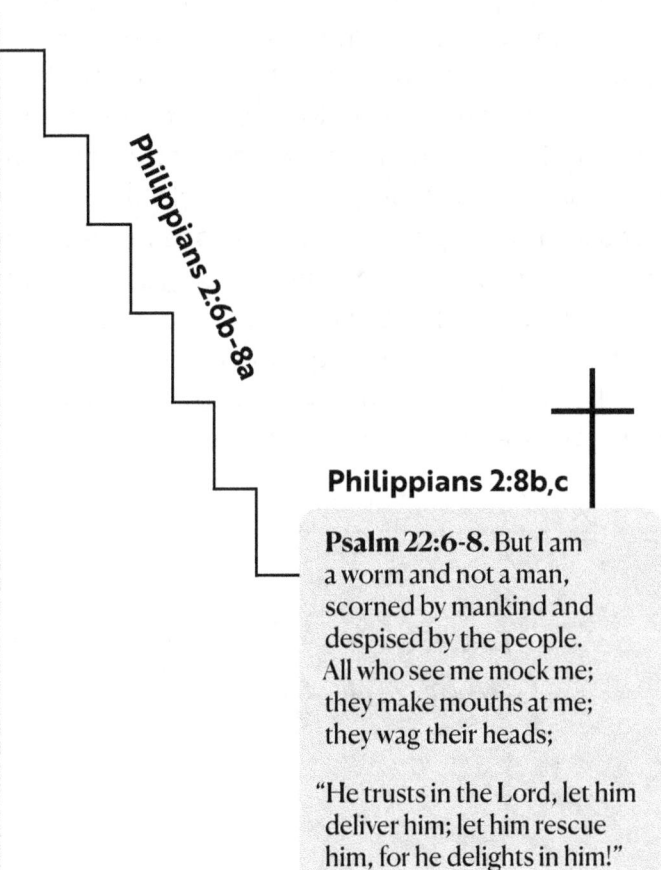

Philippians 2:6a

Colossians 1:15-17, 19. He is the image of the invisible God, the firstborn of all creation. For by him all things were created, in heaven and on earth, visible and invisible, whether thrones or dominions or rulers or authorities—all things were created through him and for him. And he is before all things, and in him all things hold together. For in him all the fullness of God was pleased to dwell,

Hebrews 1:3. He is the radiance of the glory of God and the exact imprint of his nature, and he upholds the universe by the word of his power. After making purification for sins, he sat down at the right hand of the Majesty on high,

Philippians 2:6b-8a

Philippians 2:8b,c

Psalm 22:6-8. But I am a worm and not a man, scorned by mankind and despised by the people. All who see me mock me; they make mouths at me; they wag their heads;

"He trusts in the Lord, let him deliver him; let him rescue him, for he delights in him!"

Aren't you glad the story didn't end there?

With joy in your spirit, "hear" (read) Philippians 2:9-11.

The descending staircase behind him, Jesus now faced a glorious ascension—a high exaltation—back to the right hand of His Father (Heb. 1:3). Truly, the name of Jesus is worthy of all worship! Truly, "Jesus Christ is Lord, to the glory of God the Father" (Phil. 2:11)!

As you reflect on today's lesson, think again about Lottie Moon and the well-worn path of joy, *Jesus is my paragon*. This dedicated woman took Philippians 2:5-11 to heart as she humbly set aside her affluence and joyfully served the Chinese people in obedience to God's call until her death on Christmas Eve in 1912.[15] But she also echoed the call of Paul in Philippians 2:1-4. During her 39 years in China, Lottie Moon wrote many letters to the Foreign Mission Board of the Southern Baptist denomination to enhance their understanding of needs and promote unity of purpose in reaching the lost in other countries for Christ. She persistently and boldly urged them to communicate the need with Southern Baptist churches and church members so all might be of one mind in support of mission work, sacrificially putting the needs of others ahead of their own.[16] In a way, Lottie's urging was that all would find the joy of humbly treading the path *Jesus is my paragon*.

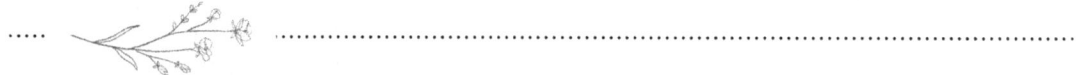

Few will be called to give their lives for Christ; however, each of us is called to live for Him daily.

Now, consider what the vision/path of joy *Jesus is my paragon* means for your own life. Few will be called to give their lives for Christ; however, each of us is called to live for Him daily. Let us purposefully and consistently choose the following: (1) I direct my thoughts to Christ's example of humility as I serve and obey God (Phil. 2:5-8), and (2) I direct my thoughts to Christ's example of humility as I honor others above myself (Phil. 2:3-5). As you envision this humble path of joy in your life, recognize its influence on your unity with other believers now and foresee its impact on the unity of believers until the day of Christ (Phil. 2:16). That potential for enduring influence for Christ ought to prompt a little enduring delight in us.

Let's fill in the chart with what we know. (Note: I placed Phil. 2:5-8 before 2:3-5 because this humility is supernatural. Without a right relationship with God first, we can't live out Paul's exhortation with respect to others.)

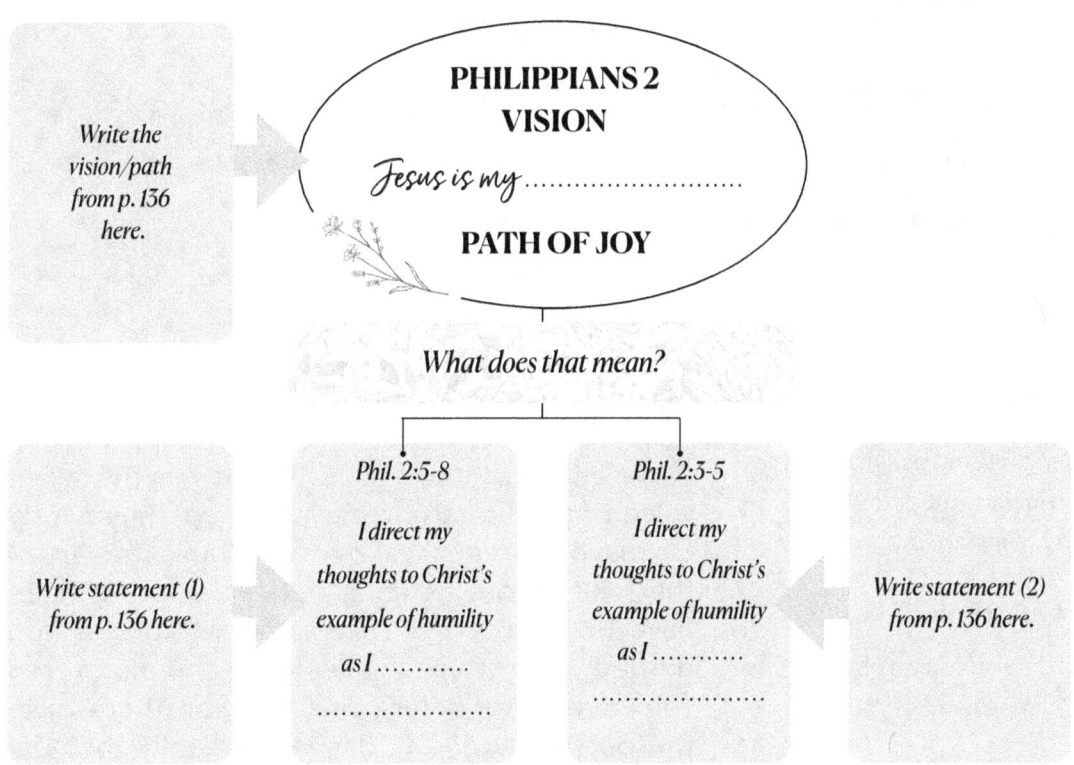

KEY VERSE: Have this mind among yourselves,
which is yours in Christ Jesus. (Phil. 2:5)

And just in case this path still makes you pause...in case emptying and serving and obedience in a self-sacrificing manner still seems like a path you would rather avoid than tread...in case you see the joy in Christ's exaltation but you're not sure how that applies to you, finish today by reading the following passage. Mark in a distinctive way what you are promised in return for your humility.

※ **1 Peter 5:6-7.** "Humble yourselves, therefore, under the mighty hand of God so that at the proper time he may exalt you, casting all your anxieties on him, because he cares for you."

Trust Him. He's got you. Just as *joy* is obedient and safe (Week 1, Days 2 and 3), these verses indicate *humility* is also. Humbly tread the path. Blessings follow obedience. What joy!

WEEK 4, DAY 3

Working out, Working in, Working for

Have this mind among yourselves, which is yours in Christ Jesus. (Phil. 2:5)

Goal for this week

❋ To understand and begin actively treading the path of joy in Philippians 2

Guiding Questions

❋ What is the vision/path of joy in Philippians 2?

❋ What does this path mean for me?

❋ What is the task that will help me tread this path?

❋ How do I execute this task effectively?

"It's empty!"

We've all heard that cry. Perhaps it was the sweet voice of a child raising her juice cup expectantly. Or maybe a teenage boy who drank the last of the milk before heading out the door. It might have been your own frustrated whisper as you hurriedly tried to get a load going and discovered you were out of detergent. Of course, there's also the possibility of any desperate family member needing rescue after failing to notice the telltale brown cardboard signaling the end of the toilet paper!

Regardless of the situation, we understand *empty*. At least, most of the time. Today, we want to begin with Philippians 2:5-11 one more time to glean another truth about our vision/path, *Jesus is my paragon*. It will help us better understand our task, *Work out my salvation*.

Read Philippians 2:5-8. Although not every version uses the word *emptied* in 2:7, the Greek verb is *kenoó* and it means "to make empty,"[17] either literally, as in the introduction above, or figuratively. What do you think the word means here?

....

....

I want us all to be very clear: This does *not* mean Christ emptied Himself of His divinity. He did not in any way cease to be God the Son at any point during His incarnation—not even on the cross. J.I. Packer explains, "When Paul talks of the Son as having emptied Himself..., what he has in mind...is the laying aside, not of divine powers and attributes, but of divine glory and dignity...The impression, in other words, is not so much one of deity reduced, but of divine capacity restrained."[18]

> Take a moment to direct your thoughts to the mind of Christ as you think about your own life.
>
> Now complete the sentences from a Christ-like perspective: When
>
> I "empty" myself by exhibiting humility, I am not ....
>
> .... Rather, I am ....
>
> ....

Emptied does not mean humbling yourself to the point you lose sight of who God created you to be. There is no joy in that! It does mean humbly yielding your desires in obedience to His. Whether this yielding requires restraining authority at home or setting aside glory at work or a more literal emptying of personal desires for godly ones, the unexplainable result is you become *more* of who God created you to be, not less, because you are becoming more like Christ. With that thought in mind and with deep delight in what holds the most significance, read Philippians 2:9-11 one more time.

Jesus was resurrected and exalted on high (Phil. 2:9). He received back the glory He had before the world was created (John 17:5). One day, at His inestimable name, all will bow and worship Him (Rev. 5:13). What incredible significance these truths hold!

From this glorious height of truth and inspiration, Paul turned his attention back to his precious Philippians: "Therefore, my beloved..." (Phil. 2:12).

What compliment does Paul pay the Philippians in 2:12? Why do you think he said this?

....

In Philippians 2:5-11, specifically in 2:8, Paul pointed out that Christ's humility led to obedience. Therefore, when Paul praised the obedience of the Philippians in 2:12, he was deftly pointing them back to *Jesus is my paragon* while also moving them forward to his next exhortation and our current task.

Read Philippians 2:12-13 and answer the following questions.

1. Paul wanted the Philippian believers to be obedient especially in his ....

2. What exhortation did Paul give near the end of 2:12 that he wanted them to obey?

    ....

    ....

Remember, Paul is making this statement in his absence to those who have *already* placed their faith in Christ. They are *already* his partners in the gospel (Phil. 1:5), so he is not dictating the need for works to gain salvation. Although we are about to dig into this more, for now consider this analogy:

> Imagine a child aligning his decisions with what you have taught him, even without your presence. His unsupervised yielding reveals trust in you and respect for your authority. Over time, the repeated "working out" of what you have "worked in" results in an emptying of childish inclinations and a maturity that brings you pleasure.

This analogy affords us a partial understanding of Paul's words in 2:12, but let's look a little deeper.

According to Philippians 2:13, who was truly working in the Philippians and why?

....

....

As he wrote, Paul's future was uncertain. He clarified that the Philippians' obedience should reflect their trust in God, not in Paul. Their growth toward spiritual maturity—toward Christlikeness—was a result of God working in them through the Holy Spirit (Rom. 8:6-8), not his leadership. Paul knew his presence was temporary, but God could and would work in them for His enjoyment (Phil. 2:13) until Christ's return (Phil. 1:6).

Think for a moment about someone you have trusted enough to willingly yield to his or her authority. Are you still acting in obedience to him? Can you hear her voice in your head? We may all smile as that person's voice seems to echo in our ears again, but the question is: Have you consciously trusted God's authority in your life and acknowledged His working in you?

Describe a time when you set aside your desires to trust God, obey Him, and grow in spiritual maturity. Are you going through something that needs this action now?

....

....

....

....

Turn to John 15:1-11 and use it to help you complete the table on the next page. We want to consider Jesus' own words as we seek to better understand what our task requires of us as God works in us.

In this analogy, what is the role of each of the following?		
God the Father (v. 1)	Jesus Christ (v. 1)	You (v. 5)

What are the responsibilities of each of the following?		
God the Father (v. 2)	Jesus Christ (Think about the analogy, not necessarily what is said.)	You (v. 5)
1.		1.
2.		2.

How do you prove you are Christ's disciple & what is the result of that proof? (v. 8)

What is the prerequisite for abiding in Christ's love? (v. 10)

Now let's tie the passages from Philippians and John together.

✳ According to Philippians 2:13 and John 15:4-5, if I try to *work out my salvation* without Christ working in me, I can accomplish **something / nothing**. (Circle the correct word.)

✳ In contrast, the result of *working out my salvation* to tread the path *Jesus is my paragon* when Christ *is* working in me is ....! (John 15:11) (Fill in the blank and mark it as we have before.)

✳ After examining the verses from John 15, what do you think Paul meant by the task "work out your own salvation" (Phil. 2:12)?

....

....

✳ Based on Philippians 2:12-13 and John 15:1-11, which of the following words or phrases accurately characterize our task, *work out my salvation*? Place a check in those boxes.

☐ Cooperative effort ☐ One-time event ☐ Becoming like Christ
☐ Individual effort   ☐ Ongoing process ☐ Earning your salvation

Last week, we saw salvation as a one-time event, God's gift accomplished without any work on our part (Eph. 2:8-9). This week, we see salvation as a cooperative process requiring our participation. This is not a contradiction. Rather, it is a key understanding for all believers: *Salvation is not one or the other; it includes both!*

Through justification, you placed your faith in Christ and were declared righteous by God. You *were saved*. Immediately, you began the process of *being saved*. For as long as you live or until Christ returns, God wants to partner with you to transform you into the likeness of His Son. Through the indwelling of His Holy Spirit, God works in you to help you empty yourself of "self," yield to Him, and become *more* of who He created you to be (Eph. 2:10). Oh, what enduring, deep delight we can find in God's love for and commitment to us. And what humility His love and commitment should provoke in us.

Our task of *working out my salvation*—the ongoing process of *being saved*—is better known as *sanctification*. Sanctification usually refers to "the process of advancing in holiness; use of the believer being progressively transformed by the Lord into His likeness (similarity of nature)."[19] Does that sound a little like the vision/path we want to tread, *Jesus is my paragon*? As you read a portion of the definition of sanctification from *Vine's Concise Dictionary of Bible Words*, underline any words or phrases that relate to your role in the process of sanctification. Circle any words or phrases that refer to God's role or His administration of the process. (Some words or phrases may have both markings.)

This sanctification is God's will for the believer,...and His purpose in calling him by the gospel...; it must be learned from God,...as He teaches it by His Word,...and it must be pursued by the believer, earnestly and undeviatingly,...For the holy character...is not vicarious, i.e., it cannot be transferred or imputed, it is an individual possession, built up, little by little, as the result of obedience to the Word of God, and of following the example of Christ...in the power of the Holy Spirit.[20]

Do you see evidence of you and God working together? What phrases in this definition stand out to you?

....

....

....

....

....

....

....

So, our task, *work out my salvation*, means we cooperate with God in the process of sanctification. I want to address the phrase "with fear and trembling" (Phil. 2:12), though, for I am concerned it might be misinterpreted. Remember that any interpretation we make needs to align both with what we know of a God who sacrificed His Son out of love for us and with Scripture. Therefore, "fear and trembling" should remind us to work in awe and reverence with a proper view of God's holiness (1 Pet. 1:16); to never take lightly the privilege of joint heirship with Christ (Rom. 8:17); and to not shirk our responsibility in the cooperative effort of sanctification (2 Cor. 7:1). Contrary to what makes earthly sense, honoring God in this manner should bring us joy because it flows from our love for Him.

As we close our day, let's tie our learning together with one final observation.

> Review what God works *for* in Philippians 2:13 and recall the roles described in John 15. Now read Philippians 1:9-11 as Paul prays for the Philippians' progress in sanctification. Write below the fruit that comes through our Vine. (Phil. 1:11)
>
> ....
>
> ....
>
> And what does that growing fruit do for our Vinedresser? (Phil. 1:11)
>
> ....
>
> ....

Sanctification is your path to abundant life on earth (John 10:10) as you grow up into Christ (Eph. 4:15). That growth in righteousness, humility, service, and obedience produces His joy in us so our joy is full (John 15:11). As a result, God receives glory and praise, and He experiences joy (2:13). We get to bring God *joy*! Amazing! Let's learn a little more about our task, *work out my salvation*, by taking a few preliminary steps over the next two days. We want to purposefully tread the path of joy *Jesus is my paragon*.

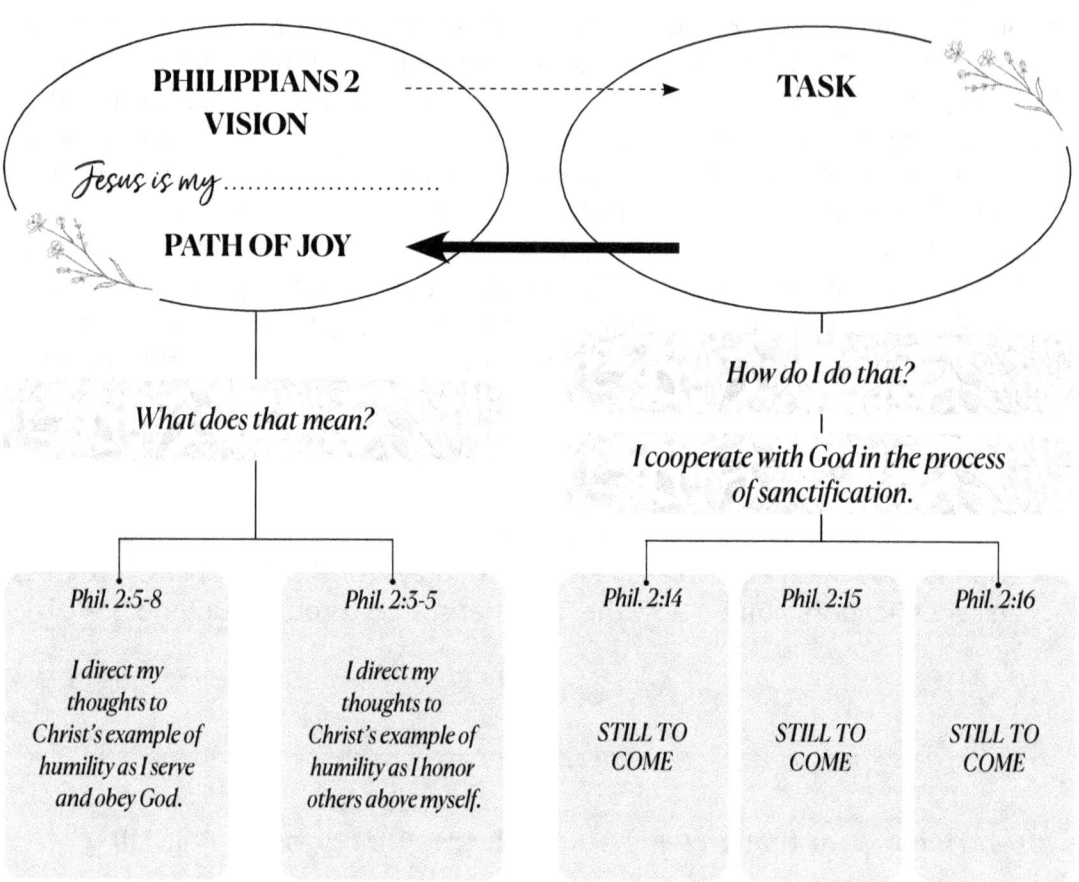

KEY VERSE: Have this mind among yourselves,
which is yours in Christ Jesus. (Phil. 2:5)

(Clarification of chart, if needed: When you have the vision *Jesus is my paragon* from Philippians 2, you desire to purposefully direct your thoughts to humility in your relationships with God and others. The task that moves this from a vision to an actual path, *work out my salvation*, requires your cooperation with God in the process of sanctification. Now, we just need to glean some clarity for this task from Paul's next exhortations.)

Joy in Sanctification

"I am being saved."

"but as he who called you is holy, you also be holy in all your conduct." (1 Pet. 1:15)

"For we are his workmanship, created in Christ Jesus for good works, which God prepared beforehand, that we should walk in them." (Eph. 2:10)

In its most basic sense, *sanctified* means to be set apart for a specific purpose. It can be used in a rather lighthearted way—"Nobody better touch my favorite coffee mug! It's *my* mug for *my* coffee!"—but usually, *sanctified* refers to something given a weightier purpose than holding coffee.

Think for a moment about something you treasure that is set apart in some sense. Consider why you have sanctified that item. (What is its purpose? How do you protect it? What does it represent?)

Technically, you were set apart at justification: set apart from the world and set apart to God. This is known as "positional sanctification."[21] Your position changed in that you were adopted as God's child, indwelt by the Holy Spirit, and set apart for His purpose. It was a one-time action tied to your justification. You are now treasured by your Father, God!

In addition, there is a one-time action known as "ultimate sanctification" tied to your glorification at Christ's return.[22] At that time, the *process* of sanctification will be complete. You will be set apart again in preparation for your eternal life in heaven.

In between those two one-time events is the sanctification we hear about most often—sometimes called "progressive sanctification."[23] It is the ongoing process whereby you "grow in the grace and knowledge of our Lord and Savior Jesus Christ" (2 Peter 3:18). As you humbly and obediently yield to God's continuous work in you through the power of the Holy Spirit, God progressively transforms you into the image of His Son and begins to use you for His purposes.

Let's read a few verses from 2 Peter 1 to gain a better understanding of the process of sanctification.

❋ **2 Peter 1:3-8.** "His divine power has granted to us all things that pertain to life and godliness, through the knowledge of him who called us to his own glory and excellence, by which he has granted to us his precious and very great promises, so that through them you may become partakers of the divine nature, having escaped from the corruption that is in the world because of sinful desire. For this very reason, make every effort to supplement your faith with virtue, and virtue with knowledge, and knowledge with self-control, and self-control with steadfastness, and steadfastness with godliness, and godliness with brotherly affection, and brotherly affection with love. For if these qualities are yours and are increasing, they keep you from being ineffective or unfruitful in the knowledge of our Lord Jesus Christ."

Because you are in Christ, you are a treasure to God. He is investing His Spirit in you to develop these qualities that will move you toward spiritual maturity and make you even more valuable in your service to Him! Yield to His efforts, for there is joy in being effective and fruitful "in the knowledge of our Lord Jesus Christ" (2 Pet. 1:8)!

As you humbly and obediently yield to God's continuous work in you through the power of the Holy Spirit, God progressively transforms you into the image of His Son and begins to use you for His purposes.

WEEK 4, DAY 4

The Task: Work Out My Salvation (Part 1)

Have this mind among yourselves, which is yours in Christ Jesus. (Phil. 2:5)

Let's start today with a game of sorts. In the following verses, the concepts of both justification (I was saved; I was declared righteous.) and sanctification (I am being saved; I am being set apart.) appear, just not in those words. Bracket the phrases referring to justification and write a number one somewhere in the bracket to symbolize a one-time, completed action (*i.e.* [1]). Under the phrases referring to sanctification, draw a wavy line with an arrow on the right to show an ongoing process (∿).

Goal for this week

✳ To understand and begin actively treading the path of joy in Philippians 2

Guiding Questions

✳ What is the vision/path of joy in Philippians 2?

✳ What does this path mean for me?

✳ What is the task that will help me tread this path?

✳ How do I execute this task effectively?

> ✳ **Galatians 2:20.** "I have been crucified with Christ. It is no longer I who live, but Christ who lives in me. And the life I now live in the flesh I live by faith in the Son of God, who loved me and gave himself for me."

> ✳ **Colossians 2:6.** "Therefore, as you received Christ Jesus the Lord, so walk in him."

It's kind of fun to read scripture and be able to recognize those differences, isn't it?! (You can check your answers on the bottom of p. 154.)

Now, let's identify some preliminary steps that move us toward the task, *work out my salvation*. In Philippians 2:14-16, Paul gives three exhortations that help us cooperate with God as He progressively transforms us into the image of Christ for His joy and ours.

Read Philippians 2:14-16. Write the exhortation found in verse 14 below.

....

Ouch...again! We said "ouch" the first week when we read that verse, then talked about the ease of firing and wiring pathways for negativity in our brains. Now, in context, we see the verse against the backdrop of Christ's humble service and obedience communicated in Philippians 2:5-11. If anybody ever had the right to grumble, it would have been Christ. Instead, He focused on His purpose for coming: "not to be served but to serve, and to give his life as a ransom for many" (Mark 10:45), and He looked to "the joy that was set before Him" (Heb. 12:2). No complaining or arguing (Phil. 2:14, NLT). Not even once.

Following Philippians 2:5-11, we notice God's joy from believers yielding to the joint work of sanctification in vv. 12-13. Now we come to Philippians 2:14 where Paul made his emphatic exhortation that "at all times they were not to murmur, or to substitute human reasonings for faith in God."[24]

Be humble. Be sanctified. Don't grumble. Why not? Isn't grumbling minor compared with other sins we might commit?

❇ Read Exodus 15:19-25. What did the people of Israel do just three days after crossing the Red Sea? (15:24)

....

❇ Now, read Exodus 16:1-8. What did the people continue to do? (16:2, 7, 8)

....

From these verses, we see how this action can easily become a habit, but not a virtuous one like the habit of joy we are trying to develop.

❇ In Exodus 16:8, who did Moses clarify as the target of their actions?

....

❇ Based on this, whether we acknowledge it or not, who is the real target of our complaining or arguing?

....

Psalm 78 retells many of God's actions on behalf of the Israelite people from the Exodus to the reign of David. It was written so future generations would know "the glorious deeds of the LORD, and his might, and the wonders that he has done" (78:4).

> Read Psalm 78:10-22. What do these verses point to as the root cause of complaining or arguing? (v. 22)
>
> ....

To draw everything together, read Psalm 78:40-41. Use the verses to fill in the blanks showing the contrast between Paul's exhorted actions in Philippians 2:12-13 and the actual actions of the Israelite people. (Reminder: I am using the ESV.)

> Instead of cooperating *with* God, the Israelite people ....
> *against* God. (v. 40) Instead of honoring God with awe and reverence, the
> Israelite people repeatedly .... and .... Him. (v. 41)
> Therefore, rather than bringing God joy, the Israelite people ....
> God. (v. 40)

When you associated complaining and arguing with rebellion against God, when you identified the root cause of these actions as a lack of trust, and when you observed that rather than bringing God joy, these actions grieved Him, did you feel grieved, as well? I did...and convicted. What I did *not* feel was joy, which tells me these actions have to go! They have far greater repercussions than I realized!

> Last week, we talked about processing in the pause. This week, we spoke of directing our mind to be like Christ's. From our exploration today, select one or two key words, phrases, or ideas you want to direct your mind to that will cause you to pause, deterring the temptation to complain or argue. Write them below.
>
> ....
>
> ....

Return to Philippians 2:14-15. In verse 15, Paul reminded the Philippians they needed to live out a treasured position or identity.

What three-word phrase gives that identity?

.... *of* ....

Whereas, in Philippians 1:27-30 Paul's words called to mind the privileges and expectations of citizenship in God's kingdom, now his message reminds us of the privileges and expectations of membership in God's family.

Read the following and delight in the significant truths that you can claim because you are His child.

Use these verses...	**...to complete these truths.**
"For you did not receive the spirit of slavery to fall back into fear, but you have received the Spirit of adoption as sons, by whom we cry, 'Abba! Father!'" (Rom. 8:15)	I have received the Spirit of .... Therefore, I know I am God's .... and I know He is my ....!
"See what kind of love the Father has given to us, that we should be called children of God; and so we are. The reason why the world does not know us is that it did not know him." (1 John 3:1)	I know the Father .... me! So much so, in fact, that He has given me the honor of being called a .... of God. And so I am!

What an amazing and privileged identity (John 1:12)! In addition to the above, you and I know we are safe in His hand (John 10:29). We are assured by the Spirit that we are His children (Rom. 8:16). We can claim to be "fellow heirs with Christ" (Rom. 8:17); to receive "every spiritual blessing in the heavenly places" (Eph. 1:3); and to be seated with Christ "in the heavenly places" (Eph. 2:5-6). Even more, we know we always have His ear just by saying, "Our Father in heaven" (Matt. 6:9).

Trace the following words and let their truth and joy flow over you as you reflect on the value of this special identity.

I am His child!

As we rejoice in the privileges of being a child of God, we cannot overlook the expectations of that role. In this chapter, we have seen that Jesus is our paragon—our ultimate example—of humble service and obedience. We have learned our task: to work out our salvation by cooperating with God in the process of sanctification. We know we are not to complain or argue. But why is that linked to our role as children of God in Philippians 2:14-15?

  ✳ According to verse 15, where are the children of God? (Notice the two "in the..." phrases.)

  ....

  ✳ In a crooked, twisted generation, why is it important for a child of God to not be conformed to that manner of living?

  ....

In Psalm 78:40, the complaining and arguing of the Israelites was considered rebellion, which makes blamelessness and innocence impossible. Thus, any child of God involved in complaining and arguing will look no different than the crooked and twisted generation in which he or she lives. Basically, these actions and attitudes hinder our witness for Christ. We are not to live conformed; rather, through the Holy Spirit, we are to live transformed by the renewing of our minds so we will know God's will (Rom. 12:2).

> Finishing our look at expectations, why is it important for a child of God to shine as a light in the world? Daniel 12:3 might help: "And those who are wise shall shine like the brightness of the sky above; and those who turn many to righteousness, like the stars forever and ever."

....

Paul's exhortations in the first century are just as applicable to us as they were to the Philippians. As children of God, we don't complain or argue, damaging our witness to the world. We do, however, honor our Father with pure actions. We shine like lights in the hope of turning many to righteousness. As God works in us, these are practical steps we can take to execute our task, *work out my salvation*, which enables us to tread the path of joy, *Jesus is my paragon*.

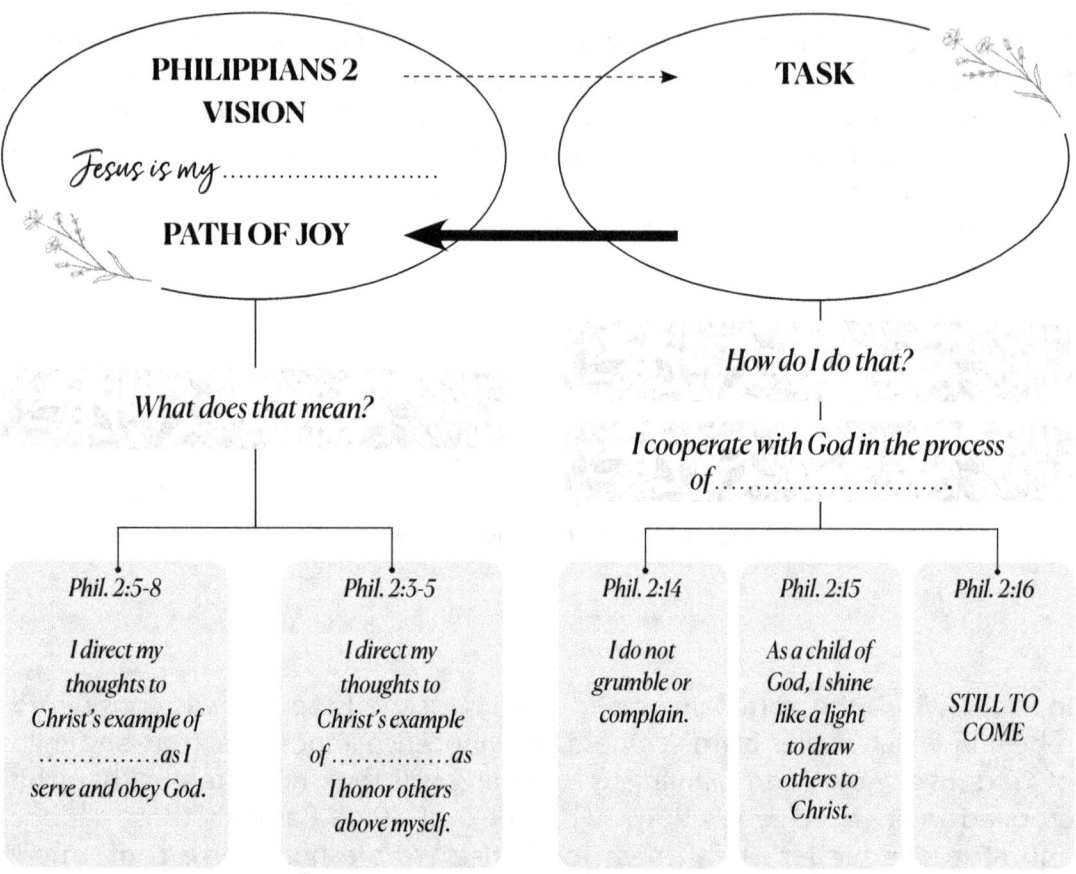

KEY VERSE: Have this mind among yourselves, which is yours in Christ Jesus. (Phil. 2:5)

Answers from today's opening "game."

Galatians 2:20. [I have been crucified with Christ.] [It is no longer I who live] but Christ who lives in me. And the life I now live in the flesh I live by faith in the Son of God, who loved me and gave himself for me.

Colossians 2:6. Therefore, [as you received Christ] [Jesus the Lord] so walk in him.

WEEK 4, DAY 5

The Task: Work Out My Salvation (Part 2)

Have this mind among yourselves, which is yours in Christ Jesus. (Phil. 2:5)

Goal for this week

✱ To understand and begin actively treading the path of joy in Philippians 2

Guiding Questions

✱ What is the vision/path of joy in Philippians 2?

✱ What does this path mean for me?

✱ What is the task that will help me tread this path?

✱ How do I execute this task effectively?

Have you ever had something that was "kind of" a bucket list goal? Something you would like to do, but it sits more in the back of your mind than the front. Something that might be rewarding but is not mandatory. That essentially describes my thoughts regarding the pursuit of a doctorate degree. At least until spring 2016. Suddenly, it was a calling I could not ignore. I just wasn't sure why.

Nevertheless, that summer I completed the extensive application process necessary to pursue a doctorate in curriculum and instruction. Those who received admission were required to work full time while taking at least six hours of classes each semester. Between the demands of work and school and family, relaxed Bible study became a sidelined luxury. Purposeful daily quiet time? Yes, but limited. Extra study for the love of the Word? Almost never. Instead, I chose to memorize Scripture. Many of the doctoral classes challenged my beliefs, so I prayed that I would know truth, and I memorized verses to plant that truth in my mind. I rehearsed those truths before I got out of bed in the morning, as I was falling asleep at night, while I got ready for work, and when I drove during the day. For three and a half years, I held fast to God's Word as my anchor in a swirling sea of demands, challenges, and—near the end—the upheaval of Covid; and I prayed.

Read Philippians 2:14-16, paying particular attention to Paul's next exhortation in verse 16.

What is Paul's exhortation in 2:16?	What is the impact on Paul if the Philippians follow his exhortations? (Remember the coaching analogy from Day 1 this week.)
Describe a time when you clung to God's Word and how His Word guided you in that situation. Is there a "Paul" in your life (a spiritual mentor) who would have been proud of your reliance on God's Word?	

Back to my story. Finally, the storm subsided. I graduated. I was ready for new opportunities. I still didn't know exactly why God wanted me to get the degree, but I was prepared to use it.

Except that is not what happened.

My husband took a new job in a new town. In October 2020, we moved from our beautiful home on the golf course to a one-bedroom apartment where we were frequently awakened by the noise in the apartment above and confronted with the smell of the trash chute down the hall. Although there were benefits to the move, I was confused. Not ungrateful or grumpy, but definitely confused. I was ironing my husband's shirts, cooking, cleaning the apartment—all good things—but I had spent a lot of time, effort, and money on a degree I was not using. Also, when we moved, I left behind a work-related identity it had taken years to cultivate. I clung to the fact that my identity is in Christ, that I am His child, but releasing the other was still a struggle. For one thing, I didn't feel like I was supposed to get another job. I felt like I was doing what God wanted me to do, but I certainly did not understand it. Then, one morning, as I was speaking the truth of Scripture before getting out of bed (a habit I had continued even after the degree), I decided to go through Philippians 2:1-11. And there it was...

"Have this mind among yourselves, which is yours in Christ Jesus, who, though he was in the form of God, did not count equality with God a thing to be grasped, but emptied himself, by taking the form of a servant..." (Phil. 2:5-7). In a very small way, God was allowing me to identify with Christ! My degree and title were not something to be grasped. I was supposed to empty myself and serve. I was to direct my thoughts to those of Christ. The confusion was gone. The identity was clear and sufficient.

And the joy overflowed! Oh, what joy!

Were there still times of discouragement and doubt? Absolutely, but I could always go back to this moment and this passage to regain my perspective. Here, I could effectively battle the discouragement and find enduring, deep delight in what holds the most significance.

That's the power of God's Word. It is "living and active" (Heb. 4:12). It "will stand forever" (Is. 40:8). It will not return to God empty but will accomplish His purpose (Is. 55:11). It is "breathed out by God and profitable for teaching, for reproof, for correction, and for training in righteousness" to equip us "for every good work" (2 Tim. 3:16-17). That's why we must hold tightly to it.

> Look up John 17:17 and notice the role of God's Word in our task. What does Jesus pray for us concerning God's Word?

....

....

Let's read again the definition of sanctification from *Vine's Concise Dictionary of Bible Words*. Notice the references to God's Word and its role in sanctification; then, answer the questions that follow.

> This sanctification is God's will for the believer,...and His purpose in calling him by the gospel...; it must be learned from God,...as He teaches it by His Word,...and it must be pursued by the believer, earnestly and undeviatingly,...For the holy character...is not vicarious, i.e., it cannot be transferred or imputed, it is an individual possession, built up, little by little, as the result of obedience to the Word of God, and of following the example of Christ...in the power of the Holy Spirit.[25]

* ❋ How does God teach sanctification? ....

* ❋ Holy character is gradually built up as the result of two actions on our part, one of which is obedience to the .... (The other action is following the example (paragon) .... which should remind us of our vision/path!)

Treading the path of joy *Jesus is my paragon* requires immersion in the Word of God. We cannot *work out our salvation* without it because we won't know what Christ is like! Hold tightly to the Word of life. Study it. Memorize it. Meditate on it. Pray it back to God. Paul said it would make him proud if the Philippians clung to the Word. I bet we might make God beam with a little pride when we do the same.

As he had done previously, Paul followed his exhortations with examples in Philippians 2:17-30. Here though, he used three human examples so the Philippians could better understand what sanctification looked like in the lives of faithful believers. As you read, you will notice a couple of joyful exhortations in these verses. Recognize them but know that our focus is on the examples and their purpose.

Read Philippians 2:17-30 and complete the following table.

Whom did Paul present as examples for working out salvation (sanctification)? Give a reason or two for why they were good examples.			
Who?	vv. 17-18	vv. 19-24	vv. 25-30
Why?			

You know, the problem with the process of sanctification is…well…it's a process! That means it is generally not fast. It may not be direct. It sometimes hits roadblocks and requires rerouting. It may get derailed by the actions of others, necessitating re-evaluation. It doesn't always take you where you thought you wanted to go. Basically, it's easy to get distracted and lose sight of your vision.

However, we have learned three practical steps that help us look past the distractions and trust our God as we work out our salvation in cooperation with Him: (1) We choose not to grumble or complain; (2) as children of God, we shine like lights to draw others to Christ; and (3) we hold securely to God's Word. The task *work out my salvation* enables us to boldly tread our path of joy with eyes focused on Jesus as our paragon, humbly yielded to God at each step.

Treading the path of joy *Jesus is my paragon*

Review

As we come to the end of the week, it's time to pause and reflect on what we have learned. Return to Day 1 and notice your interpretations of Paul's "coaching" through exhortations and examples. If you have any new insights, add them. Direct your thoughts again to Christ's example of humility in Day 2 and remember how Lottie Moon set aside privileges to follow that example. Think about humility's impact on unity and the impact of that on future believers. As you move to Day 3, ponder the importance of emptying, trusting, and obeying in becoming more like Christ. Envision the Vinedresser, the Vine, and the abiding branches with a greater understanding of working out, working in, and working for. Marvel that you get to bring God joy! From Days 4 and 5, review those three practical steps that promote your humble cooperation with God in the process of sanctification. Then, lift your head and look beyond the distractions to tread the path of joy, *Jesus is my paragon*.

A full picture

Use the chart on p. 164 to complete the full chart symbolizing how to tread our second path of joy. Remember: We're not worried about memorization, but we do want to be as familiar as possible with the truths from the Scriptures so we can hold securely to them.

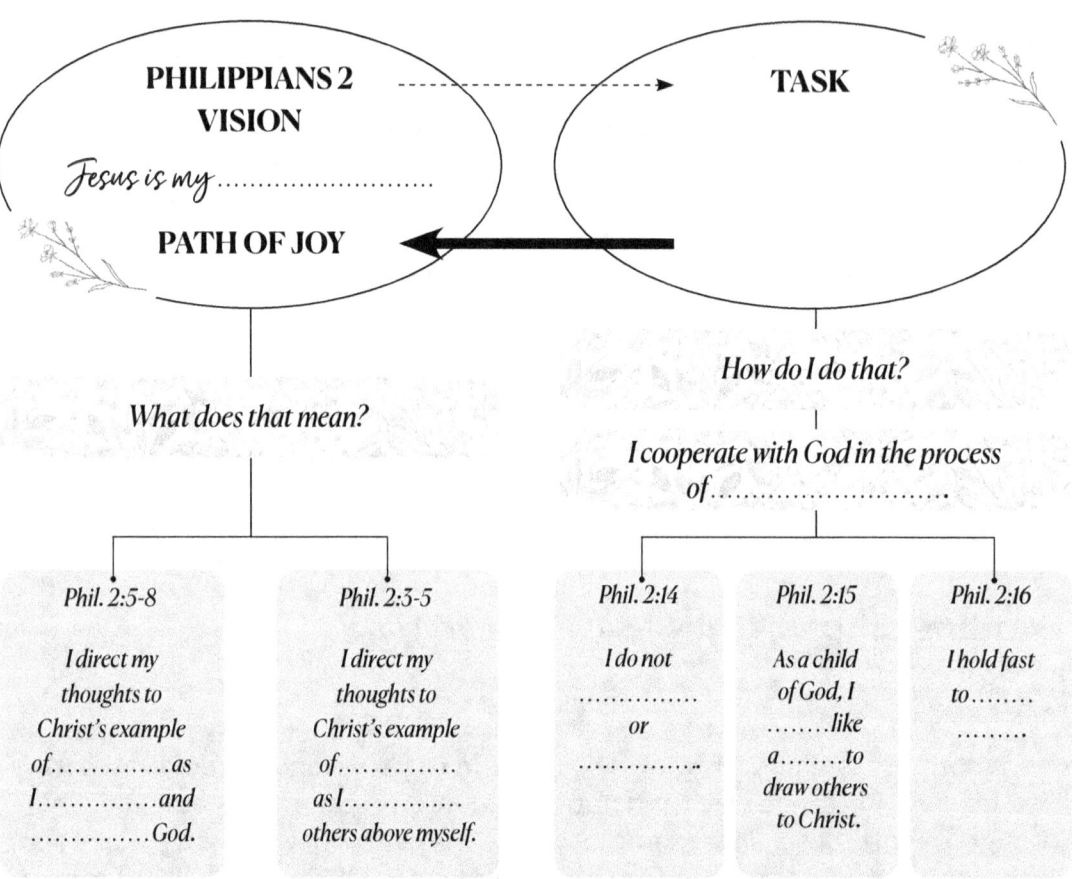

KEY VERSE: Have this mind among yourselves, which is yours in Christ Jesus. (Phil. 2:5)

Write below any thoughts you want to remember from the review and/or the chart.

....

Boots on the ground

Finally, let's try to flesh out a few practical ideas for making this path a reality. Our verses provided some thoughts listed below. Similarly to last week, put a check beside what you are already doing and an arrow beside those you want to do. Add your own thoughts and be ready to share your thoughts/actions in your group.

* God's Word is essential for sanctification. Purposefully find ways to incorporate it into your life daily. Employ your "sword of the Spirit" (Eph. 6:17) as you battle to work out your salvation and keep your eyes on Jesus as your paragon.

  * Read and study your Bible. Or pick an app that reads it to you!

  * Store Scripture in your head and heart through memorization. There are apps available to help you in this process. (*i.e.* The Bible Memory App; Versify App; Bible Memory: VerseLocker)

  * Read a single verse in the morning and meditate on it throughout the day.

  * Select a passage and pray it back to God. You can do this mentally, orally, or by writing it out as a prayer. The value of writing it out is being able to come back to it again and again.

* Ask God to equip you to live out the exhortations from this chapter. Pray specifically that He will work in you to help you

  * Live in unity with other believers.

  * Exercise humility.

  * Direct your thoughts to the mind of Christ.

  * Put away grumbling and complaining. (Honest confession to God of pain or difficulty is not grumbling or complaining. Read Psalm 13 for an example.)

  * Live as His child—aligned with Him rather than with the world.

  * Love His Word.

❋ Develop your identity as a child of God. Read Romans 8 and/or 1 John 3 and write down what you learn about being a child of God. Don't miss the privileges this position offers.

❋ Give yourself grace as you go through the process of sanctification as long as you are actively pursuing it (Rom. 8:1). Do not take it lightly, though. God is holy; He calls us to holiness, too.

❋ Acknowledge that treading the path of joy *Jesus is my paragon* will require sacrifice, but it also promises exaltation—perhaps on earth, but assuredly in heaven (1 Pet. 5:6-7; 2 Cor. 4:17-18).

❋ Rejoice that you get to bring God pleasure (Phil. 2:13).

Add your own thoughts below:

....

....

Enjoy time with your group! See you in a day or two for some joyful path-treading in Philippians 3.

The task **Work out my salvation** enables us to boldly tread our path of joy with eyes focused on Jesus as our paragon, humbly yielded to God at each step.

The Path Behind

Group Discussion of Week 4

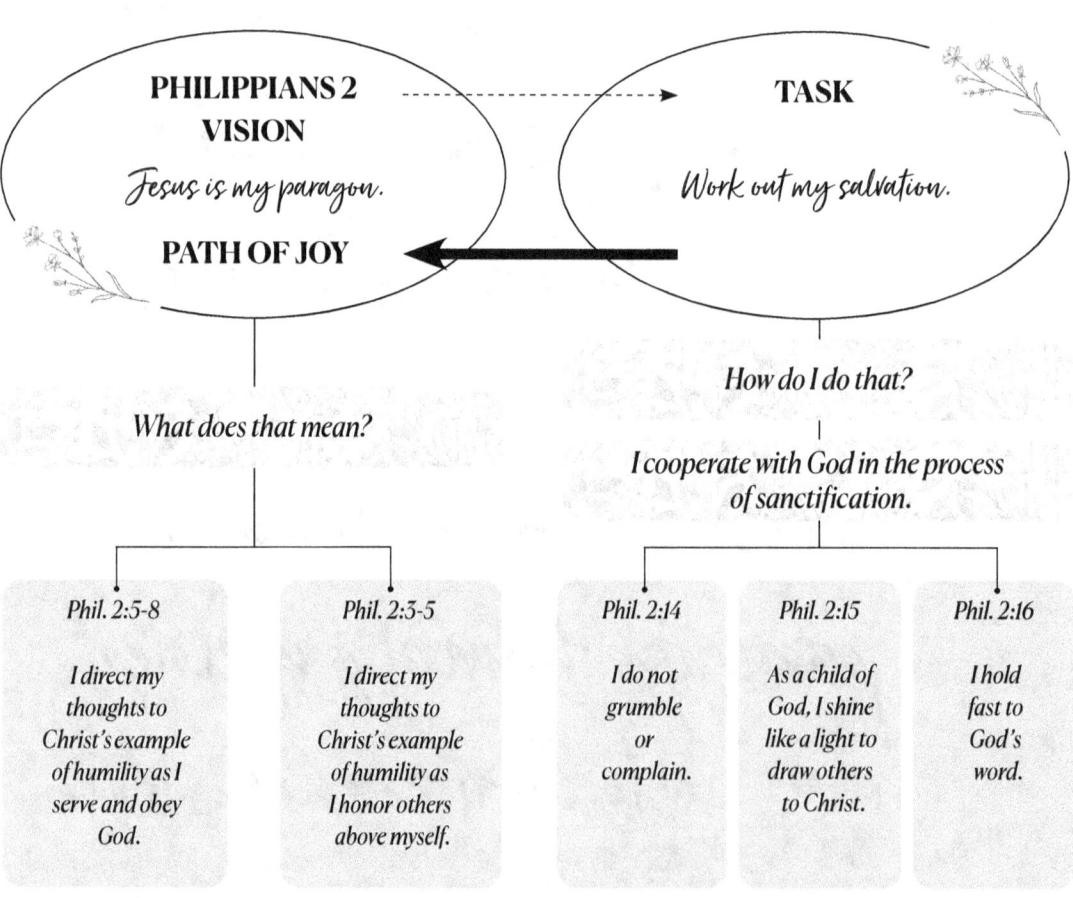

PHILIPPIANS 2 VISION

Jesus is my paragon.

PATH OF JOY

TASK

Work out my salvation.

What does that mean?

How do I do that?

I cooperate with God in the process of sanctification.

Phil. 2:5-8

I direct my thoughts to Christ's example of humility as I serve and obey God.

Phil. 2:3-5

I direct my thoughts to Christ's example of humility as I honor others above myself.

Phil. 2:14

I do not grumble or complain.

Phil. 2:15

As a child of God, I shine like a light to draw others to Christ.

Phil. 2:16

I hold fast to God's word.

KEY VERSE: Have this mind among yourselves, which is yours in Christ Jesus. (Phil. 2:5)

SESSION 5

The Path Ahead

Introductory Activity for Week 5

Part I - Group Activity

Part II - Group Discussion

WEEK 5

Treading the Path of Joy in Philippians 3

WEEK 5, DAY 1

Finding our Vision/Path in Philippians 3

Indeed, I count everything as loss because of the surpassing worth of knowing Christ Jesus my Lord. For his sake I have suffered the loss of all things and count them as rubbish, in order that I may gain Christ. (Phil. 3:8)

Another morning breaks, and the city begins to awaken. Mothers rouse their children, shop owners open early in anticipation of the afternoon heat, and merchants busily move toward the Emporium to set up their outdoor displays of food and artisan goods.[1] Quickly, but purposefully, Timothy dodges and darts through the morning traffic of Rome as he makes his way to the place of Paul's house arrest.

Even though he is arriving early to continue transcribing the letter to the church at Philippi, Timothy hears a conversation already in progress inside the house. He pauses and listens before entering. "Ah, Epaphroditus is here," he realizes. As Timothy enters, he notices Epaphroditus has gathered leftover bread and cheese from the night before, along with a few chopped figs drizzled with honey.[2] The thoughtful servant sent from the Philippians had prepared breakfast for the three men and the guard as he and Paul talked.

Paul has informed Epaphroditus of the contents of the letter thus far; so, as the men eat, the discussion now continues among the three of them. Paul brings up the current problem with the Judaizers. His letter to the Philippians had just spoken of working out salvation (Phil. 2:12), yet he knew this group of Jewish believers could take his words and twist them to a more legalistic interpretation.[3] These Judaizers could not seem to let go of their core beliefs in the Mosaic law and circumcision to fully embrace that Christ is not only necessary, He is sufficient! How could Paul protect his precious Philippians from the false teachings and false confidence in fleshly achievements this group promoted? What truths would motivate his brothers and sisters to anchor their core beliefs in the sufficiency of Christ made available by God's grace through faith? What could he say from afar that would influence the Philippians to stand strong even though the Judaizers were actually in their presence trying to sway them? Oh, what a precarious position for this dear church!

> *Suddenly, Paul paused; then his eyes began to twinkle. Timothy and Epaphroditus smiled at each other. They knew that look! God was revealing the truths Paul needed to say, and he could hardly get them out fast enough. For the next several hours, Paul spoke with enthusiasm, passion, and joy. As he relayed what God placed on his heart, Timothy quickly transcribed the inspired words and Epaphroditus prayed for his hometown believers and their reception of this powerful message.**

Today, turn first to Galatians 6:12-16 to learn a little about the Judaizers Paul will be referring to in the first four verses of Philippians 3.

Note below the reason for the Judaizers' emphasis on upholding the law.

....

....

....

....

Once again, call to mind Paul's conversion, his love for this church, and his love for his Lord. These elements are all on display in Philippians 3 as Paul's joy overflows. Yes, there is a concern, and Paul unabashedly calls a spade a spade (or in this case, a dog a dog); but he also manages to spotlight the goal rather than the problem.

Pause and ask God for His insight into the message of Philippians 3. As we have in the past, ask Him to reveal the key verse, the vision/path of joy we will tread, and the task that will establish that path.

Now place yourself in that room with Paul. As you read Philippians 3, picture Paul pacing back and forth with excitement, waving his finger in the air and animatedly declaring goals and prizes. See the changing expressions on his face as he articulates his priorities. As we did in Week 3, write below any phrases that have *Christ,* or a pronoun referring to Christ (*He, Him, His*), along with the verse number. Also make note of any words in 3:12-14 that remind you the Christian life is not a life of leisure.

---

* This story is a fictional representation of circumstances surrounding the writing of Philippians. Its purpose is to help you better relate to the context and culture. The events should not be taken as factual.

Phrases with *Christ* from Philippians 3

We glory in Christ Jesus (v. 3)

....

....

....

....

....

....

....

....

....

....

Write the words from Philippians 3:12-14 that imply Paul's efforts. (Note: Reading from the AMP, ESV, NASB, NKJV, NLT, or NIV may help with this.)

....

....

....

....

Use your notes to answer the following questions:

* What key verse seems to summarize the meaning of Philippians 3? Write the reference below.

  ....

* Fill in what you think our vision/path will be for this chapter:

  Jesus is my ....

* Look for a couple of verses that both mention the same task. As you read the chapter, note how Paul shared that he was performing this task himself. Write the task below.

  ....

Confirming your thoughts:

* The key verse is Philippians 3:8, "Indeed, I count everything as loss because of the surpassing worth of knowing Christ Jesus my Lord. For his sake I have suffered the loss of all things and count them as rubbish, in order that I may gain Christ."

* Vision/Path #3 of Joy is *Jesus is my reward.*

* The task that helps us tread that path is from Philippians 3:12-14: *Press on.* Although it may seem rather straightforward and simple, don't let it fool you. There is probably more packed in those two words than you think. This week, we will take a couple of days to fully clarify this task.

Goal for this week

* To understand and begin actively treading the path of joy in Philippians 3

Guiding Questions

* What is the vision/path of joy in Philippians 3?

* What does this path mean for me?

* What is the task that will help me tread this path?

* How do I execute this task effectively?

Use what you discovered to complete the portion of our chart that we know. Tomorrow we will gain a clearer vision for our path, *Jesus is my reward*.

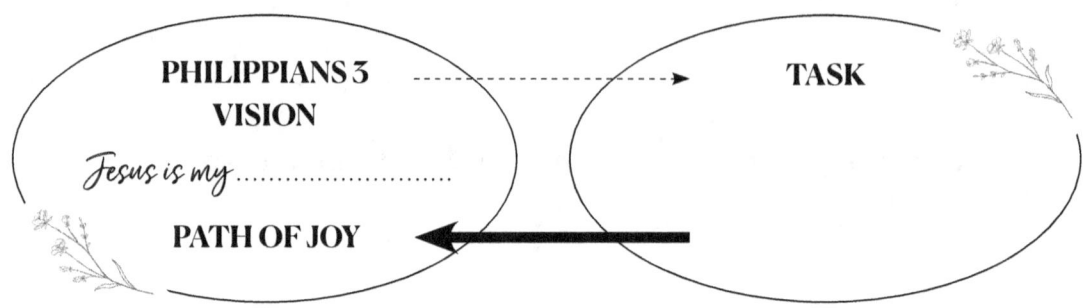

KEY VERSE: Indeed, I count everything as loss because of the surpassing worth of knowing Christ Jesus my Lord. For his sake I have suffered the loss of all things and count them as rubbish, in order that I may gain Christ. (Phil. 3:8)

Again, I include the quote below to help us remember why we need both a vision and a task.

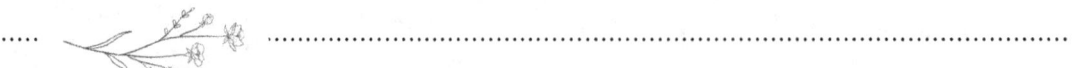

A vision without a task is but a dream.

A task without a vision is drudgery.

A vision and a task are the hope of the world.

Inscription on a church wall in Sussex England c. 1730

Onward to our joyful treading of path #3!

WEEK 5, DAY 2

Vision/Path #3: Jesus is my reward.

Indeed, I count everything as loss because of the surpassing worth of knowing Christ Jesus my Lord. For his sake I have suffered the loss of all things and count them as rubbish, in order that I may gain Christ. (Phil. 3:8)

More than a thousand people filled Valley Baptist Church in Bakersfield, California, to celebrate the life of Karen Watson—the former pool hall manager turned detention officer turned missionary to Iraq. The letter she left for her pastors in the event of her death gave the following directions for this service: "Be bold and preach the life-saving, life-changing, forever eternal GOSPEL. Give glory and honor to our Father."[4] And that is what they did.

Karen had lived a difficult life. Deep pain and loss during her childhood and early adult life left unhealed wounds. She developed a tough, independent, straightforward persona. However, when her fiancé was murdered shortly before their wedding, Karen was broken.

A Christian friend reached out to her, cared for her, and eventually led Karen to Christ in November 1995, when she was 30 years old. She recorded the following in her journal regarding her conversion: "The next morning my very first thought was of the Lord! I was so happy."[5]

Over the next few years, God worked to heal and soften Karen's heart. She was still tough enough to serve effectively as a detention officer but soft enough to see others' need for Christ. After several mission trips and active involvement with her church's Arab mission, Karen answered the call to full time missionary service in Iraq.

On March 9, 2003, Karen boarded the plane for her mission. She wrote in her journal, "For the sake of the call. Reckless abandon. Abandon it all."[6] Karen

Goal for this week

* To understand and begin actively treading the path of joy in Philippians 3

Guiding Questions

* What is the vision/path of joy in Philippians 3?

* What does this path mean for me?

* What is the task that will help me tread this path?

* How do I execute this task effectively?

didn't just write this. She lived it, having sold or given away everything that did not fit into the duffel bag she carried. She lived it as she ministered to Iraqi women, as she organized relief work, as she narrowly escaped bombings, and as threats against foreigners increased. She lived it through fear and exhaustion and turmoil.

She lived it until March 15, 2004, when the truck carrying Karen and two missionary couples to Mosul was hit with gunfire, killing four of those on board and critically wounding the other.[7]

At Karen's funeral service, one of the pastors shared the following excerpt from the letter marked for reading after her death.

Dear Pastor Phil and Pastor Roger,

You should only be opening this in the event of death.

When God calls, there are no regrets. I tried to share my heart with you as much as possible, my heart for the nations. I wasn't called to a place; I was called to Him. To obey was my objective, to suffer was expected, His glory my reward, His glory my reward...

The missionary heart:

> *Cares more than some think is wise*
>
> *Risks more than some think is safe*
>
> *Dreams more than some think is practical*
>
> *Expects more than some think is possible*

I was called not to comfort or to success but to obedience...

There is no Joy outside of knowing Jesus and serving Him. I love you two and my church family.

In His care,

Salaam, Karen[8]

As you process what you read about Karen Watson, underline what is particularly meaningful to you. Circle where she found joy.

Now, read Philippians 3:1, 7-11. Think for a moment about the treading both Paul and Karen did to make our vision/path, *Jesus is my reward*, a well-worn path of joy in their lives. What do you see in their lives that reveals their enduring, deep delight in that truth?

....

....

Such vast differences in times and cultures, yet the paths of joy Paul wrote about in the first century are the same paths believers tread in the twenty-first century. Look up Hebrews 13:8 and 1 Peter 1:25. Write below why we still tread the same paths.

....

Yes, Jesus and the Word of God remain the same. In contrast, you and I should be constantly changing...maturing spiritually as we study the Word and get to know our Savior.

But let's be honest: Sometimes the concept of spiritual maturity is joyful and motivating and beautiful (as with Paul and Karen), and other times as dull as the teacher's words on Charlie Brown ("wah-wa-wah-wa").[9] When we struggle to find meaning in the idea of maturing spiritually, it's time for a spiritual self-examination. We need to enlist the aid of the Holy Spirit and review our core identity and values. (It's not a bad idea for those who find joy in maturing, also.)

You discovered your core identity as a Christian in the last chapter: You are a child of God. What value does that position hold for you? How does this identity help you make meaning of the circumstances of your life, particularly those that are difficult?

....

....

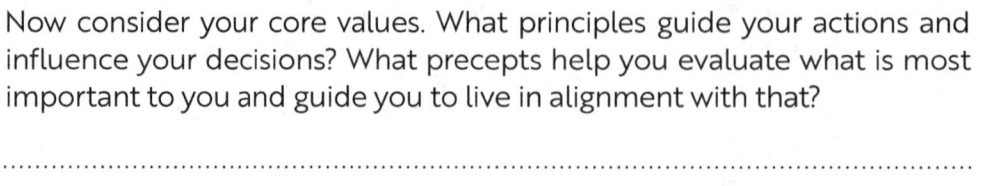

Now consider your core values. What principles guide your actions and influence your decisions? What precepts help you evaluate what is most important to you and guide you to live in alignment with that?

These questions are important. The strength of your identity as a child of God influences your core values. The core values you choose then integrate into and strengthen (or weaken) this identity.[10] The stronger your connection to your position as a child of God—the more meaning it has for you especially in difficult circumstances—the greater will be your spiritual development.[11]

Let's summarize: If you have truly repented and committed to cooperating with God in the process of your sanctification (Phil. 2:12-13) and if you truly identify as a child of God who holds securely to God's Word (Phil. 2:15-16), you should be developing the core values of knowing and becoming like Christ (Phil. 3:8, 10). These core values help you anchor your identity in Christ and strengthen you to live obediently and sacrificially for Him (maturity)...which we know results in joy!

Shifting our focus from a personal identity to a collective one, think about your local church. What are its core values and identity? The church I attend has a page on its website with its identity, mission, core values, and core strategies. As I read this page, I thought about the Philippian church. Remember, it was the first church Paul established in Europe. When he penned this letter, he had seen these people only three times, most recently about five years prior. Christianity was new. "Church" was new. The inclusion of Gentiles was new. The body of Philippian believers had no pattern to look to, no proven corporate example of Christian identity. They were basically forging uncharted territory with a leader far away in prison and deceivers in their faces.

Read Philippians 3:1 and note what Paul's words do.

* The words reminded the Philippians who they are: Paul's ....

* The words gave them a directive about their rejoicing: ....

* The words exhorted the Philippians to rejoice yet again because it was .... for them. (We used this verse in Week 1 Day 3, but the truth it states bears repeating.)

How does this one verse reinforce the Philippians' identity as being "in Christ"? How did this reminder promote safety for them?

....

....

Read Philippians 3:2-3. Paul illuminated the true identity of the Judaizers first, then the identity of the Philippians. Use the verses to complete the table below.

Identity (Judaizers)	Identity (Philippians/Us)
"Look out for..." (Phil. 3:2)	"We are the circumcision." We... (Phil. 3:3)

Gentile men typically did not bear in their flesh the mark of circumcision God commanded for Abraham and his descendants. Most Jews viewed Gentiles as outsiders; more specifically, as dogs. Notice how Paul flipped that here.[12] Imagine the joy his words brought to the Philippians, primarily Gentiles, as he made them feel included. Paul knew circumcision was now a matter of the heart (Rom. 2:29). He affirmed that this Philippian church had been living and worshiping according to truth and could continue confidently standing on their faith (core value) in Christ (identity). No fleshly accomplishments needed.

Paul continued to develop understanding. If the Judaizers thought they were "all that and a bag of chips," Paul could demonstrate that his "bag of chips" was bigger. If they thought their accomplishments carried weight, Paul's were weightier.

Read Philippians 3:4-6. Consider the options below and the scale to the right. Write the appropriate letter (either A or B) on each plate of the scale based on the information in the verses.

A. Paul's confidence in the flesh
B. Anyone else's confidence in the flesh

Ahh, but Paul is about to drive his point home. Slowly read Philippians 3:7-8 in one of the following versions: ESV, NASB, CSB, NKJV, or NIV. See the smile on Paul's face and feel the joy in his heart. Hear the emphasis in the repeated words used in each verse.

❋   How many times do the following words appear:

Count/Consider: .... Loss: ....

❋   Notice how the word *gain* referred to two different things, depending on Paul's perspective before his conversion (3:7) versus after (3:8). Write those gains below:

Paul's "gain" in 3:7	Paul's Conversion Experience	Paul's gain in 3:8

Isn't it amazing how God changes what we value?! When does He do that? Look at the verb tenses: Paul *counted* his gains as losses in 3:7, but he *counts— and keeps on counting*—everything as loss in 3:8. Do you see how those verbs point to a past action in 3:7 and continuing action in 3:8? God changed what Paul valued at justification (the point when God declared Paul righteous), and He was continuing to shape his core values throughout sanctification (the process of Paul becoming more like Christ).

Is there something that used to be important to you, but now seems less so? Record below how God has worked and continues to work in your life to establish your core values and strengthen your identity in Him. Rejoice in your spiritual growth.

....

....

....

Paraphrase the first sentence of Philippians 3:8, our key verse. Write as if the words are your own, not Paul's. Underline the core value and the phrase describing that value.

....

....

....

....

Pause and reflect. Was there a hesitancy in your spirit as you wrote those words, or did you feel joy in them as Paul did? There is no judgment or guilt here; only the opportunity for honest self-reflection as we seek to know *Jesus is my reward* and find enduring, deep delight in that knowledge.

Let's finish up with the last sentence of Philippians 3:8.

Again, consider the options below from a perspective of weight or value. In the illustration to the left, place each letter in the appropriate place based on the information in the verses.

A. All things

B. Christ

In Paul's mind now, "all things"—whatever possessions or priorities that might include—does not even deserve to be on the scale. There's only Christ. *There's only Christ.* I think Karen Watson would agree with him, don't you?

As we close today, our vision/path might be a little "fuzzy" to you still; however, it will become more defined as we move through the week. For now, we know the vision/path of joy from Philippians 3 is *Jesus is my reward.* We will use two statements to clarify what that statement means, with each statement summarizing four verses: (1) From Philippians 3:1, 3, 7, and 8, we can glean the meaning, *I glory in Christ,* and (2) from Philippians 3:3, 7, 8, and 13, we know that recognizing Jesus as our reward means acknowledging, *I count everything else as loss.* Use this information to fill in the chart below.

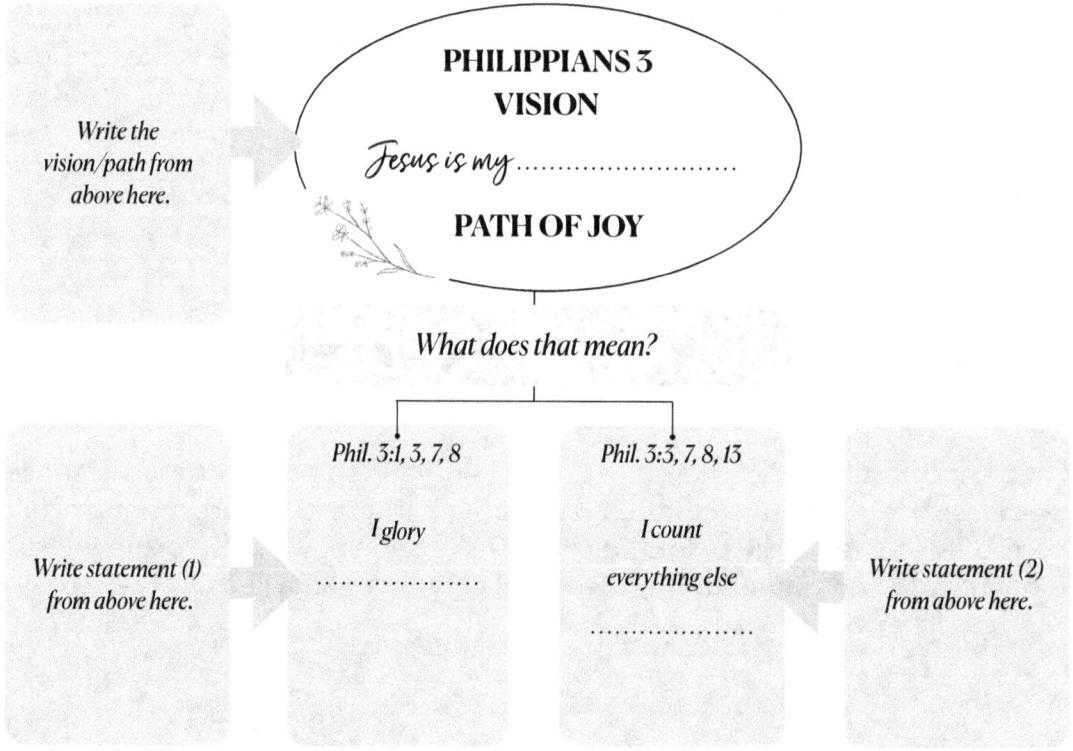

Write the vision/path from above here.

PHILIPPIANS 3 VISION

Jesus is my ....

PATH OF JOY

What does that mean?

Phil. 3:1, 3, 7, 8

I glory
....

Phil. 3:3, 7, 8, 13

I count everything else
....

Write statement (1) from above here.

Write statement (2) from above here.

KEY VERSE: Indeed, I count everything as loss because of the surpassing worth of knowing Christ Jesus my Lord. For his sake I have suffered the loss of all things and count them as rubbish, in order that I may gain Christ. (Phil. 3:8)

WEEK 5, DAY 3

A Glorious Transformation

Indeed, I count everything as loss because of the surpassing worth of knowing Christ Jesus my Lord. For his sake I have suffered the loss of all things and count them as rubbish, in order that I may gain Christ. (Phil. 3:8)

The words from Karen Watson's letter to her pastors in yesterday's lesson continue to echo in my mind. Like the peal of a bell, they ring out, beckoning me to read her story again and again. Today, it is the line near the end that calls: "There is no Joy outside of knowing Jesus and serving Him."[13]

> With this in our minds, let's read Philippians 3:8 again, but in the Amplified version. Underline the words that show Karen's statement aligned with God's Word.
>
> **Philippians 3:8.** "But more than that, I count everything as loss compared to the priceless privilege and supreme advantage of knowing Christ Jesus my Lord [and of growing more deeply and thoroughly acquainted with Him—a joy unequaled]. For His sake I have lost everything, and I consider it all garbage, so that I may gain Christ." (AMP)

Goal for this week

❋ To understand and begin actively treading the path of joy in Philippians 3

Guiding Questions

❋ What is the vision/path of joy in Philippians 3?

❋ What does this path mean for me?

❋ What is the task that will help me tread this path?

❋ How do I execute this task effectively?

Today, I had planned for us to study our task, *press on.* Yet I am halted by the paramount importance of knowing Christ. If knowing Christ is not a core value (guiding principle) in our lives, if we don't find joy in knowing Him (Phil. 3:1), there is reason to question the strength of our identity in Christ and perhaps our commitment to spiritual growth. Like Paul, I don't want any of us to fall prey to those who seek to lead people away from or dilute their faith. So let's press "pause" and sit with the verses in between for a day. We will come back tomorrow and press "on." (Ba dum tss! Get it?! *Press on*?! Sorry, I couldn't resist. [wink! wink!])

Getting to know someone requires time. Today you have time to visit with Christ. Pray and invite Him to sit with you now. As the two of you move through the verses together, recall the path of your relationship. Whether the path has been short, long, straight, crooked, bumpy, or smooth, retrace it with Him. This is a treasured opportunity to smile, laugh, cry, ask questions, express gratitude, or listen as you pause to connect with your Savior. Find joy in the time!

As Paul continued, he followed his excited exclamation about the "supreme advantage of knowing Christ Jesus my Lord" (Phil. 3:8, AMP) with three verses that help us understand how to know Christ. You will find two of those verses review familiar themes from the last couple of weeks.

Start by reading Philippians 3:8-9 in the Amplified version if it is available. Philippians 3:9 refers to

☐ Justification   ☐ Sanctification   ☐ Glorification

(A past event: I have been saved. God has declared me righteous because of my faith in Christ.)

(An ongoing process: I am being saved. I am being set apart to become more and more like Christ.)

(A future event: I will be saved. God will permanently and eternally remove sin from my life.)

You cannot know Christ in the present without having placed your faith in Him in the past—without having experienced justification. On that basis, Paul could consider earthly achievements and attempts at righteousness through keeping the law worthless because he had been made righteous through faith in Christ. God had transferred Christ's righteousness to Paul! Paul never took that truth for granted. He compared who he could have been without Christ with who he was in Christ, and the current position consistently sparked awe and wonder. His identity was anchored in what Christ had done for him. Paul rejoiced that he had been saved.

As God did for Paul, He has done for you. God has transferred Christ's righteousness to you. When you admitted you were a sinner; believed the death, burial, and resurrection of Christ atoned fully for your sins; and confessed Christ as Lord of your life, you were justified! Reflect on what it means to you that God has declared you righteous. Make justification personal. If needed, turn back to Week 3 Day 3 and find wonder again in the gospel. Write what you would like to say to Jesus as you think about who you could have been and who you are. If you struggle to find joy in this or your identity feels a little insecure, tell Him. Ask Jesus to reveal why that is and to help you make the changes needed for a stronger connection with Him.

....

....

....

....

....

....

Now move on to Philippians 3:10, again in the Amplified version if possible. Philippians 3:10 refers to

☐ Justification

(A past event: I have been saved. God has declared me righteous because of my faith in Christ.)

☐ Sanctification

(An ongoing process: I am being saved. I am being set apart to become more and more like Christ.)

☐ Glorification

(A future event: I will be saved. God will permanently and eternally remove sin from my life.)

Paul continued by communicating again his core values to know Christ and be more like Him (sanctification). Although his joy was evident, this is not a light-hearted verse. Paul did not sugarcoat what he was willing to experience during the process of sanctification lest he diminish the truth of his message: He wanted to know Christ so completely that there would be no aspect of Christ's life where he would have to say, "I missed knowing that part of You." Paul rejoiced that he was being saved.

If you need to, pause again and ask Christ to join you. Think about your personal sanctification. As you know, during sanctification the Holy Spirit reveals Christ to you (1 Cor. 2:10-16) and guides you to be more like Him (1 John 3:3; Rom. 8:16-17). How has the Spirit matured you through the practice of prayer, Bible study, and Christian fellowship? How have your priorities changed as you have grown? Have you come to know Christ through suffering and/or experiencing His power in your life? Are knowing Christ and becoming increasingly more like Him included in your core values? Again, share your answers to any of these questions as if you are sharing them with Christ. As you write, are you rejoicing that you are being saved?

....

....

....

....

....

....

....

In Philippians 3:11, notice that Paul looked beyond justification and sanctification. He was pursuing knowing Christ and Christlikeness for a particular purpose.

Let's read both Philippians 3:11 and 3:21 to aid our understanding. The Amplified version is still quite helpful if it is available. What did Paul want to attain? (3:11).

....

In these verses, Paul described the final stage of salvation: glorification. Sanctification may be hard, but Paul knew that "through many tribulations we must enter the kingdom of God" (Acts 14:22). He was convinced "that the sufferings of this present time are not worth comparing with the glory that is to be revealed to us" (Rom. 8:18). Paul rejoiced that he will be saved!

Finish your conversation with Jesus. Think about what heaven will be like and express gratitude that you will always be with Him (1 Thess. 4:17). Thank Him that He has chosen you for the incredible privilege of knowing Him (Is. 43:10-11).

....

....

....

....

....

....

Our goal today was to view Paul's life as a model for knowing Christ and finding joy in that relationship. We walked Paul's steps by personally looking to Christ in each stage of our salvation. We sought to recognize the relationship we have with Him and to make knowing Him a priority—a core value.

And what about the joy? Because Paul knew Christ, he found enduring, deep delight in his salvation: in justification, when he was saved from the penalty of sin; in sanctification, as he was in the process of being saved from the power of sin; and in glorification, when he would be saved from the presence of sin.

Pause for a minute and do the same: Find enduring, deep delight in your salvation as you fill in the following blanks with *I was, I am, or I will be*. Once complete, read it out loud once or twice. Rejoice in the Lord for this is evidence of our ultimate "safety"! (Phil. 3:1)

In justification, ... saved from the penalty of sin. In sanctification, ... in the process of being saved from the power of sin. In glorification, ... saved from the presence of sin.

Oh, such joy in knowing Christ!

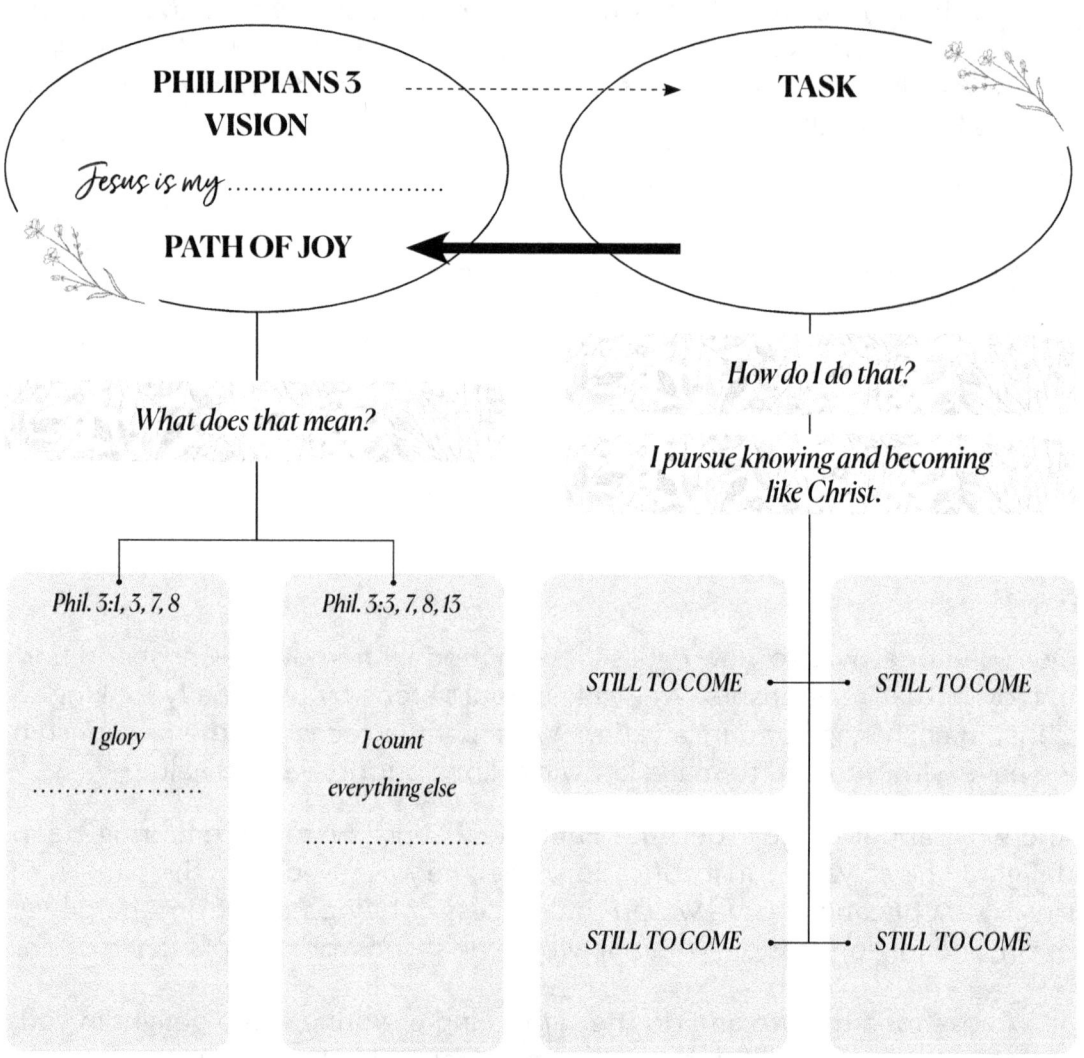

KEY VERSE: Indeed, I count everything as loss because of the surpassing worth of knowing Christ Jesus my Lord. For his sake I have suffered the loss of all things and count them as rubbish, in order that I may gain Christ. (Phil. 3:8)

Joy in Glorification

"I will be saved."

"But our citizenship is in heaven, and from it we await a Savior, the Lord Jesus Christ, who will transform our lowly body to be like his glorious body, by the power that enables him even to subject all things to himself." (Phil. 3:20-21)

"For everything there is a season, and a time for every matter under heaven." (Eccl. 3:1). This first verse of Ecclesiastes 3 begins a passage well known even to non-Christians. Solomon's rhythmical words sketch a picture of the time-bound seasons of life. Seasons of dark and light. Seasons that appear, disappear, and reappear like the flashing of fireflies. Seasons as relevant to us today as to Solomon's contemporaries almost 3,000 years ago.

Our familiarity with this passage typically extends through the first part of Ecclesiastes 3:11: "He has made everything beautiful in its time." Oh, but don't miss the curious words of the second part that point us beyond time: "Also, he has put eternity into man's heart" (Eccl. 3:11b). Man's heart that beats in the present also has a sense of the eternal! Still, in a striking parallel to our daily lives, that phrase about the eternal often gets eclipsed by a focus on times and seasons.

We weren't designed to live like that! All humans were created with eternity in their hearts. They sense there is something—or Someone—beyond the temporal. As Christians in this temporal existence, we *know* the best is yet to come! The God of the universe has given us the Holy Spirit as a guarantee that (1) we will be with Him forever in heaven AND (2) we will experience the ultimate fulfillment of our salvation—glorification. Sin will be removed from our lives permanently. Read these verses with joy!

> **1 Thessalonians 4:17.** "Then we who are alive, who are left, will be caught up together with them in the clouds to meet the Lord in the air, and so we will always be with the Lord."

> **1 Corinthians 15:51-53.** "Behold! I tell you a mystery. We shall not all sleep, but we shall all be changed, in a moment, in the twinkling of an

eye, at the last trumpet. For the trumpet will sound, and the dead will be raised imperishable, and we shall be changed. For this perishable body must put on the imperishable, and this mortal body must put on immortality."

1 John 3:2. "Beloved, we are God's children now, and what we will be has not yet appeared; but we know that when he appears we shall be like him, because we shall see him as he is."

Sometimes, we tend to focus on the "new body." God is not satisfied with just giving us a new body, though. In that "twinkling of an eye" moment, what we attempted as "good faith efforts" on earth—knowing Christ and becoming more like Him—He will accomplish for us. Glorification is the reality of fully knowing and being like Christ as we live forever in that transformed body in His presence...forever separated from the presence of sin. Oh, the hope of glorification! It is a confident hope that compels us to live with a view of the eternal while our hearts beat in the temporal. A confident hope that compels us to find enduring, deep delight in what truly holds immeasurable significance even amid trying times and seasons! What joy!

1 Corinthians 15:57-58. "But thanks be to God, who gives us the victory through our Lord Jesus Christ. Therefore, my beloved brothers, be steadfast, immovable, always abounding in the work of the Lord, knowing that in the Lord your labor is not in vain."

Glorification...

...a confident hope that compels us to live with a view of the eternal while our hearts beat in the temporal.

WEEK 5, DAY 4

The Task: Press On (Part 1)

Indeed, I count everything as loss because of the surpassing worth of knowing Christ Jesus my Lord. For his sake I have suffered the loss of all things and count them as rubbish, in order that I may gain Christ. (Phil. 3:8)

My son is a coach, specifically girls' cross country and track. He can talk your ear off about all kinds of warm-ups and drills that prepare runners for different types of races. He gets really excited about what aspect of someone's race a drill will improve. (I mean really, *really* excited.)

His girls who are repeatedly doing those drills? Eh, not so much.

And yet, those high school girls know their coach. They know he has their best interests at heart. They appreciate his knowledge and enthusiasm (even though he does earn a few "eye rolls" now and then). However, because they don't know all the benefits of the drills, or they don't see immediate improvement, they often wish they could move on to something else. Admittedly, they may tire of the battle, both physically and mentally. And yet, if they want to gain strength and stamina, if they want to eliminate the bad techniques and gain the good, if they want to succeed in the race, they must put the weariness out of their minds, refocus, and continue to pursue the goal. They must press on.

Goal for this week

❋ To understand and begin actively treading the path of joy in Philippians 3

Guiding Questions

❋ What is the vision/path of joy in Philippians 3?

❋ What does this path mean for me?

❋ What is the task that will help me tread this path?

❋ How do I execute this task effectively?

Our Christian lives are somewhat different because, more or less, we are training as we run the race. Nevertheless, do you see any parallels between the training above and the "training" we go through to be more like Christ? Note the parallels below.

....

....

Paul knew the Philippians were facing a mental and spiritual battle. He needed to give them a mental picture with which they could identify. As he did in other letters (*i.e.,* 1 Cor. 9:24-27; 2 Tim. 2:5), Paul used language that would call to mind an athlete in a demanding race, knowing that athletes would have been admired by both Greeks and Romans.[14]

Similarly to yesterday, the Amplified version fleshes out some of the ambiguities, so the verses are easier to understand. If you can access that version, use it to read Philippians 3:8-14. Write the phrase that appears in both 3:12 and 3:14.

....

Here, we find our task for this week: *Press on.* Typically, we might think of this phrase as promoting perseverance, but that is not the case in this instance. The Greek word translated here as *press on* is *diókó,* and it means "to put to flight, pursue, by implication to persecute."[15]

Use a thesaurus to find synonyms for perseverance and pursuit. Write down two or three of the given synonyms for each word.

Synonyms for perseverance	Synonyms for pursuit

What differences in meaning do you notice?

....

....

While maintaining pursuit does require perseverance, the meaning here is that Paul is pursuing or chasing after something specific. The focus is on the goal, not the challenges of the path.[16]

Toward what was Paul "pressing on"? What is it he had not yet obtained? (This is where the Amplified version is particularly helpful!)

....

Like the questioning of a naïve child to a beloved parent away on a business trip, the Philippians may have asked Paul, "Are you there yet?" Lest there be any confusion, Paul clarified at the beginning of both 3:12 and 3:13 that indeed, he was not "there." He was still in the process of sanctification—not "already perfect" and not "Christlike." Oh, but he was chasing it with focused intensity!

Think about this phrase: .... pursuit.

Give three adjectives that could fill the blank and convey the meaning we typically associate with pursuing something.

....

Why do you think Paul emphasized pursuit in this verse instead of endurance or perseverance? He encouraged endurance and perseverance in other letters. Why was *pursuit* the message here?

....

....

....

Let's explore that question together. Paul had given a brief personal testimony in 3:9-11. Do you think he was still remembering his conversion experience? Notice the last part of 3:12: "…Christ Jesus took hold of me and made Him His own" (AMP). Call to mind the urgency, passion, and focus of Paul's trip to Damascus to persecute Christians. As he was thinking about Christ taking hold of him for a purpose on that road, did the memory influence his choice of words? Look at the following two verses. The verbs are the same, conjugated differently for first- and second-person usage, but the same verb.

※ **Acts 22:7.** "And I fell to the ground and heard a voice saying to me, 'Saul, Saul, why are you persecuting (*diōkeis*) me?'"

※ **Philippians 3:12.** "Not that I have already obtained this or am already perfect, but I press on (*diōkō*) to make it my own, because Christ Jesus has made me his own."

Paul's previous pursuit had the goal of eradicating Christianity, but Christ "took hold of" him. Paul's current pursuit was the goal of knowing and becoming like Him in every way possible with equal, if not surpassing, urgency, passion, and focus. This message was one of fervency and action in the pursuit of a goal. It was meant to inspire others to passionately pursue that goal, as well.

Does Paul's message inspire you? As Christians, should we all feel urgency, passion, and focus to become like Christ? Is one of our threats the deception of Satan that there is no hurry? How do we combat that?

As he moved into Philippians 3:13-14, Paul placed the idea of pursuit in a relatable context. He described himself as an athlete who does one thing: *presses on* toward a specific goal for the resulting reward. To accomplish that one thing, Paul again emphasized that he did not look back. Instead, he leaned forward with everything he had for that finish line![17]

Let's read that again. We don't want to get so focused on *press on* that we miss another key phrase. Do you see it? How many things is Paul doing?

☐ One thing   ☐ Two things   ☐ A few things

One thing. *One thing!*

Imagine that you are an Olympic sprinter preparing to run the 100-meter dash. (You can smile at that thought but stay with me.) Do you fixate on the girl in the next lane who beat you the last time? No, you focus on one thing: the finish line. Do you hear the crowd and allow the noise to annoy you? No, you focus on the tape. Do you get distracted by the memory of another race? An unkind comment? Somebody's uniform that's cuter than yours? No, no, no. Do you let frustration pierce your thoughts by dwelling on a bad day at practice? A fuss with your spouse? A weather delay? A bad hair day? Again—all no. You have trained for this. You know how to run your race. You get into those blocks and look down the track with complete tunnel vision, focused on the tape at the end. And when the starting gun sounds you have forgotten what's behind, and you are striving for what's ahead. You are pressing on for that tape and leaning forward with every ounce of strength!

Why is it important for us to look so closely at the phrase *one thing*?

....

We live in a world of distractions and activities. The phrase *one thing* does not ask us to relinquish our activities and only go to church and Bible studies all the time! It does, however, call us to examine ourselves and our activities. We spoke earlier of identities and core values. Take a minute to evaluate if your activities align with and support your identities and core values. Your commitments should not contradict the desire to be Christlike or distract from your efforts in that direction.

With that in mind, is there something you need to release to focus on your *one thing* of pressing on toward Christlikeness?

....

You know, part of the beauty of Philippians 3:13-14 is how these verses make visible the passionate dedication Paul expressed in Philippians 3:10-11. He manifested his commitment to sanctification and desire for glorification when he described himself leaning wholeheartedly into what the future holds. The question is: What does the future hold? I think we know Paul *pressed on* toward the goal of Christlikeness, but for what prize?

Even though Paul spoke of his resurrected, glorified body in both 3:11 and 3:21, I don't think that is the prize in 3:14. Yes, after all our strivings to subdue our flesh and become Christlike here on earth, Christ will accomplish in heaven what we could not. That is the "goal" Paul spoke of. We can assuredly look forward to a new body and to being made like Christ and find joy in that. But if that's the prize, then the prize would be about *us*. Let's consider the following verses. What is the common theme?

❇ **John 17:3.** "And this is eternal life, that they know you, the only true God, and Jesus Christ whom you have sent."

❇ **1 Corinthians 13:12.** "For now we see in a mirror dimly, but then face to face. Now I know in part; then I shall know fully, even as I have been fully known."

❇ **1 John 3:2.** "Beloved, we are God's children now, and what we will be has not yet appeared; but we know that when he appears we shall be like him, *because we shall see him as he is.*" (emphasis mine)

Did you see it? We will *know* Him! We will get to gaze into the face of our Savior, fully comprehending who He and God the Father are. Although our temporal life has been a battle to progressively forget earthly things and know Christ as much as possible, our eternal life will be an effortless and immediate understanding because Christ will reveal Himself to us. We will "see him as he is" (1 John 3:2). Truly, *Jesus is my reward*! Let us find joy in this path and joy in the task of *pressing on*!

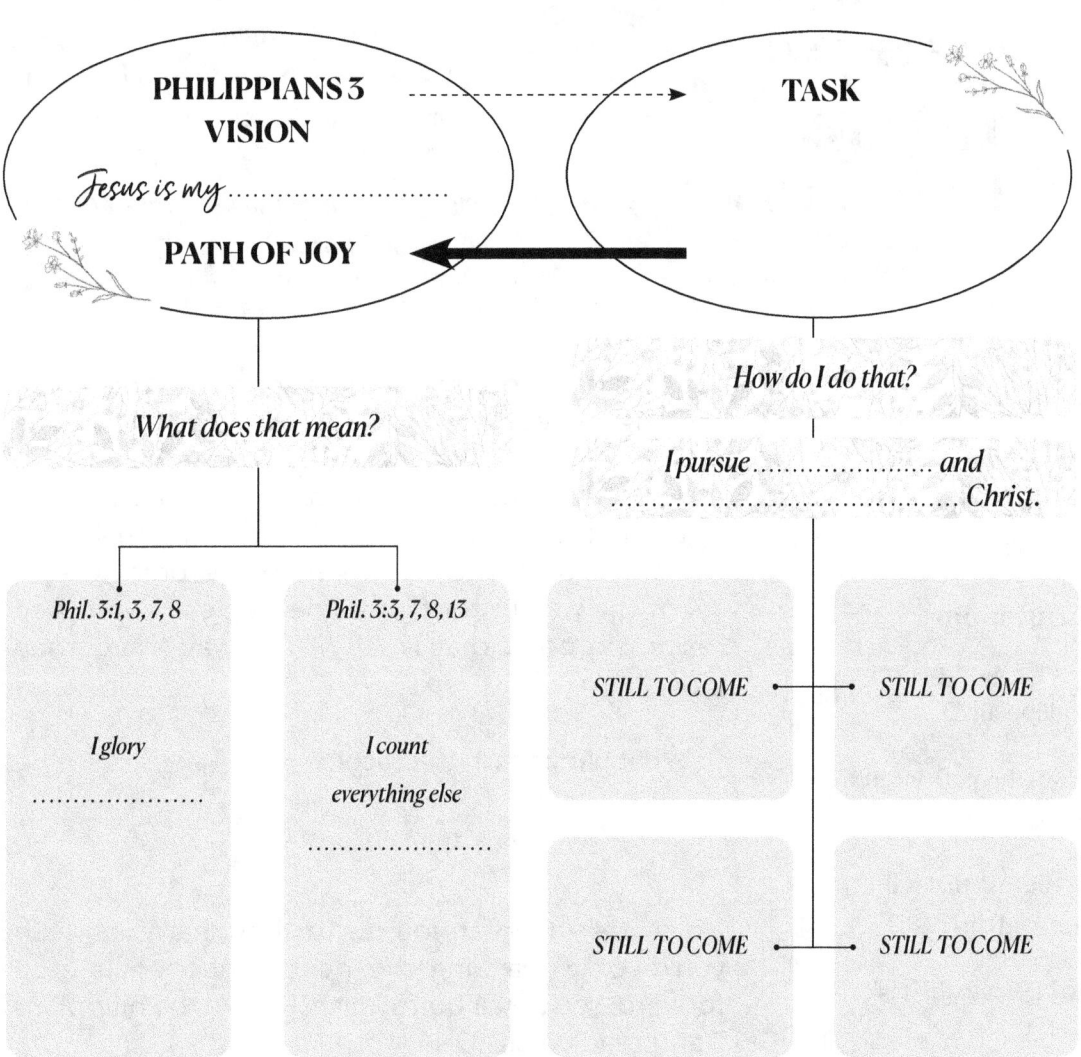

KEY VERSE: Indeed, I count everything as loss because of the surpassing worth of knowing Christ Jesus my Lord. For his sake I have suffered the loss of all things and count them as rubbish, in order that I may gain Christ. (Phil. 3:8)

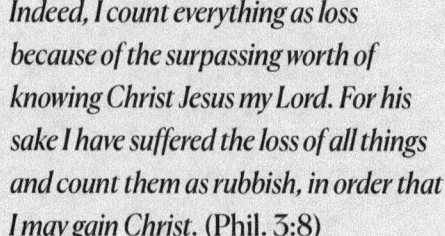

WEEK 5, DAY 5

The Task: Press On (Part 2)

Indeed, I count everything as loss because of the surpassing worth of knowing Christ Jesus my Lord. For his sake I have suffered the loss of all things and count them as rubbish, in order that I may gain Christ. (Phil. 3:8)

Goal for this week

❋ To understand and begin actively treading the path of joy in Philippians 3

Guiding Questions

❋ What is the vision/path of joy in Philippians 3?

❋ What does this path mean for me?

❋ What is the task that will help me tread this path?

❋ How do I execute this task effectively?

Let's return to our race metaphor again. You're still running and you're still pursuing the goal. Now think more like a mathematician than an athlete. (You may need to smile again...just don't cringe!) To get to the finish line in a race, you must first reach the half-way point. Then, you get to the point that is 3/4 of the way to the finish line. Logically, you then reach the point that is 7/8 of the way there...then 15/16...then 31/32...then...[18]

What happens in this race?

....

No matter how far you run or how hard you lean, you're only reaching the next fraction of a step forward. You never quite finish! Return to Philippians 3 and read verses 12-16.

How do these verses relate to the race described above?

....

....

....

Paul's goal in Philippians 3:14 was Christlikeness. Imagine him running toward the finish line, yearning to break that tape...but he can't! Not in this lifetime, anyway. In Philippians 3:12-13, Paul emphasized spiritual perfection is not achievable on earth. If trying to accomplish that has been stressing you out, you can just take that off your plate. The race we run here mimics the unfinishable race above. We *press on* toward Christlikeness, but we are living in a place where sin is ever-present. We still give in to our flesh even as we try to live in the Spirit. Guess what? God knows that. In His eyes, we have infinite opportunities to experience His grace and forgiveness in our lives. Don't take it lightly by any means; but humbly and joyfully accept it by all means (James 4:6).

Now, although Paul emphasized that he had not yet achieved Christlikeness (Phil. 3:12-13), he also recognized he had achieved something in his spiritual walk.

Fill in the blank below using Philippians 3:15.

"Let those of us who are .... think this way,"

This verse allows us to make a reassuring deduction:

1. Paul had not achieved spiritual perfection (3:12, 14).

2. Paul had achieved spiritual maturity, as had others (3:15).

3. Therefore, spiritual maturity is not spiritual perfection.

Let's say that one more time: Spiritual maturity is not spiritual perfection.[19] In fact, it is in spiritual maturity that we discover how far from perfect we are. (Note Paul's gentle warning in the second half of 3:15.) Like a mature sunflower bows its head and readily yields its seeds, so a mature Christian humbly bows before God and willingly yields more and more of himself to become as much like Christ as possible. It is an act of love filled with joy.

Earlier this week, we admitted that the idea of *spiritual maturity* may feel dull (Day 2) at times. We examined our identity and core values to combat that. Today, we acknowledge there may be times when it seems ambiguous and distant. Let's find a way to make it clearer and more accessible.

Spiritual maturity is rooted in relationship: You must have placed your faith in Christ. You need to know you have a connection to God even if it feels weak. Now, recognize that all strong relationships require time and the intentional effort of both parties. Below is a table that shows a few of God's investments in His relationship with you. God designed opportunities for Christians to invest in their relationship with Him through the practice of actions and attitudes known as *spiritual disciplines.*

Do a search for *spiritual disciplines* on your phone and write five or six examples below. Circle ones that you will immediately begin (or continue) to strengthen your connection to God.

God's investment in His relationship with you...	Opportunities for your investment in the relationship through spiritual disciplines
❋ He chose you. ❋ He allowed His Son to die for you. ❋ He placed His Holy Spirit in you. ❋ He adopted you as His child. ❋ He made available several ways for you to connect with Him through spiritual disciplines.	
You can rest in the fact that God loves you and has an unbreakable connection to you!	**Draw near to God, and he will draw near to you. (James 4:8)**

Logically, these disciplines don't develop by accident or "luck."[20] In particular, the disciplines of prayer and time in the Word of God (reading, studying, memorizing, meditating, etc.) should be purposed, daily priorities. So, yes, spiritual disciplines require time and intent, but you are investing in a relationship with your heavenly Father! And the more you know Him, the more precious that relationship becomes. Joy permeates the process for you are finding enduring, deep delight in this most significant relationship. Love and trust for your Father overflow into the desire to become like Christ which leads to spiritual maturity. It is a process, but all maturing is a process. Stay the course.

> *Stay the course* is a paraphrase of the message of Philippians 3:16, but translations vary widely in their wording of this verse. Write the wording from your translation below. If you have time, look up another version and note it, as well.

....

....

....

Regardless of the wording, the meaning is to stay on the purposefully chosen path toward becoming like Christ.[21] It is easy to be deceived into compromise. Don't. Be laser-focused on your goal. Don't run backward or step out of your lane. Hold true to the path. Faithfully practice the spiritual disciplines. The Holy Spirit will use them to refine your core values and strengthen your identity, which we know will lead to spiritual maturity (Week 5, Day 2). Not spiritual perfection, but maturity!

> Read Philippians 3:17-19 and recognize Paul's revisiting of two topics, one in 3:17 and one in 3:18-19.

Again, Paul reminded the Philippians of the value of watching and learning from the lives of committed Christians. Again, he warned the Philippians of those who could mislead them. His repeated emphases for them should not be lost on us today. Ask yourself the following:

* ❋ Is there a woman in my church or circle of contacts whom I can observe as a Christian role model? (Look for someone who, though imperfect, has an obvious love for and commitment to her Lord. Your church may have an established mentorship program where you could meet with a personal mentor.)

✳ Are the messages I hear, whether in church or through media, in alignment with Scripture? (Be discerning about those who distort or dilute the gospel, for "there will be false teachers among you, who will secretly bring in destructive heresies" (2 Pet. 2:1).)

Did you notice the tone of 3:18-19 when you read those verses? The words were almost hard to read. No joy. Nothing enduring. Nothing delightful. Oh, but notice the contrast as you move to the next two verses. What a way to finish the week!

Read Philippians 3:20-21. Jot below any words or phrases you would classify as *enduring* or *delightful*.

....

....

....

Paul was enthusiastically guiding this beloved church to stand united in the truth of who they were in relation to who Christ is and what He had done for them.

And what He *will* do!

As we near the end of our racing analogies, I think I will "pass the baton" to C.S. Lewis for the "last leg" of our study this week. He clarifies how knowing what is ahead should impact us as we live on earth. Underline what is meaningful to you.

[A] continual looking forward to the eternal world is not...a form of escapism or wishful thinking, but one of the things a Christian is meant to do. It does not mean that we are to leave the present world as it is. If you read history you will find that the Christians who did most for the present world were just those who thought most of the next. The Apostles themselves, who set on foot the conversion of the Roman Empire, the great men who built up the Middle Ages, the English Evangelicals who abolished the Slave Trade, all left their mark on Earth, precisely because their minds were occupied with Heaven.[22]

Remember our citizenship truly is in heaven. One day, our Savior will come, and He will rescue us from this earthly race—breaking that finish line tape for us and standing us firmly in His presence. Let us *press on* toward Christlikeness daily here on earth, knowing that *Jesus is my reward* for eternity. What a reason to rejoice in the Lord!

Treading the path of joy *Jesus is my reward*

Review

You're probably getting pretty good at this by now. Pause and think through this week, remembering that Philippians 3 captures Paul's efforts to guide the Philippians toward establishing individual and collective identities and core values. These identities and values would strengthen them to withstand the sway of false teaching and move them toward spiritual maturity. Reread your notes from Day 1. Remind yourself again of the vision/path, the task, and the key verse. From Day 2, admire the commitment of Karen Watson and Paul as they walked their well-worn path, *Jesus is my reward*. Ponder the core values and identity that gave them strength to leave all behind to know and gain Christ. How can we, as Christians (individually) and churches (corporately), hold true to our path in the challenges we face today? Review your time with Jesus from Day 3 and find joy in knowing Christ. As you move to Day 4, envision a race in your mind. See yourself *pressing on* toward Christlikeness with urgency, passion, and focus, knowing that spiritual perfection and an eternity of fully knowing Christ await! Finally, be purposeful to stay on the path to Christlikeness. Use spiritual disciplines, mentors, and the truth of glorification to maintain your pursuit. Know that, in the sufferings of this earthly life, there is joy on the path *Jesus is my reward*.

A full picture

As in previous weeks, we want to complete the chart that represents this path of joy. I have filled in today's steps since they are new. Once you are done, take the time necessary to make the truths of this chart familiar so your treading will be easier!

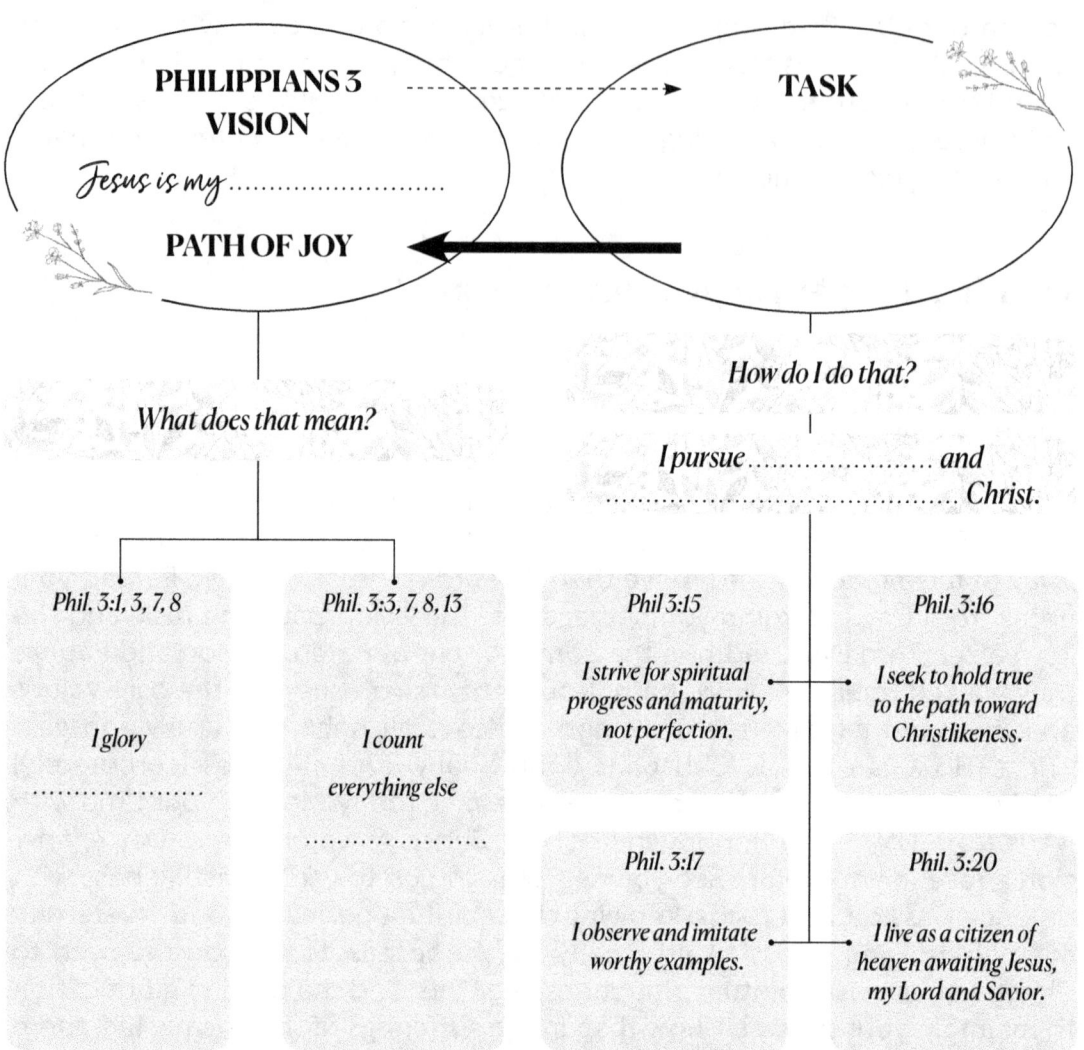

KEY VERSE: Indeed, I count everything as loss because of the surpassing worth of knowing Christ Jesus my Lord. For his sake I have suffered the loss of all things and count them as rubbish, in order that I may gain Christ. (Phil. 3:8)

Write below any thoughts you want to remember from the review and/or the chart.

Boots on the ground

Finally, I offer the following practical ideas for *pressing on* as you tread the path of joy *Jesus is my reward*. As we have in the previous weeks, put a check mark beside those you are already doing and an arrow beside those you wish to do. Be ready to discuss your thoughts and actions in your group.

* Fervently pursue knowing Christ personally and becoming like Him.

    * Faithfully practice spiritual disciplines, prioritizing Bible study and prayer daily.

    * Read Psalm 18 with the intent to discover how David knows God. It will leap off the page! Write down what vv. 1-3 would be if you were writing a similar psalm.

    * Read *The Scarlet Thread Through the Bible* by W.A. Criswell. It is currently a free e-book through Lifeway. You will see how the whole Bible reveals Jesus, not just the New Testament.

    * Read *Lives Given, Not Taken: 21st Century Southern Baptist Martyrs* by Erich Bridges. This book contains the story of Karen Watson and others who have recently given their lives for the cause of Christ. They are worthy examples.

    * Make a list of experiences that have revealed Jesus to you and helped you know Him. Keep it somewhere safe and add to it as you know Him better.

    * Pay attention to the examples of godly women around you and learn from them.

* Clarify the identities you have because you are in Christ. Here are a few examples. You are:

    * A child of God (or children of God) (John 1:12)

    * Chosen (Eph. 1:4)

    * A temple of the Holy Spirit (1 Cor. 3:16)

✳ An ambassador (2 Cor. 5:20)

✳ A vessel of honor (2 Tim. 2:21)

✳ Part of the Body of Christ (corporate identity) (Rom. 12:5; 1 Cor. 12:12)

Do you see yourself as each of these? If not, pick one and begin to establish that as part of your identity. Read the verse and pray: "God, I know that I am .... because Your Word says so. Please help me to believe this, to know what it means, and to live it out for Your glory. In Jesus' name, Amen."

✳ Make a list of your core values. Identify values that define who you are, influence your decisions, and help you act in alignment with what holds the most significance in your life. You can do a search for "Christian core values" online to help you get started.

✳ Rejoice in the Lord as you find joy in your salvation—justification, sanctification, and glorification! Use that joy and the understanding of who you are in Christ as motivation to press on to greater spiritual maturity.

Add your own thoughts below:

....

....

....

Enjoy time with your group! See you for some joyful path-treading in Philippians 4 soon!

Notes from this week

....

....

....

....

....

....

....

....

....

....

....

....

....

....

....

....

....

The Path Behind

Group Discussion of Week 5

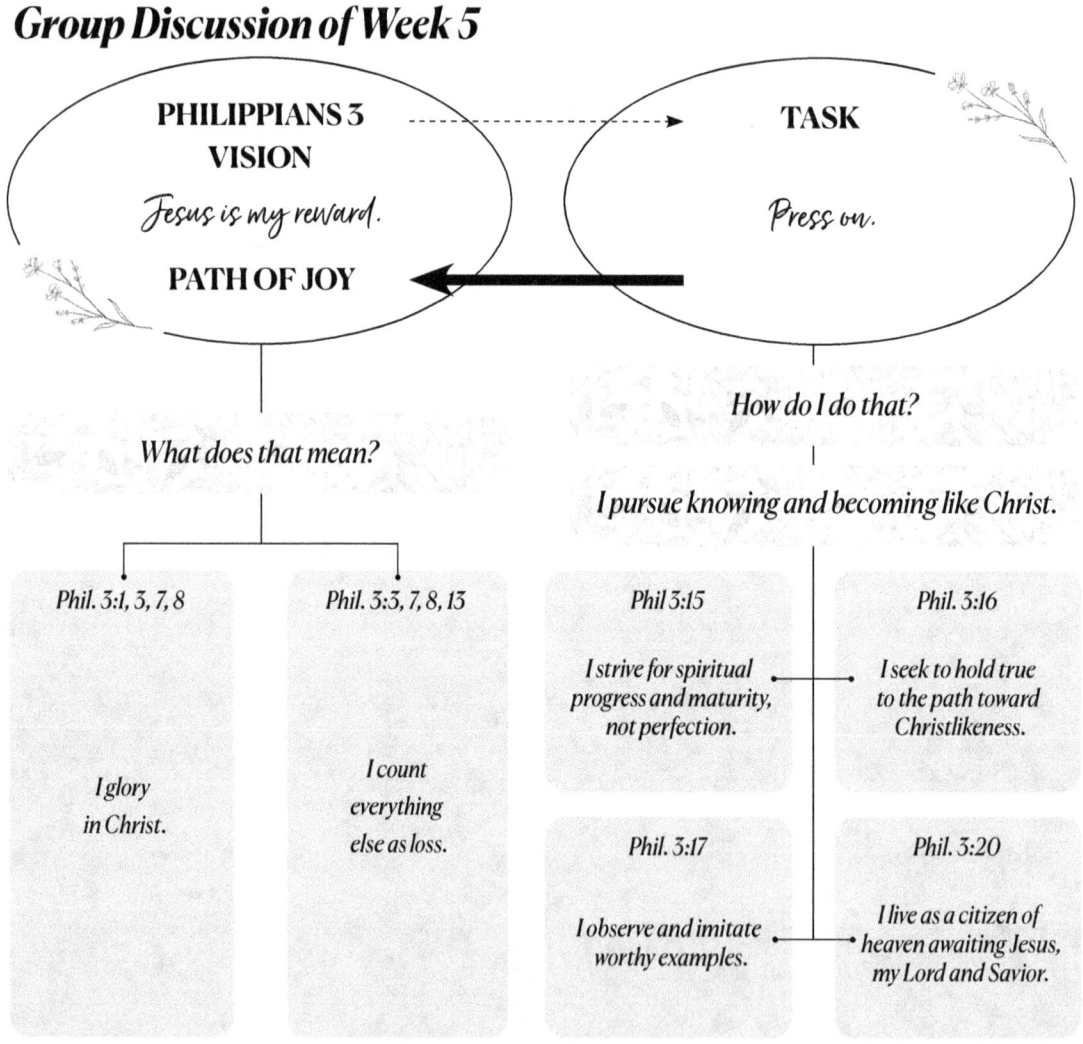

PHILIPPIANS 3 VISION

Jesus is my reward.

PATH OF JOY

TASK

Press on.

What does that mean?

How do I do that?

I pursue knowing and becoming like Christ.

Phil. 3:1, 3, 7, 8

I glory in Christ.

Phil. 3:3, 7, 8, 13

I count everything else as loss.

Phil 3:15

I strive for spiritual progress and maturity, not perfection.

Phil. 3:16

I seek to hold true to the path toward Christlikeness.

Phil. 3:17

I observe and imitate worthy examples.

Phil. 3:20

I live as a citizen of heaven awaiting Jesus, my Lord and Savior.

KEY VERSE: Indeed, I count everything as loss because of the surpassing worth of knowing Christ Jesus my Lord. For his sake I have suffered the loss of all things and count them as rubbish, in order that I may gain Christ. (Phil. 3:8)

SESSION 6

The Path Ahead

Introductory Activity for Week 6

Part I - Group Activity

Part II - Group Discussion

WEEK 6

Treading the Path of Joy in Philippians 4

WEEK 6, DAY 1

Finding our Vision/Path in Philippians 4

I can do all things through him who strengthens me. (Phil. 4:13)

The sun cast its morning rays across an awakening Rome once again. Emotion filled the heart of Epaphroditus as he looked down into the weathered face of the man he would be leaving today. The lines in that face gave the appearance of someone older than mid-fifties, but those deep etchings also told the story of passionate commitment to God and God's calling. Years of travel by foot and by boat, beatings and imprisonment, doing without what most would consider the basic needs of food and clothing—these things had marked Paul's face, but not his spirit. His steadfast spirit radiated love and joy.

Even now, as Paul stood tethered to the ever-present Roman guard, Epaphroditus could see love and joy in Paul's tear-filled eyes...feel them in the firm grip of Paul's hands on his upper arms...hear them in the tender, yet intense timbre of Paul's voice as he prayed for the impending journey. What a blessing this time had been! How grateful Epaphroditus was that his home church in Philippi had sent him to serve Paul during his imprisonment! It had not been without risk, but endeavors for the Lord rarely, if ever, are. He had learned that from Paul. He had also learned the secret to facing those risks: reliance on the sufficiency of Christ.

Today, Epaphroditus would step out in faith yet again as he began the almost 800-mile journey[1] back to Philippi. For a moment, his mind darted to the treasured letter safely packed in his small bag. He could hardly wait to read Paul's words to his fellow believers in Philippi. They would know Paul valued them, for the message opened with Paul's gratitude to God for his partners in the gospel (Phil. 1:3, 5) and closed with his gratitude to the Philippians for their generosity—"a fragrant offering, a sacrifice acceptable and pleasing to God" (Phil. 4:18). They would know Paul was aware of their situation because, in between, he never minimized their suffering; yet somehow communicated that joy in Christ was always possible when living with the humility of Christ, recognizing the incredible salvation God

> *provided in Him, seeking above all else to know Him and be like Him, and living in the assurance of His sufficiency in all things.*
>
> *As was his custom, Paul bid Epaphroditus farewell with "a holy kiss" (Rom. 16:16). Then, with what felt like leaden feet, Epaphroditus turned to begin the journey to Philippi. The final words of the letter accompanied his first steps and brought bittersweet joy to his heart as Paul called after his "brother and fellow worker and fellow soldier" (Phil. 2:25): "The grace of the Lord Jesus Christ be with your spirit" (Phil. 4:23).**

As we continue the Day 1 pattern we have followed each week, again seek God's guidance before reading Philippians 4. Ask Him for understanding of the message as you seek to identify the key verse, the final vision/path of joy we will tread, and the task for establishing that path. It is the end of the letter, so prepare yourself: Paul poured himself into this passage to such an extent that it may be difficult to settle on just one verse, vision, or task. That's okay. I would rather you hear the joy (and, in this chapter, the peace) in Paul's voice than to get the "right answers." No stress!

The opening paragraphs describe a possible scenario when Epaphroditus left for Philippi. As you begin reading today's passage, imagine your own setting for Paul as he finishes dictating his letter. You will benefit from reading Philippians 3:20-4:23 to remember the message leading into Chapter 4. Consider what Paul might have been feeling when communicating these potentially final words to the church he loved—the church that dearly loved him. Notice his repeated use of "all-inclusive" words like *always, all, every, no, whatever,* etc. Write below the final exhortations Paul gave to the Philippians. Also, note any phrases that have either *God* or *Christ Jesus,* along with the verse number.

---

* This story is a fictional representation of circumstances surrounding the writing of Philippians. Its purpose is to help you better relate to the context and culture. The events should not be taken as factual.

Exhortations from Ch. 4 - Paul's encouraging commands to the Philippians

Stand firm in the Lord (v. 1)

....

....

....

....

....

....

Phrases with God or Christ Jesus from Philippians 4

....

....

....

....

....

....

....

This is the last chapter of Philippians, so let's not change things now. Use your notes to help you identify a key verse, a vision/path of joy, and a task from Philippians 4. This one may be a little tougher than the others because Paul is trying to squeeze in all his last few thoughts!

❋ What key verse seems to summarize the meaning of the chapter? Write the reference below.

....

❋ Fill in what you think our vision/path will be:

Jesus is my ....

(Hint: Look at Philippians 4:12, 13, and 19. The word does not appear there, but it summarizes what is said.)

❋ Look for a couple of verses that provide a task. Paul shared that he had been performing this task himself. Write the task below.

....

....

Confirming your thoughts:

❋ The key verse is Philippians 4:13, "I can do all things through him who strengthens me."

❋ Vision/Path #4 of Joy is *Jesus is my sufficiency.*

❋ The task that helps us tread that path is from Philippians 4:11: *Learn to be content.*

Goal for this week

❋ To understand and begin actively treading the path of joy in Philippians 4

Guiding Questions

❋ What is the vision/path of joy in Philippians 4?

❋ What does that path mean for me?

❋ What is the task that will help me tread this path?

❋ How do I execute that task effectively?

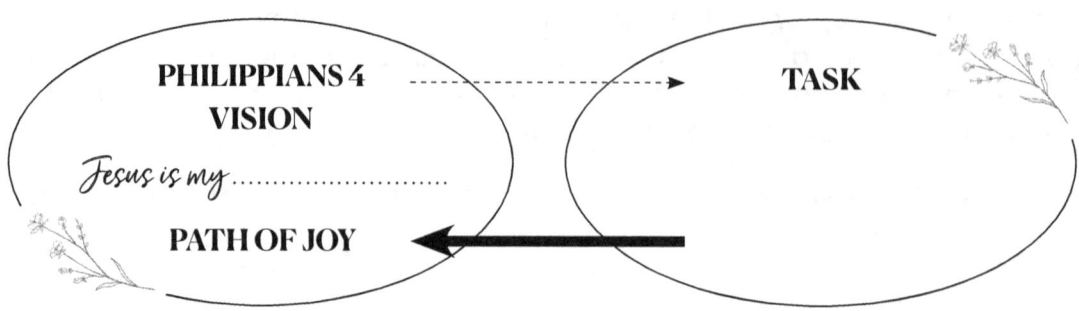

KEY VERSE: I can do all things through him who strengthens me.
(Phil. 4:13)

Are you ready to find joy in knowing Jesus as your sufficiency? Let's start treading that path!

WEEK 6, DAY 2

Vision/Path #4: Jesus is my sufficiency.

I can do all things through him who strengthens me.
(Phil. 4:13)

Goal for this week

❋ To understand and begin actively treading the path of joy in Philippians 4

Guiding Questions

❋ What is the vision/path of joy in Philippians 4?

❋ What does that path mean for me?

❋ What is the task that will help me tread this path?

❋ How do I execute that task effectively?

The teacher lovingly surveyed her classroom of female students, each cutting out a dress using the same simple pattern.[2] She was in her seventies now, yet Mama wa Mputu (Mother from Far Away), as her Congolese students called her, still felt such joy for the opportunity to instruct these girls. She had redeemed many of them from slavery by bartering, using whatever the Lord provided, including scissors, fabric, and salt. Now, they lived with her in the Pantops Home for Girls. She had used both donations and her own funds to build this home—a setting where she and other missionaries could provide the girls with a basic education of reading, writing, and arithmetic, as well as instruction in the skills of homemaking and gardening. Most importantly, this home was a place to daily share principles of the Christian faith.[3]

Mama wa Mputu began her life as Maria (pronounced *Mariah*) Fearing. Born July 26, 1838, to parents enslaved on a plantation near Gainesville, Alabama, Maria was taken from her family at a very young age to be a house servant.[4] As she grew, part of her responsibilities included helping with the young children of the household. Thus, when the children's mother told them stories of Bible characters or of missionaries to Africa, Maria learned, too.[5] The stories stirred Maria's young heart, but no one could have imagined how the Lord would use these early experiences to prepare her for His calling.

Life began to change for Maria with her emancipation in 1865. At first, she left the plantation and worked as a paid, live-in maid for five years. Then she learned that African American adults could attend literacy classes at an American Missionary Association school in Talladega, Alabama. The opportunity held such value for Maria that she traveled by foot or wagon the 150 miles to Talladega College. (This "college" was a school for basic education and teacher training, not a college according to our current use of the word.) Although she had to begin her studies as the classmate of young children—who sometimes mocked her lack of literacy at 31 years of age—she was determined to learn.[6] By age 33, she had completed the ninth grade and begun training to become a teacher.[7]

Maria spent 23 years at the school, first as a student, then a staff member.[8] During this time, she also taught in a nearby school in Aniston, Alabama. She gained financial stability and was able to purchase her own home.[9] How meaningful these accomplishments must have been for the woman born into slavery who could not read until her early thirties.

Even so, God had greater plans for Maria. In 1894, William Sheppard, an African American missionary, came to Talladega College and spoke about his mission work in the Congo in Africa. Maria brightened, recalling the compelling stories heard years before on the plantation. Oh, how she longed to be a part of sharing Christ with the people of the Congo! Maria immediately volunteered. However, her age of 56 years and her inadequate level of education for missionary work led the Foreign Mission Committee of the Presbyterian Church to deny her application.[10]

Maria was undeterred. With steadfast determination to follow God's call, she sold her home, combined money from the sale with a $100 donation from a group of ladies at Talladega College, and traveled to Africa with William Sheppard and the other missionaries. She soon learned the language and helped translate hymns. Within two years, she became a paid missionary. For eighteen additional years, Maria faithfully and joyfully continued her ministry in the Congo, paying the cost to free young slaves, maintaining the home for girls, and impacting lives beyond her tenure as she taught the girls of their worth and purpose in the eyes of Christ.[11]

> *Jesus is my sufficiency*! Do you see the truth of that on display in the events of Maria's unlikely story? Read Philippians 4:12-13, 19. Write below some examples of the sufficiency of Jesus in Maria's life.

> ....

> ....

As we begin today, let's notice a subtle, but important, distinction between provision and sufficiency. Provision is about the action of supplying—giving what one has. Sufficiency is about the supply—having available whatever is needed. Provision depends on sufficiency. In Christ, God has abundant riches available to us (Phil. 4:19) and He has blessed us "with every spiritual blessing in the heavenly places" (Eph. 1:3), so Christ is sufficient. If we have trouble recognizing His sufficiency in our lives, we may be focused on and expecting a different provision than we are receiving. Whenever we struggle with releasing our expected provision and trusting that Jesus is enough, this path of joy is where we need to be. So, let's learn more about the sufficiency of Jesus to help us tread this path.

The following verses testify to Jesus' sufficiency regarding different *resources*. Although we are only identifying a few, this sample will draw our minds to the joy of knowing *Jesus is my sufficiency*. As you read, notice the resources Jesus has or is full of and write them in space provided.

Verse	Resource(s)
"When he saw the crowds, he had compassion for them, because they were harassed and helpless, like sheep without a shepherd." (Matt. 9:36)	
"And the Word became flesh and dwelt among us, and we have seen his glory, glory as of the only Son from the Father, full of grace and truth." (John 1:14)	
"Peace I leave with you; my peace I give to you. Not as the world gives do I give to you. Let not your hearts be troubled, neither let them be afraid." (John 14:27)	
"These things I have spoken to you, that my joy may be in you, and that your joy may be full." (John 15:11)	
"But he said to me, 'My grace is sufficient for you, for my power is made perfect in weakness.' Therefore I will boast all the more gladly of my weaknesses, so that the power of Christ may rest upon me." (2 Cor. 12:9)	

Although we recognize Jesus' sufficiency in His resources, we don't want to stop there. Our confession *Jesus is my sufficiency* is possible because of His *experiences*, also.

❋   Read Hebrews 2:9-18. Then, complete the following sentences.

❋   *Jesus is my sufficiency* because He has suffered ....
.... (v. 9), so that "He might experience death for [the sins of] everyone" (Heb. 2:9 AMP).

❋   *Jesus is my sufficiency* because He was perfected through .... (v. 10), as am I (James 1:2-4).

❋   *Jesus is my sufficiency* because He came in human form, sharing in my .... and .... (v. 14).

❋   *Jesus is my sufficiency* because, through His death, He .... (v. 14) the one who has the power of death and .... (v. 15) me from lifelong slavery.

❋   *Jesus is my sufficiency* because He is my merciful and faithful ....
.... (v. 17), serving God and interceding on my behalf (Heb. 7:25).

❋   *Jesus is my sufficiency* because He .... (v. 18) when He was tempted; therefore, He is able to help me when I am tempted.

Jesus came to earth and lived in the limitations of flesh. He participated in suffering and death so He could have the experiences necessary to be your sufficiency (Is. 53:10-12). His suffering made Him sufficient to save you and to help you in your sufferings and temptations. How amazing...and humbling.

Oh, but we can't stop yet. We discovered Jesus is sufficient because of His resources and His experiences, but we don't want to miss the truth that He is also sufficient simply because of *who He is*!

> With joy and awe, read the passage below. Underline any phrases that convey Christ's sufficiency based on who He is. Then answer the question.

> **Colossians 1:15-20.** "He is the image of the invisible God, the firstborn of all creation. For by him all things were created, in heaven and on earth, visible and invisible, whether thrones or dominions or rulers or authorities—all things were created through him and for him. And he is before all things, and in him all things hold together. And he is the head of the body, the church. He is the beginning, the firstborn from the dead, that in everything he might be preeminent. For in him all the fullness of God was pleased to dwell, and through him to reconcile to himself all things, whether on earth or in heaven, making peace by the blood of his cross."

> Which phrase took on new or renewed meaning to you? Why do you think that phrase resonated with you?
>
> ....
>
> ....

Yes, Christ is sufficient in His resources to equip you for His calling. He is sufficient in His experiences to sustain you in any circumstance. But, above all, He is sufficient because of who He is! There is never a time when Christ is not enough. John MacArthur states it like this: "To have Him is to have everything, not to have Him is to have absolutely nothing at all. All joy, peace, meaning, value, purpose, hope, fulfillment in life now and forever is bound up in Christ. And when a person receives Jesus Christ as Lord and Savior, they enter into an all-sufficient relationship with an all-sufficient Christ."[12]

> With the sufficiency of Jesus in mind, read Philippians 4:10-20.

Do you smile with sympathetic understanding at Paul's tap dance with words? Like we seek to avoid misunderstanding in a text or email, Paul labored to express a message with unmistakable meaning. (Anybody else suddenly grateful for the backspace key?) He knew the Philippians never lacked concern for him. He didn't want them to feel guilty for not meeting a need.[13] Truly, he was grateful for their repeated, sacrificial giving. Yet he also wanted them to understand the truth of the sufficiency of Christ.

Although Paul may have wrestled with a portion of the message, he knew exactly how to communicate his main point. Notice his cleverness in piquing the curiosity of the Philippians. Using Philippians 4:12, check the box beside the word that correctly fills the blank of the following paraphrase.

"I have learned the .... of facing any situation."

☐ Truth   ☐ Secret   ☐ Lord's Prayer

Can you see Paul's eyes sparkle as he dictates these words in his little house? Can you imagine the beloved Philippians anxiously leaning forward in anticipation as they listen? I think I hear murmurs of "What's the secret?!" and "Don't keep us in suspense!"

Well, don't keep them in suspense! (wink!) Write Paul's secret below. (Hint: It's our key verse, Philippians 4:13.)

....

....

....

The Amplified version magnifies the meaning of this verse with the words "I am ready for anything and equal to anything through Him who infuses me with inner strength and confident peace" (4:13 AMP). Read those words again as if that truth is yours, ladies. Because it is.

We may not yet state this truth as boldly as Paul. After all, he had had years of intense practice by this writing. His path, *Jesus is my sufficiency,* was well-worn through reliance on Christ's infusion of strength in a multitude of circumstances. We know we will face "a multitude of circumstances" ourselves (though probably not like Paul's), so let's begin choosing to rely on Christ's infusion of strength. As we learned from Paul, the result is a life marked by strength, peace, satisfaction, and joy. I like the sound of that, don't you?

Before leaving Philippians 4:13, let's expose a couple of misinterpretations. First, a focus solely on the initial phrase leads to reliance on personal resources, not on Christ. The common expressions "Believe in yourself" and "You can do whatever you set your mind to" are trappings of this world and distortions of God's truth. Second, overemphasis on the second phrase can potentially lead to claiming Christ's strength and barging into something without a calling. Correct interpretation affirms that, in His strength, we can face whatever He allows in our path and accomplish whatever He calls us to do. He is sufficient to strengthen us; and, infused with His strength, we are sufficient! Find joy in this truth as you read the following scriptures.

> **2 Corinthians 3:5.** "Not that we are sufficient in ourselves to claim anything as coming from us, but our sufficiency is from God."

> **2 Corinthians 9:8.** "And God is able to make all grace abound to you, so that having all sufficiency in all things at all times, you may abound in every good work."

Is there an area of your life where you need to recognize *Jesus is my sufficiency*? What expected provision might you need to release to live in Christ's sufficiency and know you have "all sufficiency in all things at all times" (2 Cor. 9:8)?

You know, the goal is to hop on this path when our feet hit the floor in the morning and joyfully tread it all day long. At times, though, something specific in our lives will compel us to intentionally state this path out loud and stead-fastly stand in the middle of it until Jesus, in His sufficiency, helps us move forward. If that resonates with you, state the truths of our chart aloud as you complete them. Seek to find enduring, deep delight in their meaning.

Our vision/path of joy for Philippians 4 is *Jesus is my sufficiency.* Today, we recognized Jesus' sufficiency simply because of who He is, and we saw His sufficiency applied to us through His resources and His experiences. Therefore, saying *Jesus is my sufficiency* means (1) *I trust Jesus to sustain me in every circumstance* (4:13), and (2) *I trust God to supply my every need according to His riches in Christ Jesus* (4:19).

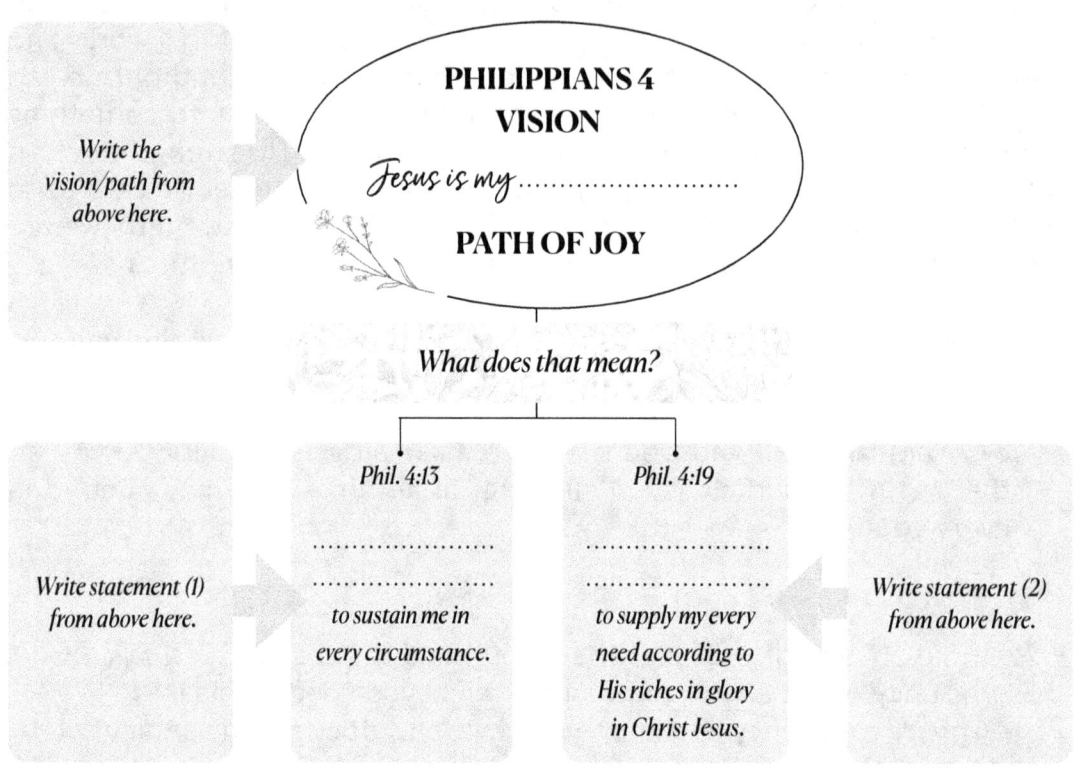

Write the vision/path from above here.

PHILIPPIANS 4 VISION

Jesus is my ....

PATH OF JOY

What does that mean?

Phil. 4:13

....
....
to sustain me in every circumstance.

Phil. 4:19

....
....
to supply my every need according to His riches in glory in Christ Jesus.

Write statement (1) from above here.

Write statement (2) from above here.

KEY VERSE: I can do all things through him who strengthens me.
(Phil. 4:13)

WEEK 6, DAY 3

I have learned...

I can do all things through him who strengthens me. (Phil. 4:13)

Since our title today is "I have learned," and since we are in the last chapter of Philippians, let's take a minute to review our visions/paths of joy and the accompanying tasks. We will start with the quote to remind ourselves we must have a task—an action—to bring the vision of a well-worn path to reality.

"A vision without a task is but a dream.

A task without a vision is drudgery.

A vision and a task are the hope of the world."

Fill in the following portions from our charts.

Goal for this week

❋ To understand and begin actively treading the path of joy in Philippians 4

Guiding Questions

❋ What is the vision/path of joy in Philippians 4?

❋ What does that path mean for me?

❋ What is the task that will help me tread this path?

❋ How do I execute that task effectively?

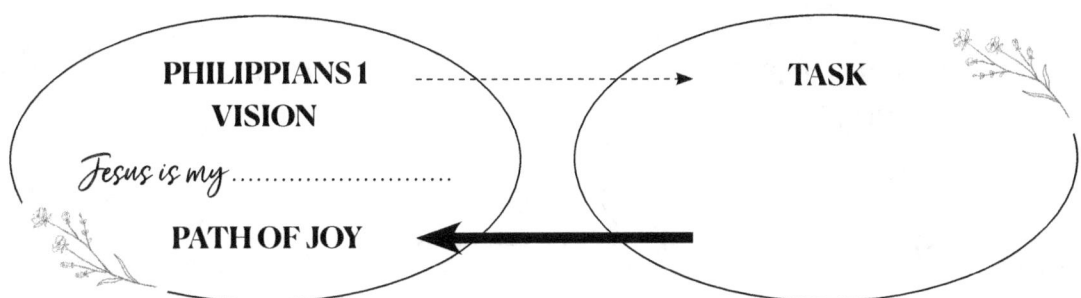

KEY VERSE: For to me to live is Christ and to die is gain. (Phil. 1:21)

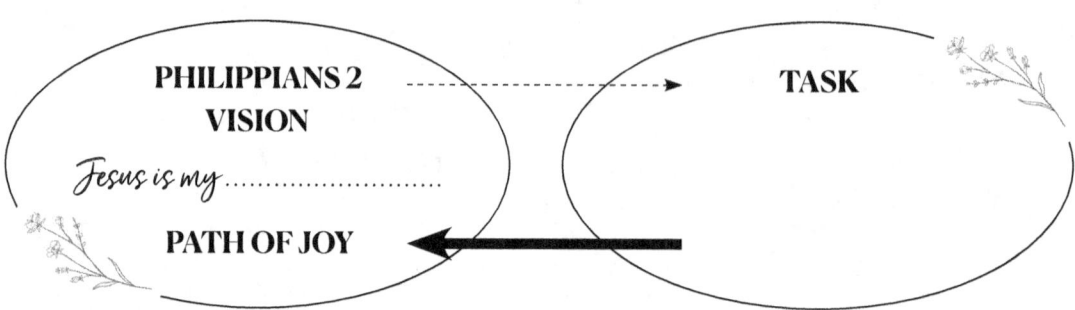

KEY VERSE: Have this mind among yourselves, which is yours in Christ Jesus. (Phil. 2:5)

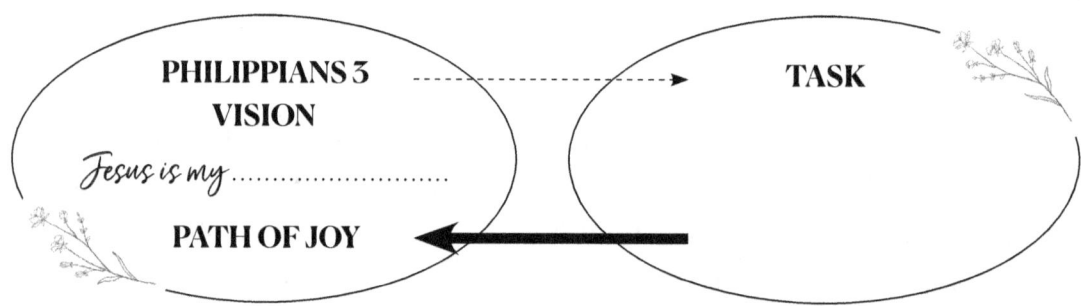

KEY VERSE: Indeed, I count everything as loss because of the surpassing worth of knowing Christ Jesus my Lord. For his sake I have suffered the loss of all things and count them as rubbish, in order that I may gain Christ. (Phil. 3:8)

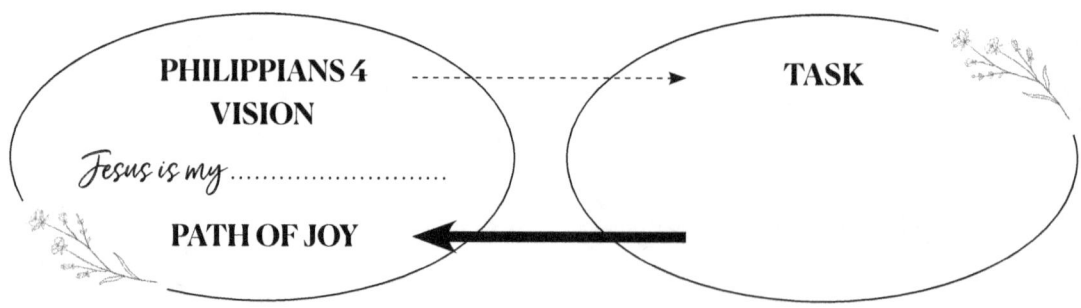

KEY VERSE: I can do all things through him who strengthens me. (Phil. 4:13)

Look at those together for a minute. Read through them slowly. Think about what you have learned and the well-worn paths you are trying to accomplish. Just look at all that precious, joyful treading!

Although studied individually, we don't want to miss a key understanding from the paths as a whole: Jesus can only be *my life, my paragon,* and *my reward* because He is sufficient to be so. When we undertake the task to *learn to be content,* we are impacting our ability to *live worthy of the gospel, work out my salvation,* and *press on (toward Christlikeness).* On a personal level, learning contentment in the sufficiency of who Christ is and how He applies His sufficiency in your life will produce steadfastness (2 Tim. 1:12), which increases the likelihood your paths of joy will become well-worn.

Let's shift our study to the concept of *contentment.*

> Read Philippians 4:10-20; then use 4:11 to complete the sentence in your own words.

> "I have learned ...."

> For most of us, our lives consist of areas of contentment with Christ's sufficiency and areas where we waver. Record some of those in the table below. Thank God that you recognize His sufficiency in some areas, then ask Him to move you toward contentment in areas of wavering.

Areas of contentment	Areas with a lack of contentment

Content in Philippians 4:11 is the adjective *autarkés* and is used only here in the Bible. Surprisingly, it refers to *self*-sufficiency.[14] Plot twist! Was Paul really saying he was sufficient within *himself* to be content in any situation?

> Reread 4:11-13. Recognize Paul's efforts to catch people's attention in vv. 11-12 to set them up for the big reveal in v. 13. (We talked about the "attention grabber" in v. 12 yesterday.) On what basis did Paul claim to be "self"-sufficient?
>
> ....
>
> ....

In essence, Paul was saying, "I have learned to be self-sufficient in any situation. I can handle whatever is thrown at me. Wanna know my secret?" (Pause for dramatic effect.) *"Jesus is my sufficiency*!" Whereas self-sufficiency typically implies *you* have the strength within to satisfy your needs, Paul knew the strength within him was through the *Spirit.* The power at work in him was from the One "who is able to do far more abundantly than all that we ask or think" (Eph. 3:16, 20). What sufficiency!

> In what ways do we seek contentment through our own self-sufficiency? (Buying a designer coffee to settle my emotions rather than pausing to pray comes to my mind. Again, no guilt; just acknowledging the struggle. We can't make changes without awareness of a problem.)
>
> ....
>
> ....
>
> ....

> In the following verse from the writer of Hebrews, circle the phrase *be content with what you have*; then, write what you have in the blank. (Hint: It's not material possessions.)

Hebrews 13:5. "Keep your life free from love of money, and be content with what you have, for he has said, 'I will never leave you nor forsake you.'"

I have ....

What do we have? We have Christ! Like Paul, we can rest in His complete sufficiency which is much more satisfying than anything we listed on p. 226.

How do I know this? Allow me to share a little. I mentioned in Week 4 that we moved to a new town in the fall of 2020 when my husband took a new job, and I was without a job after pursuing a costly degree. Within three weeks of the move, my daughter was hospitalized with Covid. She still has long Covid and has had to quit her job and move in with us. We eventually bought a house, but we had to do so when the market was crazy; thus, it lacked the square footage, lot size, and eye appeal of our previous home. After a year, my husband took another job, so another bit of upheaval. A few months later, I fell and broke my foot, requiring surgery and extended elevation. Consequently, we had to cancel our long-anticipated vacation. When adding concerns for other family members and aging parents in this mix, you could almost wonder where God was in all of this.

But I don't wonder. I see Christ's sufficiency and God's provision over and over. When our daughter became sick, we lived within twenty minutes of her apartment rather than four hours. We were available to carry her to the hospital, pray for her in the hospital parking lot (we couldn't go in), and stay with her after her release. God knew we needed to be here, and He knew I didn't need the demands of a job. Also, although we did overpay for a home, we were no longer in the smelly apartment. Plus, the new house had a large room with a bathroom above the garage that we thought would probably be a guest space. Guess what? When our daughter moved in a few months later, her apartment furnishings fit perfectly. God knew we would need that space for Rachel's Retreat. The job my husband took? It was within driving distance of the house, so we didn't have to move, and the salary increase was sufficient to cover the added living expenses of our daughter. When I found out my foot was broken, for some reason I didn't console myself with a designer coffee. I drove home from the doctor, propped my foot up, and continued reading through the Psalms. I was on Psalm 94. Do you want to see the sufficiency of Christ in action? Read the following verses.

Psalm 94:18-19. "When I thought, 'My foot slips,' your steadfast love, O LORD, held me up. When the cares of my heart are many, your consolations cheer my soul."

Exactly the words I needed to hear! And even though the vacation may seem minor, God knew we needed a break. My brother-in-law offered us his lake house for a week. It was only an hour and a half from our home, so I could easily keep my foot elevated on the trip. In addition, we rejoiced at the birth of two sweet grandsons during this time—exclamation points emphasizing God's sufficiency and grace!

Are all our problems solved? No. Is my daughter still sick and unable to work? Yes. Does our house still pale in comparison with the other one? Yes, so we don't compare. (More on that topic later.) We have had more people visit and spend the night with us here than in any house we have ever owned. Sometimes it's a mad rush to change the sheets between guests, but we are grateful God uses this house.

Hopefully, we better understand that with Christ in us through the power of the Holy Spirit, we can intentionally *learn to be content.* We can stomp out weeds of fear and doubt and tread with calm assurance the joyful path *Jesus is my sufficiency.* We just need a plan of action.

To develop that plan, let's go back to the beginning of Philippians 4...or just a bit further. Since there weren't divisions originally, we'll begin with the last verses from chapter 3.

Read Philippians 3:20-4:1, remembering how excited Paul was as he shared about glorification. You can feel that excitement flow into 4:1 as Paul expresses his love and joy for the Philippians by referring to them in four different ways.

Let me paraphrase a little: *Oh, I can hardly wait! One day our Savior, the Lord Jesus Christ, will return! By His power, He will transform us from our pitiful estate into the glorious image of His resurrected body. Then, we will take up residence in the territory of our citizenship: heaven! In light of this, you—you for whom my joy and affection overflow beyond expression—you stand firm in the Lord! It will be so worth it!*

Paul closed this enthusiastic exclamation with another exhortation. It would be difficult to learn contentment without choosing to act on these few words from 4:1. Write them below.

....

....

Near the end of chapter 1, Paul used words that prompted thoughts of the Philippians' citizenship and their need to stand firm in unity for the faith of the gospel (1:27). As Paul prepared to close his letter, he did the same. Recall that Roman soldiers had been encouraged to settle in Philippi. Therefore, when Paul spoke of enemies (3:18), when he reminded the Philippians directly of their heavenly citizenship (3:20), and when he called them again to "stand firm" (4:1), he was using language that resonated with his audience. Their minds were likely filled with thoughts of battle against enemies, defense of the place of citizenship, the necessity of unity, the importance of standing firm without thought to personal harm, and the unquestionable value of confidence and trust in the commanding officer.

We may not relate as easily, but we certainly need to reflect on these concepts ourselves. As Christians, we fight battles in our minds and spirits every day. One of those is the battle to be content.

> What do you see or do frequently that has the potential to threaten your contentment?
>
> ....
>
> ....

Daily we face advertising, social media, home renovation shows, and other avenues that may be harmless...or may subtly prompt us to make comparisons. Be aware of any dissatisfaction that tries to creep in, for comparison undermines contentment. In fact, Theodore Roosevelt is credited with this comment that seems relevant to us: "Comparison is the thief of joy."[15]

Nope! No deal! Let's not give *comparison* that kind of power in our lives! We've come too far on our paths of joy to lose ground now. Instead, let's find truth in God's Word.

Look up 1 Timothy 6:6 and fill in the blanks below.

"But................................. with .... is great gain."

I have often used this verse to redirect my thoughts when I have been self-ishly veering toward comparison and discontent. *Godliness* reminds me to look beyond myself and reflect Christ's character; while *contentment* calls me to exhibit faith in Christ's sufficiency, to stand firm in the Lord.

As we close, we need to emphasize a key point regarding our task.

Write below how Paul acquired his contentment.

....

Contentment is neither natural nor easy. We must learn it. When I taught, I had a poster on the wall with one of those pithy bits of life-impacting wisdom all teachers hope to impart to their students: *The only place where "success" comes before "work" is in the dictionary.* Learning is work. It requires effective practice. It also produces success in that you are eventually able to stand firm in what you know while building on that knowledge to gain deeper under-standing. The result is an ever-developing expertise that benefits others as well as yourself.

Modifying those last four sentences to fit our context yields these thoughts: Learning contentment is work. (It is our *task* after all.) It requires effective practice. It also produces peace in that you are eventually able to stand firm in *Who* you know while building on that spiritual knowledge to gain deeper understanding. The result is an ever-developing joy in the sufficiency of Jesus that benefits others as well as yourself. (And a bonus in this context: It glorifies God!)

We will build that knowledge base as before, by identifying and enacting practical, preliminary steps. For this chapter, the steps will aid us in standing firm as we learn contentment. I think Paul knew the difficulty of this concept because he left us plenty of opportunities for practice. No excuses for not gaining ground if we do the work in the power of the Holy Spirit. Paul wanted us to know the peace of contentment so we can successfully tread the path *Jesus is my sufficiency.*

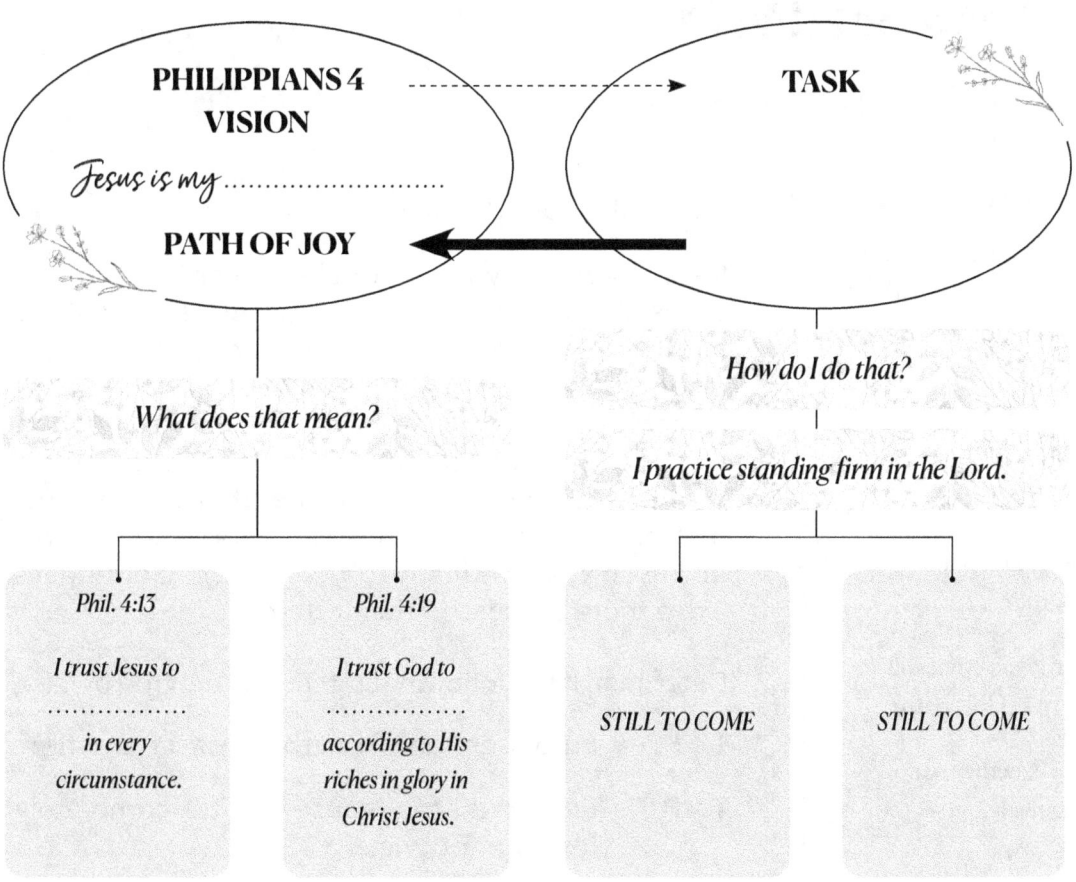

PHILIPPIANS 4
VISION

Jesus is my ....

PATH OF JOY

TASK

What does that mean?

How do I do that?

I practice standing firm in the Lord.

Phil. 4:13

I trust Jesus to
....
in every
circumstance.

Phil. 4:19

I trust God to
....
according to His
riches in glory in
Christ Jesus.

STILL TO COME

STILL TO COME

KEY VERSE: I can do all things through him who strengthens me.
(Phil. 4:13)

WEEK 6, DAY 4

The Task: Learn to be content (Part 1)

I can do all things through him who strengthens me.
(Phi. 4:13)

Goal for this week

❋ To understand and begin actively treading the path of joy in Philippians 4

Guiding Questions

❋ What is the vision/path of joy in Philippians 4?

❋ What does that path mean for me?

❋ What is the task that will help me tread this path?

❋ How do I execute that task effectively?

"Let's talk about the facts."

It's a statement you would likely hear in my home as we discuss something that upset us. That statement reminds us to calm our emotions and seek resolution for the moment. We may not be able to solve the problem, but we can discuss the situation reasonably and eventually shift our focus to what should hold our attention: the things that truly matter in our lives. It is our small effort to stand firm in the Lord as we learn to be content. (Some days we're more successful than others.)

Determine if the following statements are true or false.

T F   Emotions can strengthen us to stand firm.

T F   Emotions can cause us to completely lose our footing.

T F   Emotions can focus our minds and move us toward a goal.

T F   Emotions can distract us to the point of not knowing which way to go.

Those are all true statements. Emotions are God-given. We are supposed to feel them, but we are also supposed to control them. Robin Kramer writes, "Emotions are like toddlers. You can't put them in the trunk, but you can't let them drive the bus either."[16] Well, if they have to ride with us, I guess we better learn to buckle them securely in their safety seats. To do so, we will look today at how Paul urged the Philippians to handle emotions and how he handled an emotionally charged situation.

> Read Philippians 4:1-9; then, write below the exhortation in 4:1 we discussed near the end of yesterday's lesson.
>
> ....

Paul shifted from an exciting, inspiring message in 3:20-21 to an area of local concern in 4:2-3. Philippians 4:1 is his transition verse. As we said yesterday, these words reassured them yet again they were all dearly loved and called them together to stand firm.

Then, Paul named names.

Paul had called for unity, humility, and a focus on Christ throughout this letter. He had set the stage to directly address the unity disrupting that concerned him. Without taking sides or commanding them to yield strongly held beliefs, Paul addressed two ladies by name (Phil. 4:2). What was their problem? We don't know. It did not merit Paul naming it.[17]

It is interesting that the Greek verb used in 4:2 for "to agree," *phroneó*, is the same verb used in Philippians 2:2, 2:5, and 3:19[18] when we looked at verses that talked about directing the mind.

> Turn back to Philippians 2:2-3. Based on these verses, what did Paul expect of these ladies?
>
> ....
>
> ....

Typically, in arguments, emotions run high. We can't see issues clearly, and the point of argument often trumps what is true or most important. Paul directed these ladies to re-establish a Kingdom focus and value each other. Then, he asked an unnamed, but trusted, companion to help them. He also reminded all of them of two key facts: (1) They had worked together in the gospel, and (2) their names were written in the book of life. Directing their minds to these eminent matters would allow them to stand firm in the Lord and tame the emotions threatening the effectiveness, or possibly the existence, of the church—not to mention impacting the ladies' personal relationships with Christ (Ps. 66:18).

Have you ever observed or been involved in a similar situation? Was a strategy like this used to bring reconciliation? If not, how might this approach—diverting focus from self to a bigger goal, esteeming each other, and recognizing commonalities that hold greater value—have helped mediate the situation?

....

....

Paul spent only a brief two verses here before he moved on. (Note to self: I think I need to learn something from Paul's "address it, but don't dwell on it" approach. I might be guilty of harping on something after I needed to move on. Anybody with me?)

Now, we start taking our practical steps that help us stand firm so we can *learn to be content.* Paul is in rapid-fire mode as he nears the end of the letter, so get ready!

In Philippians 4:4, we see our overarching theme of joy come up again.

Fill in the following blanks using this verse.

What do we do? ....

In whom? ....

When? ....

Those three blanks should re-emphasize in our minds that joy is not an emotion like happiness. As we said in Week 1, there *is* an emotional aspect to it when we consider joy to be a virtue—a habit that directs our thoughts, *feelings*, and actions toward what God intends—but by now, we know joy is more complex than we originally thought. Restating the definition we have used, joy is enduring, deep delight in what holds the most significance. Therefore, joy is not a downward concentration on current circumstances, but an upward and outward devotion to what maintains long-term value. It does not come and go but is rooted in the truth of who God is and displayed as evidence of His Spirit in us. When viewing joy from this perspective, we can *always* rejoice in the Lord.

In the next verse, let's use the Amplified version to examine another exhortation. It gives us several options for a word that must be rather difficult to translate. Approach this verse as an encouragement for quiet, controlled strength, not for subservience.

> **Philippians 4:5 (AMP).** "Let your gentle spirit [your graciousness, unselfishness, mercy, tolerance, and patience] be known to all people. The Lord is near."

Underline the words above that clarify what a gentle spirit is. Is it a spirit dominated by emotion or calm intent? How do people respond to someone who has a gentle spirit?

....

....

Now consider how God views a gentle spirit. Underline any phrases that describe a gentle spirit in the verse below.

> **1 Peter 3:3-4.** "Do not let your adorning be external—the braiding of hair and the putting on of gold jewelry, or the clothing you wear—but let your adorning be the hidden person of the heart with the imperishable beauty of a gentle and quiet spirit, which in God's sight is very precious."

Oh, ladies, we want our spirits to look like that in God's eyes! In Psalm 18:35, David said God's gentleness made him great. David recognized that God's tender grace and mercy had raised him up. May we recognize God's gentleness in our lives. May we allow it to develop "the imperishable beauty of a gentle and quiet spirit" (1 Pet. 3:4) in us. And may we then let that spirit be known to all so God can use us to impact our families and others for Him.

In the process of learning to be content thus far, we know to stand firm in the Lord by rejoicing (v. 4) and having a gentle spirit (v. 5). In v. 6, we add *praying with gratitude*. Simple enough, right?

Or not. Did you catch the first phrase of Philippians 4:6? If not, read it again. Does that feel like an impossible task?

As we approach this sensitive topic, I do not want to discount any anxiety-related struggles you or your loved ones experience. However, with a heart full of compassion and with gentleness that longs to lift you up, I also need to acknowledge we live in a world where feelings are becoming more relevant than facts, which does not align with God's Word.

Look up the following scriptures and fill in the blanks.

Jeremiah 17:9. "The heart is .... above all things."

2 Timothy 1:7. "For God gave us a spirit not of .... but of power and love and ...."

Our emotions can deceive us. If our focus is on our emotions, we will be "riding the wave" rather than standing firm. Faith calls us to stand firm on what we know to be true. If we follow the prevailing wisdom of the world, our emotions can drive our lives. From Philippians 4:6, it is obvious that is not what God wants.

Write the second phrase of Philippians 4:6 below—the one about gratitude.

....

....

....

So, is Paul saying, "Just pray with gratitude. All your anxiety will be gone. Poof!"? No, he's not. He is trying to point us in a direction that will help, though. Although Paul was probably more aware of the positive impact of gratitude on the *spirit* when he wrote, there is now a great deal of research on the physical benefits of gratitude, as well. Like the research on the negative impact of complaining we examined on Week 1, Day 4, there is significant research on the positive impact of gratitude—impact on quality of life, in general, and on anxiety, in particular. Briefly, your brain has a difficult time thinking about both positive and negative occurrences. Therefore, the more you focus on gratitude, the fewer anxious thoughts you will have.[19] Over time, as we discussed previously, your brain can fire and wire to make gratitude a well-worn path, as well.

Of course, Paul's perspective of the spiritual impact should also be considered. Prayers and requests offered with thanksgiving, particularly those anchored in the promises of Scripture, can only strengthen our spirits. Therefore, gratitude helps us stand firm and promotes contentment. It is not easy, and it won't be immediate. In fact, it may be a daily battle. Still, I pray you will recognize growth and find peace in that.

As we mention peace, let's move to verse 7. Do you feel more secure and settled just reading this verse?

> According to this scripture, what do you experience when you practice the exhortations we have studied today?
>
> ....
>
> And what does the above do for you?
>
> ....
>
> ....

Wait a minute! Didn't we just read that the heart was deceitful (Jer. 17:9)?

Yes, but that was "the" heart, the fleshly seat of emotions. This is "your" heart "in Christ," the spiritual place where Christ dwells by faith (Eph. 3:17).

We want to spend our last few minutes exploring the guarding of our hearts and minds.

Look up the scriptures in the table below and use them to answer the questions.

Guarding the heart	Guarding the mind
Why do you guard your heart? (Prov. 4:23)	Why do you guard your mind? (1 Pet. 5:8)
How do you guard your heart? (Prov. 3:5-6)	How do you achieve "perfect peace"? (Is. 26:3)
How do you align your heart with God? (Ps. 37:4)	How do you align your mind with God? (Col 3:2)

How do these verses support what we have learned this week? Why do you think it is important to understand the role your heart and mind play in learning contentment and knowing Jesus as your sufficiency?

....

....

As I'm sure we know—but it's still worth saying—the world cannot give this peace (John 14:27). Man cannot bestow this peace by making a "V" with his first two fingers. A piece of jewelry cannot exert this peace when adorned with the well-known circular symbol. No, this peace comes from God. It is peace that passes understanding. It is peace that guards our hearts and minds. And it is critical to standing firm and *learning to be content*. So, rejoice! Have a gentle spirit. And pray with thanksgiving. The vision/path of joy, *Jesus is my sufficiency*, needs some treading!

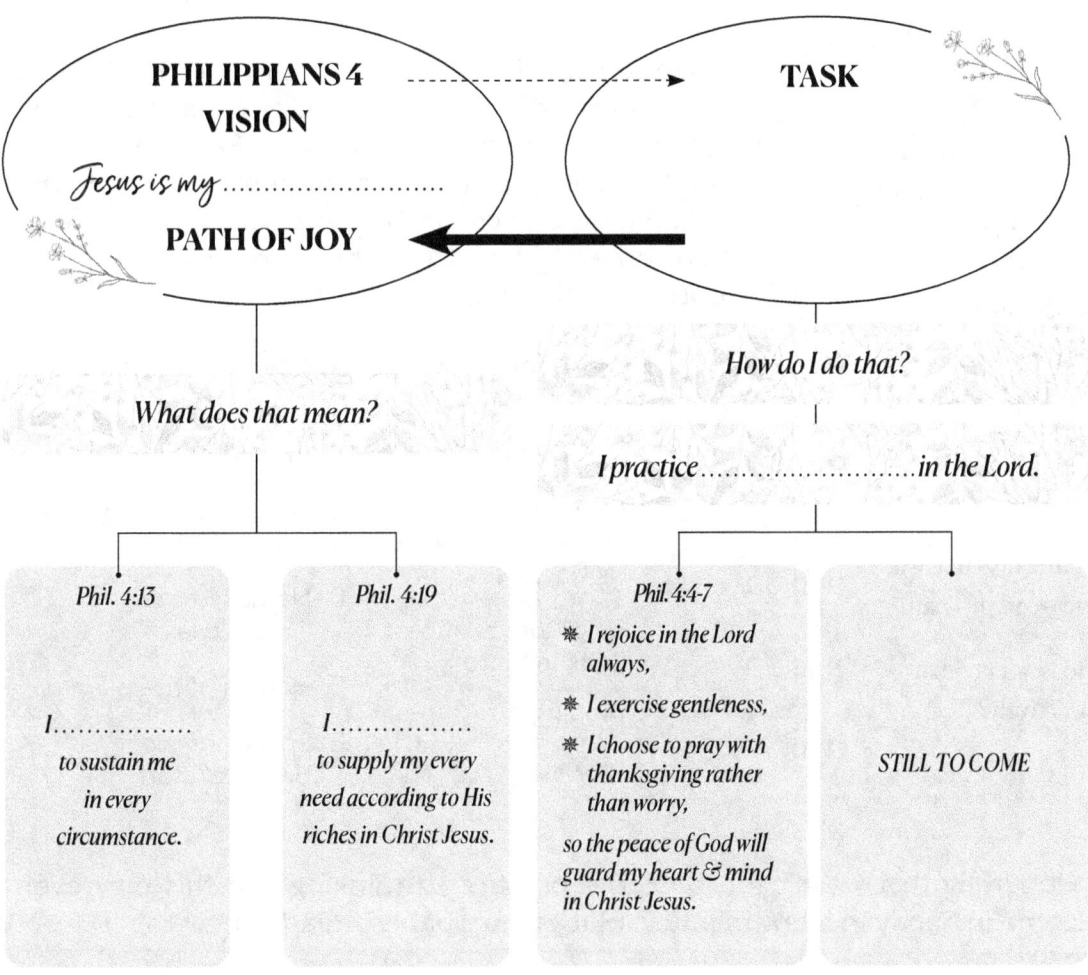

KEY VERSE: I can do all things through him who strengthens me.
(Phil. 4:13)

WEEK 6, DAY 5

The Task: Learn to be content (Part 2)

I can do all things through him who strengthens me.
(Phil. 4:13)

Goal for this week

❋ To understand and begin actively treading the path of joy in Philippians 4

Guiding Questions

❋ What is the vision/path of joy in Philippians 4?

❋ What does that path mean for me?

❋ What is the task that will help me tread this path?

❋ How do I execute that task effectively?

Anybody up for a good mnemonic challenge? (A mnemonic device is a pattern that helps you remember something specific.) See how many of the following you can remember. Match the mnemonic device on the left with what it helps you remember on the right. (The answer is at the bottom of the page.)

.... 1. Every Good Boy Does Fine.

.... 2. All Cows Eat Grass.

.... 3. My Very Excellent Mother Just Served Us Nachos.

.... 4. Ring Out Your Great Bells In Victory.

.... 5. HOMES

.... 6. PEMDAS

A. Colors of the rainbow

B. Order of operations in mathematics

C. Lines of the treble clef staff

D. Names of the Great Lakes

E. Names of the planets

F. Spaces of the bass clef staff

Hopefully that wasn't too bad. The practice in thinking like this may even come in handy in a few minutes. (But you probably already knew that.)

Answers: C / F / E / A / D / B

Reread Philippians 4:1-9 again, focusing on vv. 8-9.

Yesterday, we closed with guarding our hearts and minds. However, most of yesterday's learning was tied more to the mind and the impact of emotions. We begin with the mind again today, so I want to clarify once more that the mind is not the brain. The mind allows you to focus and make decisions. Without peace, you cannot evaluate things correctly or make appropriate decisions. Furthermore, Satan's arena is the mind.[20] The last thing he wants is the peace of God guarding your mind.

2 Corinthians 10:3-5 addresses our battle with Satan. Read the verses below and answer the question.

> **2 Corinthians 10:3-5.** "For though we walk in the flesh, we are not waging war according to the flesh. For the weapons of our warfare are not of the flesh but have divine power to destroy strongholds. We destroy arguments and every lofty opinion raised against the knowledge of God, and take every thought captive to obey Christ."

According to this verse, how do we do battle in our thought life?

....

....

And what does that mean exactly? Philippians 4:8 holds the answer. Paul reminded the Philippians to anchor their thoughts so they could stand firm in trials and callings. He wanted, for them, what we want for ourselves: to direct our minds to Christ and His sufficiency, not *be* directed by our emotions. (Emotions don't get to drive, remember?) This verse is a beautiful exhortation, but rather difficult to remember. Let's read Philippians 4:8 first; then, we'll work on getting it into our minds.

> **Philippians 4:8.** "Finally, brothers, whatever is **true**, whatever is **honorable**, whatever is **just**, whatever is **pure**, whatever is **lovely**, whatever is **commendable**, if there is any **excellence**, if there is anything **worthy of praise**, think about these things." (emphasis mine)

Do you see the beauty in the rhythm? Do you also see all. the. words.? Well, let's start by changing *worthy of praise* to *praiseworthy*, then switch the order a bit to create the following mnemonic: "I think on things...**T**hat **L**et **H**is **J**oy & **P**erfect **P**eace **E**xceed **C**omprehension." In this manner, the first letter of each of the last eight words gives us the things to dwell on and allows us to clump the words into two groups of four. Even learning the sentence should bring a little peace to your mind. Think about how this can impact the firing and wiring pathways of your brain!

	True	Lovely	Honorable	Just	Pure	Praiseworthy	Excellent	Commendable
I think on things...	That	Let	His	Joy &	Perfect	Peace	Exceed	Comprehension

Spend the next few minutes trying to get the mnemonic and/or the actual verse stored in your memory. This effort will be worth your time as you prepare to do a little firing and wiring, training your brain to capture errant thoughts so notions of contentment can freely flow.

Now that you have made some progress, let's move to Philippians 4:9. Paul again reminded the Philippians to follow his example. It's a rather bold statement, but we need to remember, the Philippians had few role models for living as Christ-followers. Thus, Paul volunteered for the job. He remains a worthy example 2,000 years later.

As we finish our practical steps for standing firm, look one more time at verses 7 and 9.

Fill in the blanks using the given verses.

❋ **Philippians 4:7.** "And the .... of .... will guard your hearts and your minds in Christ Jesus."

❋ **Philippians 4:9.** "...and the .... of .... will be with you."

What is the significance of the differences between the two promises?

....

....

The God of peace is with us as the peace of God stands guard. How abundantly sufficient is that?! Contentment and joyful path treading, here we come!

Finally, we can't end our study without spending just a minute on the closing verses.

Scan Philippians 4 and get a feel for the flow since we were not particularly linear in our study this week. Then focus on the last four verses, Philippians 4:20-23.

What a beautiful picture of the church as the worldwide body of believers. Believers' greetings echoing back and forth (vv. 21-22) across land and sea, glory shining out (v. 20) and grace flowing in (v. 23). It's a complete picture, and a very fitting way for Paul to end this letter to the church he loved.

Treading the Path of Joy *Jesus is my sufficiency*

Review

Aaahhhh. Breathe. Settle your thoughts as you review Paul's last words to the Philippian church. In your Week 6, Day 1 notes, think about what Paul shared and why, given his current circumstances. Don't miss the significance of the vision/path, the task, and the key verse to your life. As you begin Day 2, reflect on the life of Maria Fearing and her treading of the path *Jesus is my sufficiency.* Recall that Christ is sufficient in resources and experiences, and because of who He is; in Him, you are sufficient, as well. Day 3 called us to work as we realized we must **learn** to be content, while Day 4 began with Paul's call to agree in the Lord. From there, Days 4 and 5 gave us practical steps for having the peace of God that comes from the God of peace guarding our hearts and minds. That peace strengthens us to stand firm and establishes the task of learning contentment, which produces the joyous, treasured, and well-worn path, *Jesus is my sufficiency.*

A full picture

Use the chart on p. 248 to help you complete this chart symbolizing how to tread our final path of joy. Take a minute for these truths to sink in.

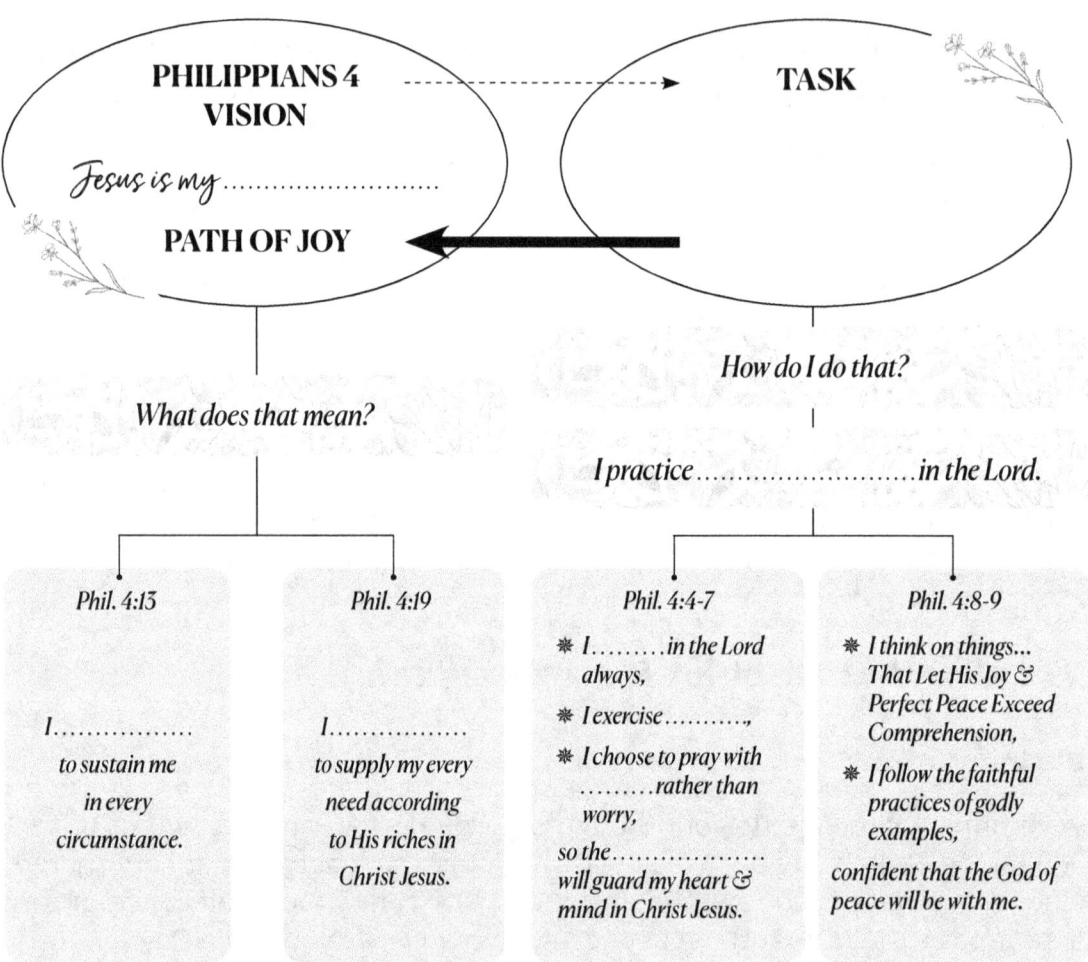

PHILIPPIANS 4 VISION

Jesus is my ....

PATH OF JOY

TASK

What does that mean?

How do I do that?

I practice ....*in the Lord.*

Phil. 4:13

I..................
*to sustain me
in every
circumstance.*

Phil. 4:19

I..................
*to supply my every
need according
to His riches in
Christ Jesus.*

Phil. 4:4-7

❊ *I*..........*in the Lord
always,*

❊ *I exercise*.........,

❊ *I choose to pray with
.........rather than
worry,*

so the...................
*will guard my heart &
mind in Christ Jesus.*

Phil. 4:8-9

❊ *I think on things...
That Let His Joy &
Perfect Peace Exceed
Comprehension,*

❊ *I follow the faithful
practices of godly
examples,*

*confident that the God of
peace will be with me.*

KEY VERSE: I can do all things through him who strengthens me.
(Phil. 4:13)

Write below any thoughts you want to remember from the review and/or the chart.

....

Boots on the ground

If we're going to *Learn to be content*, we need effective opportunities for practice. This week, I focused mainly on Paul's exhortations and brainstormed a few practical actions that support the development of our path. As usual, put a check mark beside those you are already doing and an arrow beside those you wish to do. Then do a little brainstorming of your own and be ready to discuss this page with your group.

* *Promoting faith in the sufficiency of Christ:* I know we've said this every week, but there is no substitute for Bible study. Learn the truths of Scripture that will allow you to stand firm when Satan is really trying to rock your emotional boat. Learn to trust Him and to rest in Him.

* *Focusing on contentment:* Try a media fast. It doesn't have to last for days. It might mean you intentionally skip your favorite TV show and purposefully use that hour to meet another's need or pray for your family.

* *Standing firm*

   * *Rejoice in the Lord:* Throw a party, even if it's just for your family, and provide opportunities for each person to express joy in something God has done. For children, I think about providing M&Ms or some other "treat"—one for each joy they share. What a great opportunity to teach children to think longer term!

   * *Exercise gentleness:* Read or listen to the book *Amazing Grace: William Wilberforce and the Heroic Campaign to End Slavery* by Eric Metaxas. You will be amazed at what one sincerely devoted man with a good group of praying friends can accomplish.

   * *Pray with thanksgiving:*

* Create a gratitude journal. Daily, write 3 things you are thankful for. Add any meaningful scriptures on gratitude. Use this to supplement your prayer time so you are praying with thanksgiving.

* Remember that thinking about both positive and negative things is very difficult for your brain. Choose to use your brain power on positive thoughts.

❋ *Think on these things:* Memorize either Philippians 4:8 or the mnemonic: I think on things...**T**hat **L**et **H**is **J**oy & **P**erfect **P**eace **E**xceed **C**omprehension! (*i.e.* things that are true, lovely, honorable, just, pure, praiseworthy, excellent, and commendable)

❋ *Follow godly examples* (I think we've covered this well in previous weeks!)

Add your own thoughts below:

....

....

Enjoy time with your group! See you shortly for our final week!

The God of
peace is with
us as the
peace of God
stands guard.

GROUP

The Path Behind

Group Discussion of Week 6

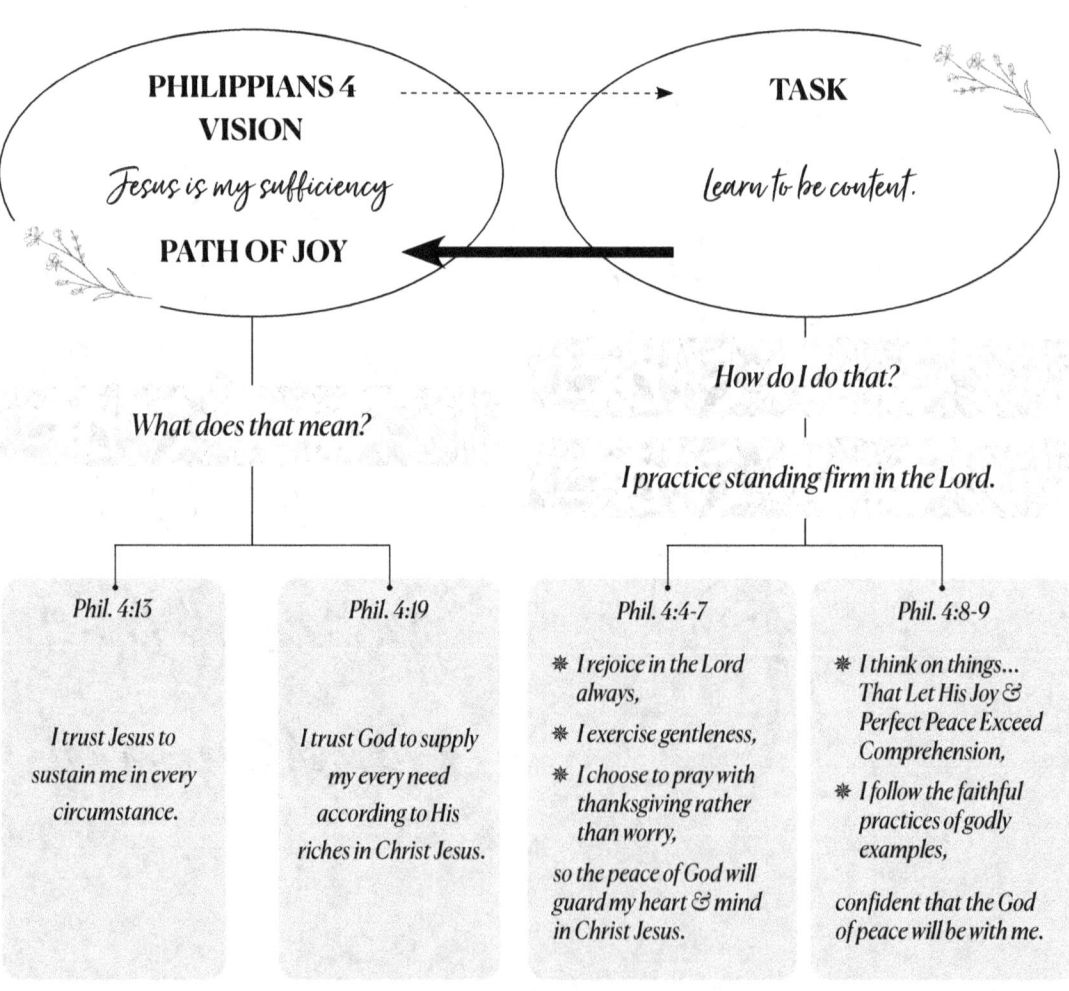

PHILIPPIANS 4 VISION

Jesus is my sufficiency

PATH OF JOY

TASK

Learn to be content.

What does that mean?

How do I do that?

I practice standing firm in the Lord.

Phil. 4:13

I trust Jesus to sustain me in every circumstance.

Phil. 4:19

I trust God to supply my every need according to His riches in Christ Jesus.

Phil. 4:4-7

* *I rejoice in the Lord always,*
* *I exercise gentleness,*
* *I choose to pray with thanksgiving rather than worry,*

so the peace of God will guard my heart & mind in Christ Jesus.

Phil. 4:8-9

* *I think on things... That Let His Joy & Perfect Peace Exceed Comprehension,*
* *I follow the faithful practices of godly examples,*

confident that the God of peace will be with me.

KEY VERSE: I can do all things through him who strengthens me.
(Phil. 4:13)

SESSION 7

The Path Ahead

Introductory Activity for Week 7

Part I - Group Activity

Part II - Group Discussion

PART 4
Successful Treading of Joyful Paths

Well, brave, committed, and joyful path treaders, we have made it to the final week of our study of joy. Give yourself a high five and a fist bump! In this short time, you have done a lot of stomping in an effort to tread rightly the paths of joy we have discussed. I hope you feel like you are well on your way to making joy a delightful habit. Keep the picture on the left as a vision in your mind, for eventually, as you keep treading, those well-worn paths will more fully emerge.

This week, we will take advantage of the opportunity to reflect on the visions/paths of joy and the tasks we have learned. It is a slower pace, designed to let the Holy Spirit awaken your spirit to matters of significance in which you can find enduring, deep delight. Be sure to start each day with a brief prayer, an acknowledgment that you are a child of God, and a desire to know Christ better.

This week may represent our last steps together, but don't leave this study without establishing in your mind the intent to continue making joy a virtue, a delightful habit that directs your thoughts, feelings, and actions to what God intends. My prayers go with you, dear ladies, as you purposefully tread well-worn paths of joy!

WEEK 7

Establishing and Guarding Our Paths of Joy

WEEK 7, DAY 1

The Joy of Philippians

The joy of the LORD is your strength.
(Neh. 8:10)

"Today is the day!" Lydia smiled to herself. There would be no selling of purple cloth on this day. All work was set aside for food and fellowship and news from Rome. Epaphroditus was back with stories to tell of his travels and the mission on which the church had sent him. And he had a letter from Paul to read to them!

Lydia was pulled from her thoughts by the sound of laughter. She wasn't the only one excited about these impending events. Her whole house-hold was buzzing as they were getting ready, and she could sense their joy in anticipation of what the day would hold. Oh, how these precious family members had grown in their faith since Paul's first trip more than ten years ago. Her eyes grew moist as she gratefully acknowledged the amazing blessings God had bestowed on her and her family, blessings that began because of Paul's obedience to come to Macedonia and share Christ with a group of women by the river.

As Lydia and her family stepped out the door and into the street, her gratitude only grew. Men, women, and children of all ages and all walks of life were making their way to the church. The seeds Paul had planted were producing a flourishing crop of believers—"saints," as Paul called them (Phil. 1:1). Little did any of them know this church would be the start of a long-lasting Christian community that would influence the people and culture of Philippi for more than five more centuries—until the early 7th century AD when an earthquake would destroy the city.[1]

As they entered the church, Lydia's family members spotted their friends and moved to sit with them. A couple with rather drab attire but joyful countenance waved at Lydia from near the front. It was the old Philippian jailer and his wife smiling and motioning for her to join them. They had saved her a seat. Although the couple and Lydia were distant in social standing, they were united in Christ. Together, they had started this church. Together, they had prayed for this church. Together, they had worshiped. Together, they had grown in their knowledge of Christ. Together, they had shared in supporting Paul. Together.

And now, they sat together, ready to listen. Carrying a small bag, Epaphroditus was making his way through the crowd. Although he looked a bit tired from his long trip, there was no mistaking his joy as he navigated a path to the chair where he would sit to speak. Epaphroditus would be sharing stories of hardships when traveling, severe illness, and Paul's imprisonment, yet his demeanor foreshadowed that this would be a time of rejoicing. Yes, they would rejoice!

Lydia, the Philippian jailer, and the rest of this precious church settled in to listen as Epaphroditus prefaced the reading with the events since he had left. Then he moved to get his small bag, withdrew the parchment he had so carefully packed, and began to read. Even the children were quiet as Epaphroditus spoke Paul's words. Lydia smiled through her tears as she listened. It may have been Epaphroditus she was watching, but it was Paul's voice she was hearing in this treasured message of love and encouragement and exhortation...and joy!*

If you are in a place where you can read Philippians aloud, I encourage you to do so. It will only take fifteen minutes to read all four chapters (I timed it), and it will be worth your time. As we have each week, pray God will bless the reading of His Word and help you keep your mind focused. Whether aloud or silently, read the letter without stopping, as the Philippians would have heard it. Resist the urge to take notes or answer your phone. Just read. Let the message of this joy-filled book soak into your spirit.

Pause, pray, and read Philippians out loud.

* * * * * * * · * * * * * * * * * *

Goals for this week

❋ To reflect on our study of Philippians

❋ To move some of what we know from information to revelation

❋ To learn how to guard our joy

❋ To prepare for more joyful path-treading!

* This story is a fictional representation of circumstances surrounding the writing of Philippians. Its purpose is to help you better relate to the context and culture. The events should not be taken as factual.

Does your mind feel a little like this after reading?

I hope your mind is full of Jesus and joy. What a great way to start the week.
This space is available for thoughts, verses, prayers, or poems if you wish to use it.

....

....

....

....

....

....

....

....

WEEK 7, DAYS 2 & 3

Your paths of joy

The joy of the LORD is your strength.
(Neh. 8:10)

Yesterday, we ended our day with this image that may represent the thoughts in your mind. As we begin today, we want to think *about* these thoughts:

Would you classify the thoughts filling your mind as information or revelation?

Your answer to this question is important. Information is gained or lost easily. We want *revelation*! We want God-revealed truths we can hold to and apply to our lives. We want heart-understanding, not head-knowledge. We want deep-down-in-our-soul comprehension the world cannot cloud, and Satan cannot steal.

Goals for this week

※ To reflect on our study of Philippians

※ To move some of what we know from information to revelation

※ To learn how to guard our joy

※ To prepare for more joyful path-treading!

Deuteronomy 29:29 says, "The secret things belong to the Lord our God, but *the things that are revealed belong to us and to our children forever,* that we may do all the words of this law" (emphasis mine). Don't you love the thought of God taking us into His confidence? Of Him sharing with us secret things that belong to and help us live aligned with Him? What a privilege! And what a promise: The secret things will be "ours" forever, impacting our lives and the lives of our family members.

So, let's take some time to process. Although I pray the Holy Spirit has revealed truths to you throughout this study, they may have come at you too quickly to really absorb...too hastily to be able to call them "yours." The purpose of this time is to let them settle and find their home in you. The truths that become yours as you tread these paths of joy will help you know Christ better, strengthening your relationship with Him.

Today and tomorrow, you have space to review Weeks 3-6. There is a page for each path of joy—*Jesus is my life, Jesus is my paragon, Jesus is my reward,* and *Jesus is my sufficiency.* You may focus on one or two paths that seem particularly important right now or you can review all four. You may go in order or out of order. Primarily, what you want to do is *understand* and *remember.* You don't want to miss God's revelation or forget a time when His revelation became real. Spend some concentrated time with these pages, but also just leave them open and available to write as God brings thoughts to your mind throughout the days. Use the following questions to guide your thoughts.

Guiding Questions for Reviewing Paths

When have you known Jesus in this way (as life, paragon, reward, or sufficiency)? What did you learn about Him? Were there scriptures that anchored you? Was there support from fellow Christians that Jesus used to help you through? Write a brief testimony so you don't forget.

What did Christ use from this study to speak to your heart? (Scriptures, stories, aspects of salvation, etc.) Write down any information or revelation you want to remember. Sometimes information becomes revelation later as the Holy Spirit continues to work.

Identify one or two specific actions you will take now to facilitate the tasks that make well-worn paths of joy a reality for you and an influence on your family. (The *Boots on the ground* pages will help with ideas.)

What questions do you still have? Don't let lack of clarity keep you from all God has for you.

Review Week 3 and the questions on the previous page. Pray for revelation. Record your insights.

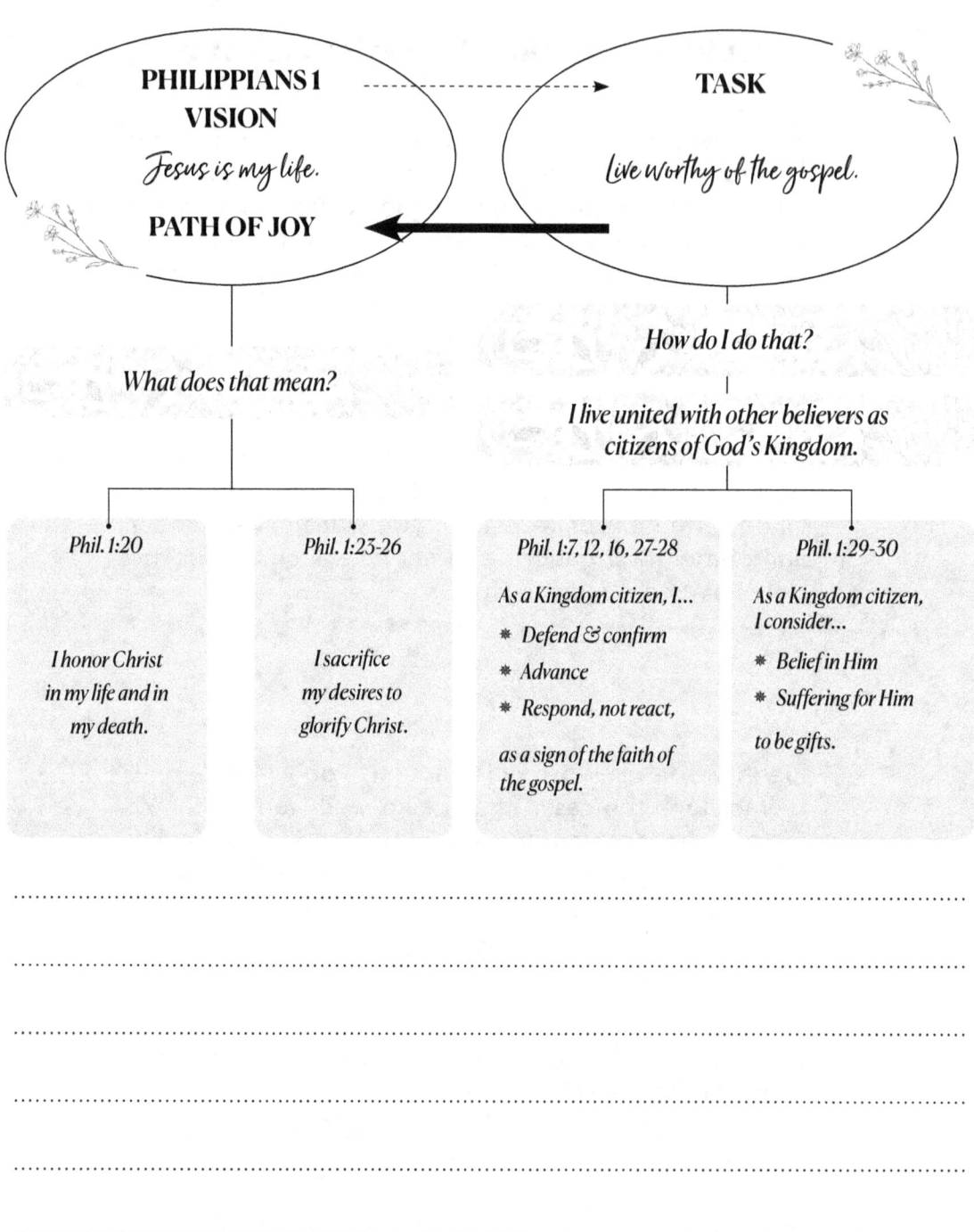

PHILIPPIANS 1 VISION

Jesus is my life.

PATH OF JOY

TASK

Live worthy of the gospel.

What does that mean?

How do I do that?

I live united with other believers as citizens of God's Kingdom.

Phil. 1:20

I honor Christ in my life and in my death.

Phil. 1:23-26

I sacrifice my desires to glorify Christ.

Phil. 1:7, 12, 16, 27-28

As a Kingdom citizen, I...
* *Defend & confirm*
* *Advance*
* *Respond, not react,*

as a sign of the faith of the gospel.

Phil. 1:29-30

As a Kingdom citizen, I consider...
* *Belief in Him*
* *Suffering for Him*

to be gifts.

....

....

....

....

....

....

Review Week 4 and the questions on p. 259. Pray for revelation. Record your insights.

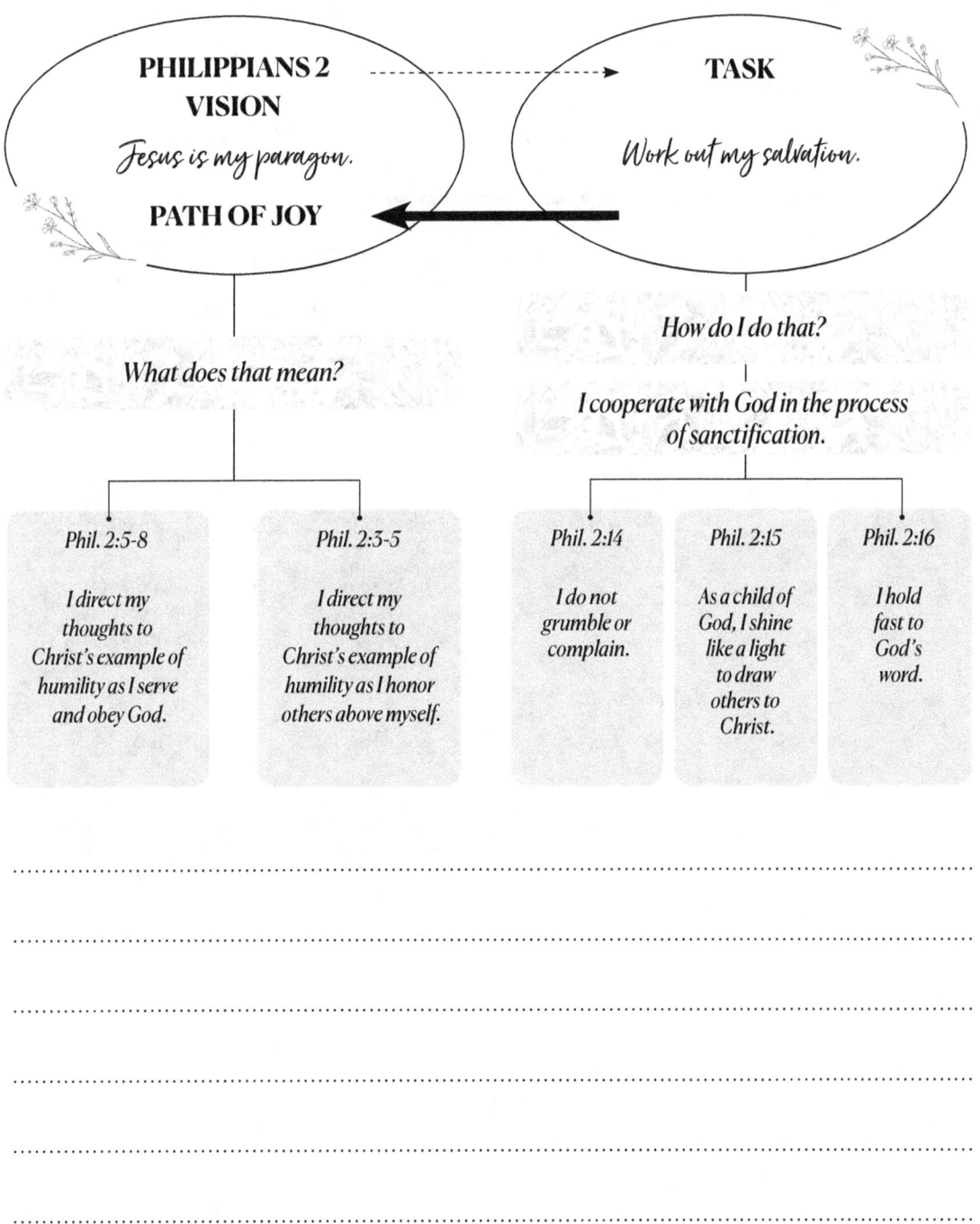

PHILIPPIANS 2
VISION

Jesus is my paragon.

PATH OF JOY

TASK

Work out my salvation.

What does that mean?

How do I do that?

I cooperate with God in the process of sanctification.

Phil. 2:5-8	Phil. 2:3-5	Phil. 2:14	Phil. 2:15	Phil. 2:16
I direct my thoughts to Christ's example of humility as I serve and obey God.	*I direct my thoughts to Christ's example of humility as I honor others above myself.*	*I do not grumble or complain.*	*As a child of God, I shine like a light to draw others to Christ.*	*I hold fast to God's word.*

....

....

....

....

....

....

Review Week 5 and the questions on p. 259. Pray for revelation. Record your insights.

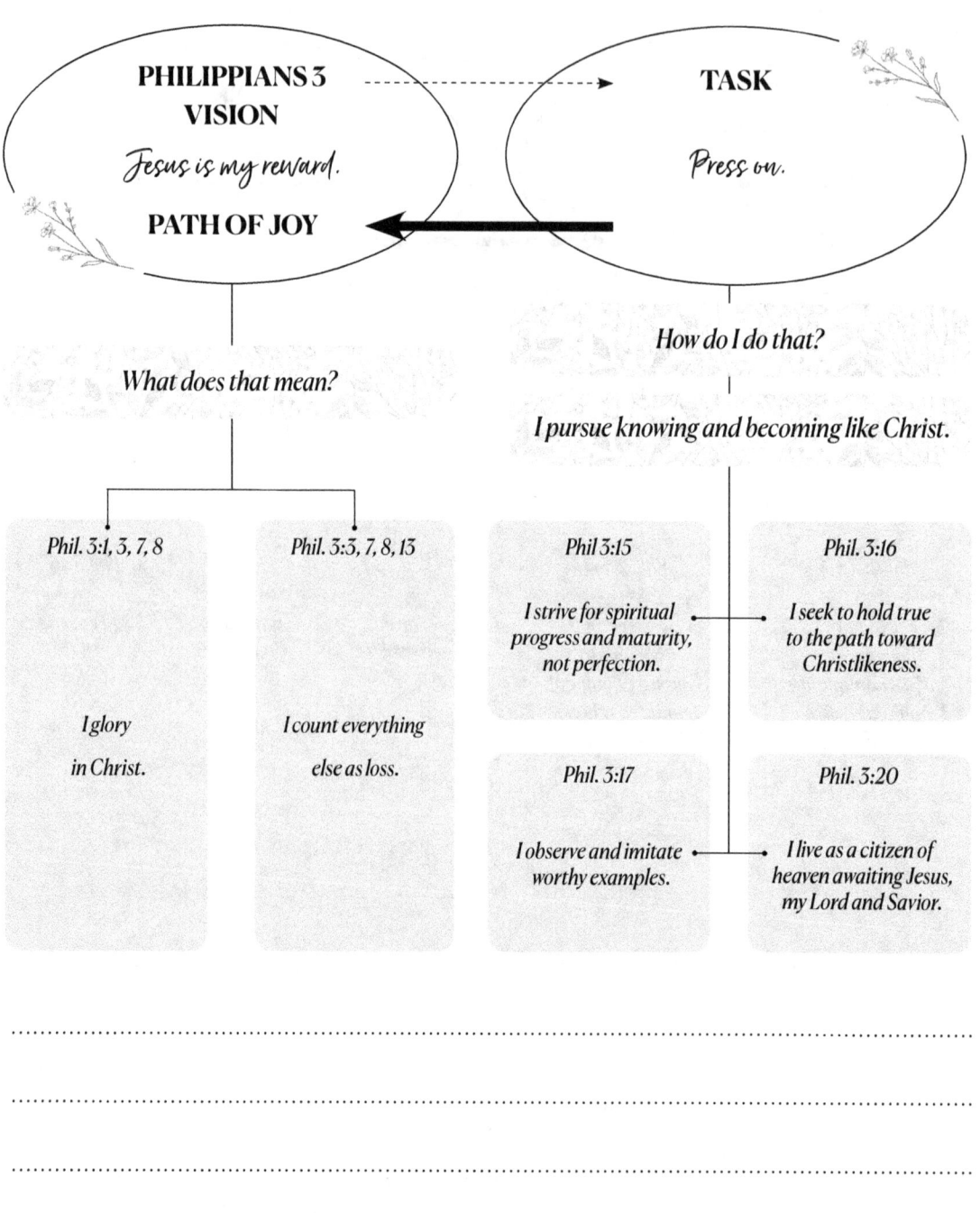

....

....

....

....

Review Week 6 and the questions on p. 259. Pray for revelation. Record your insights.

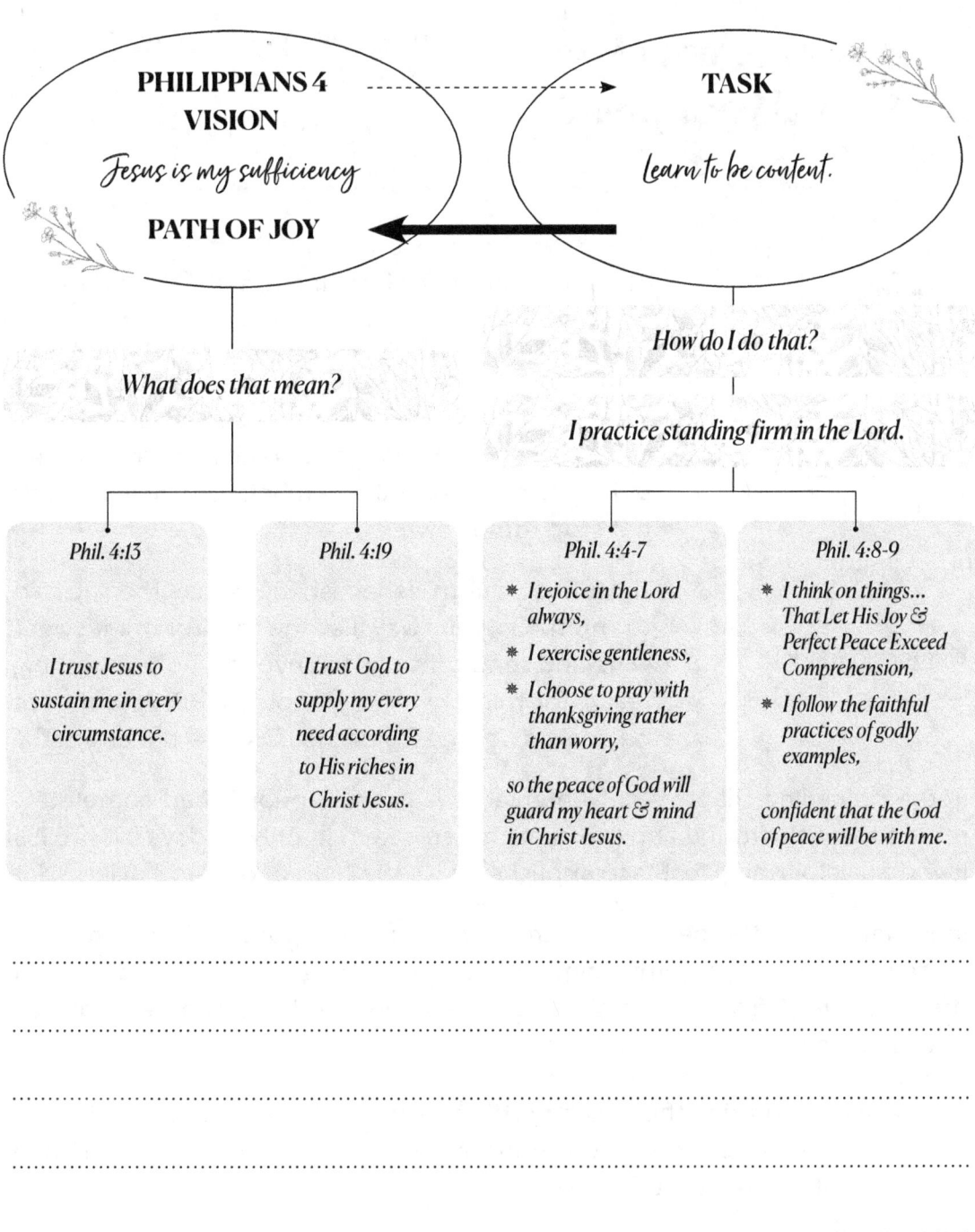

PHILIPPIANS 4 VISION

Jesus is my sufficiency

PATH OF JOY

TASK

Learn to be content.

What does that mean?

How do I do that?

I practice standing firm in the Lord.

Phil. 4:13

I trust Jesus to sustain me in every circumstance.

Phil. 4:19

I trust God to supply my every need according to His riches in Christ Jesus.

Phil. 4:4-7

* *I rejoice in the Lord always,*
* *I exercise gentleness,*
* *I choose to pray with thanksgiving rather than worry,*

so the peace of God will guard my heart & mind in Christ Jesus.

Phil. 4:8-9

* *I think on things... That Let His Joy & Perfect Peace Exceed Comprehension,*
* *I follow the faithful practices of godly examples,*

confident that the God of peace will be with me.

WEEK 7, DAY 4

A closing warning: Guard your joy!

The joy of the LORD is your strength.
(Neh. 8:10)

Goals for this week

* To reflect on our study of Philippians

* To move some of what we know from information to revelation

* To learn how to guard our joy

* To prepare for more joyful path-treading!

"The joy of the LORD is your strength." (Neh. 8:10)

It seems like a verse we should have used *somewhere* in this study. But there's more to this verse than meets the eye, and it will serve us well to consider it now as we prepare to guard the joyful paths we have worked so hard to get started. (Remember: Your treading does not stop tomorrow!)

The full verse from Nehemiah 8:10 reads, "Then he said to them, 'Go your way. Eat the fat and drink sweet wine and send portions to anyone who has nothing ready, for this day is holy to our LORD. And do not be grieved, for the joy of the LORD is your strength.'"

In the preceding chapters of Nehemiah, the Israelite people had completely rebuilt the wall around and the gates of Jerusalem in only 52 days (Neh. 6:15)! It was an astonishing feat "accomplished with the help of our God" (Neh. 6:16).

In Nehemiah 8:1, the people gathered "with a unified purpose" (NLT): to celebrate their amazing accomplishment with the reading of God's Word. As Ezra, the priest, read from the scrolls, the words convicted the people, and they began to weep.

Why do you think this was a problem? Isn't God's Word supposed to be convicting? Doesn't the Holy Spirit use it to guide us toward repentance and a life more aligned with God's will?

> Although repentance is necessary, is it possible to focus so much on our sin that we miss God's forgiveness and fail to bring Him glory? How does that impact our joy?
>
> ....
>
> ....

As stated above, the people of Israel had accomplished an amazing feat as God worked through them. The purpose of this time was to recognize God's help and glorify Him. It should have been an opportunity to feel strong in Him. Yet, Ezra and Nehemiah could probably see the strength and energy draining from the crowd as focus shifted from God to self. One of those leaders (scholars differ on who) made the statement that ended with the familiar phrase, "the joy of the LORD is your strength" (Neh. 8:10).

Since His joy is our strength, what does that imply if we do not have His joy?

....

....

If our strength is affected by the presence of His joy (or the lack thereof), we need to consider what hinders joy. We can see examples in Philippians as we consider the hindrances of spiritual attack, trials, and sin.

In the same way a soldier needs to know his source of attack so he can fight well, we need to correctly identify our source of attack to battle it effectively. A spiritual attack, our first hindrance to joy, can come from more than one source (James 4:1-7).

Use the following verses to identify the sources of spiritual attack. Write them below each verse.

Romans 7:18, 25. "For I know that nothing good dwells in me, that is, in my flesh. For I have the desire to do what is right, but not the ability to carry it out...Thanks be to God through Jesus Christ our Lord! So then, I myself serve the law of God with my mind, but with my flesh I serve the law of sin."

....

1 John 2:16. "For all that is in the world—the desires of the flesh and the desires of the eyes and pride of life—is not from the Father but is from the world."

....

Ephesians 6:11-12. "Put on the whole armor of God, that you may be able to stand against the schemes of the devil. For we do not wrestle against flesh and blood, but against the rulers, against the authorities, against the cosmic powers over this present darkness, against the spiritual forces of evil in the heavenly places."

....

So, the flesh battles against our spirit (internal), the world draws us away from God with its allures (external), and Satan seeks to turn us from Christ through deception. All of these prohibit joy. Let's look at examples of these in Philippians.

Source of attack	Example	Reference	Problem	How to fight the attack
Flesh	Euodia & Syntyche	Phil. 4:2-3	Personal disagreement	Re-establish a Kingdom focus, agree in the Lord
World	Paul in prison	Phil. 1:12-18	Others preaching from false motives	Release control, trust God
Satan	The Philippian church	Phil. 3:2-3	The Judaizers distorting the gospel	Prioritize knowing Christ & becoming like Him

Did you notice the last column? We need to know what action Paul recommended or took to fight spiritual attacks and protect Christ's joy in us! Although the column has specific actions, you can summarize them using

Paul's words in Philippians 4:1: *Stand firm*! Remember from 4:1-9, standing firm included rejoicing, having a spirit of gentleness, praying with gratitude rather than being anxious, and thinking thoughts That Let His Joy & Perfect Peace Exceed Comprehension (our mnemonic for 4:8). Standing firm is an effective strategy to resist a spiritual attack in any form and to guard your joy when enduring it.

The second hindrance to joy can be trials. Just to be blunt, trials can be frustrating, exhausting, difficult, and depressing. They can cause anxiety, anger, sadness, and feelings of isolation. However, the book of Philippians and the information in this study should provide a better perspective of the role of trials in our lives—one that can help mitigate those unwanted feelings. We have learned that opposition unites us (Phil. 1:27-28); suffering for Christ is a gift (Phil. 1:29); rejoicing should occur when we sacrifice for the faith of others (Phil. 2:17); knowing Christ is the result when we partake in His sufferings (Phil. 3:10); and, whatever the circumstances we find ourselves in while doing the will of God, we can learn to be content (Phil. 4:11).

There's a beautiful passage from the Old Testament that also illustrates this viewpoint. In the following, underline the trials, circle the two *I will's*, and mark *joy* and *rejoice* as you have done previously.

Habakkuk 3:17-19.

"Though the fig tree should not blossom,
  nor fruit be on the vines,
the produce of the olive fail
  and the fields yield no food,
the flock be cut off from the fold
  and there be no herd in the stalls,
yet I will rejoice in the LORD;
  I will take joy in the God of my salvation.
GOD, the Lord, is my strength;
  he makes my feet like the deer's;
  he makes me tread on my high places."

Though separated by more than six centuries, Habakkuk and Paul had a common response to trials. Habakkuk wrote, "Yet I will rejoice in the LORD" (Hab. 3:18). Paul stated, "Rejoice in the Lord always; again I will say, rejoice" (Phil. 4:4). On a side note, did you notice Habakkuk had some treading going on in that last line? When we follow the model of these men, trials no longer stand in the way of joy.

So, what about our third hindrance to joy—sin? Maybe a better question to start with is, *What is sin?*

Circle the words below that answer the question "What is sin?"

James 4:17. "So whoever knows the right thing to do and fails to do it, for him it is sin."

This verse clarifies that *sin* does not include spiritual attacks and trials, per se. However, if you succumb to a spiritual attack or if your trial is the result of knowing the right thing but not doing it (James 4:17), then sin is the cause of your lack of joy.

Paul specifically mentioned two sins in Philippians 2:3—selfish ambition and conceit. He also provided a strategic action to guard against these sins.

What strategic action did Paul state specifically in Philippians 2:3, then provide Christ as the example of in 2:5-11?

....

....

We would all agree that humility before God is a strategic action against sin and a powerful guardian of our joy. But what if it's too late? What if we have already sinned?

Humility still answers the call. Underline the action we perform in the following verse.

1 John 1:9. "If we confess our sins, he is faithful and just to forgive us our sins and to cleanse us from all unrighteousness."

Technically, *humility* does not appear in that verse. Still, is it possible to sincerely confess our sins *without* humility before a holy and righteous God who gave His only Son to pay the penalty for our sins? I don't see how. I believe that, through humble confession of sin with a sincere and contrite heart, God restores us to joy (Is. 57:15) just as strongly as I believe humble obedience to God protects us from sin and maintains our joy.

I believe that, in part, because I see it in the encouragement in Nehemiah to accept God's forgiveness and move forward: "And do not be grieved, for the joy of the LORD is your strength" (Neh. 8:10). I believe it in full because I know the assurance of justification. I know this past, one-time action of God declared me righteous by grace through faith in Christ. At that time, my sin debt was canceled for both past and future sins. I still need to confess for I am being set apart for God's purpose through sanctification, the process of being conformed to the image of Christ. Unconfessed sin hampers both that process and my relationship with God. But confession restores through God's promise of forgiveness (1 John 1:9). Therefore, on the basis of God's faithfulness, I choose to accept His forgiveness and live joyfully!

So don't move forward without confession. But once you have done so with a humble, sincere spirit, rejoice that you are forgiven and go forward in the strength of the Lord.

To summarize today...(because, by now, you know how much I like charts and tables)...

To guard your joy...	
Recognize the hindrance	**Know the strategy that overcomes the hindrance**
Spiritual attack (flesh, world, Satan)	Stand firm! (Phil. 4:1-9)
Trials	Rejoice! (with the proper perspective of trials) (Phil. 4:4)
Sin	Be humble! (in submission & confession) (Phil. 2:3-11)

Now that we can recognize hindrances to joy, we can also take action to ensure consistency in living out "the joy of the LORD is my strength" (Neh. 8:10).

I think we are ready for our send-off tomorrow!

WEEK 7, DAY 5

These boots were made for joyful treading

The joy of the LORD is your strength.
(Neh. 8:10)

Goals for this week

❊ To reflect on our study of Philippians

❊ To move some of what we know from information to revelation

❊ To learn how to guard our joy

❊ To prepare for more joyful path-treading!

Question: What does a buffalo say when his kid goes to college?

Answer: "Bison"

(Question: Are you rolling your eyes at me...again?)

We started with a joke, so we ought to close with one, right? Jokes may not bring us joy according to our definition, but they can lighten the mood, helping us lift our heads and look beyond our circumstances. So, in your continued treading, enjoy some fun and silliness. God created us with senses of humor. Recognize laughter (or eye rolling) as His gift and use it to refocus on Him. A God-centered focus will always lead to joy.

Following our initial joke on Week 1, Day 1, we began exploring four questions:

❊ What is joy?

❊ Why frame the learning process as "treading paths" of joy?

❊ Why tread paths of joy?

❊ With all the references to joy in the Bible, why focus on Philippians?

Do you remember being unsure in your responses? If the answers to those questions are more meaningful and memorable than in Week 1, give yourself a fist bump. You've done some effective treading! Let's take another quick stroll through the questions, but in reverse order. The joy of fresh insight and new commitment awaits.

With all the references to joy in the Bible, why focus on Philippians?

At this point, you may think, "Ummm...why would you *not* focus on Philippians?" The theme of joy is obvious throughout. Its message of intentional rejoicing, both encouraging and challenging. I hope your affinity for this book is stronger than when you began for its words are as relevant to us as to the church at Philippi.

Speaking of the church at Philippi, is there a tug at your heart as you think about not spending your days with Paul, Timothy, Epaphroditus, and this beloved church? How much we have learned from them. Their lives were not easy, but they stood firm in the Lord and rejoiced. (On a side note: We're not actually leaving them. We can return and have a joyful visit anytime. The welcome mat is out.)

Finally, this book lays out beautifully the joy of our salvation—joy in justification, sanctification, and glorification—as it points us to a deeper connection with our Savior. The joy we discover when we know Jesus as our life, our paragon, our reward, and our sufficiency confirms our choice to focus on this book.

Why tread paths of joy?

We found three answers to this question in Week 1:

* Rejoicing is obedient. It leads us to abide in Christ's love and experience His joy to the full.

* Rejoicing in the Lord is safe. It drives us to rely on God regardless of circumstances.

* Rejoicing is logical. It promotes our mental (and spiritual) health, protecting us from negativity as we set our minds on things of the Spirit.

A better question at this point: Why will you *keep* treading paths of joy?

We have supported our initial reasons throughout this study, but something else may also give you purpose in persisting. What have you learned that will motivate continued treading? Write that motivating factor in the blank below.

Rejoicing is ....

Why does this make you want to keep treading paths of joy?

....

....

For me, our original reasons became even stronger motivators as we studied. *Rejoicing is obedient* was evident in Paul's willingness to remain on earth for the faith of others in Philippians 1 and gloriously displayed with Christ's example in Philippians 2 (and Heb. 12:2). The joy of justification, sanctification, and glorification reminded me that *rejoicing is safe*. These phases of salvation all came together in Philippians 3 to show us how we are truly saved from the penalty, power, and presence of sin. Then, in Philippians 4, we saw several examples of *rejoicing is logical/healthy*: Paul's contentment, the impact of praying with gratitude, the peace of God that guards our hearts and minds, and the guidelines of Philippians 4:8. However, I would also add *rejoicing is honoring*. Out of love for my Lord, I long to keep rejoicing simply to honor and glorify Him.

Be ready to share your justification for persistence in establishing well-worn paths of joy.

Why frame the learning process as "treading paths" of joy?

At this point, we have seven weeks of treading paths under our belts. The well-worn paths on the cover and on pages throughout the study have been a powerful image reminding us of the paths of joy we walk with Jesus. The two-track road visually testifies to an intentional, repeated practice we desire to mimic as we further develop the delightful habit of joy that directs our thoughts, feelings, and actions to what God intends. We want to keep firing and wiring those pathways, ladies!

To do that, let's identify a couple of things that promote firing and wiring. The likelihood of establishing desired habits (those aligning with our core values) increases when the habits tie to our identities.[2] So, let's find actions we can take to support us in the successful establishment of our habit of joy.

Make paths of joy part of your identity

Do you remember the primary identity you have in Christ? Oh, the privilege of being a child of God! However, that is not your *only* identity. Below, I have rewritten the visions and tasks in terms of identities to increase the likelihood of living out the paths of joy. Pick one of the following, write it on a notecard, and read it every day for the next month. This practice may help you find delight in significant matters a little more easily.

I am a person who lives worthy of the gospel because Jesus is my life.

I am a person who works out my salvation because Jesus is my paragon.

I am a person who presses on (toward Christlikeness) because Jesus is my reward.

I am a person who learns to be content because Jesus is my sufficiency.

Identify core values in the paths of joy

Remember, core values are the principles that guide your actions and influence your decisions. They help you act in alignment with what holds the most significance in your life. Earlier, we emphasized two primary core values: to know Christ and to become like Him. Now we identify some additional ones to guide and influence us. On p. 275, the bottom, light gray boxes in our charts are each written as a core value. As you prepare to keep your boots treading rightly on paths of joy, choose one or two as anchors for your actions and decisions. Focus on making those core values in your life.

Use the paths of joy to develop spiritual maturity

In Week 5, Day 2, we learned that our core values need alignment with and integration into our identity as a Christian. We further stated that, as the strength of our connection to that identity increases, so does our spiritual maturity. So make this personal. Know that when you seek to make a habit of joy, you

are purposefully aligning that habit with your core values and strengthening your identity. Hold to the truth that treading the paths of joy from
this study will produce growth in you that leads to (or increases) spiritual
maturity (2 Pet. 1:8).

What is joy?

When you read that question, did you smile at how meaningful joy is now?
I bet your answer would be quite different today than it was on Week 1, Day 1.

After trying to define joy in our own words on that initial day, we examined
a definition from the research of Dr. Pamela Ebstyne King. We adopted it for
this study so we would all have the same perspective of joy.

> Fill in the blanks below according to the definition of joy we have
> been using.

> Joy is ...., ... delight in what

> holds the ....,

> What are some matters you would classify as holding the "most
> significance"? Remember, this term represents a category of items,
> not a single item. Take a moment to find joy in what you wrote.
>
> ....
>
> ....
>
> ....

Hopefully, the beauty, depth, and relevance of this definition have enhanced
your understanding of joy. As you keep treading, maintain the concept of joy
as a virtue—a purposefully developed habit directing thoughts, feelings, and
actions toward what God intends. Keep your awareness that joy is a characteristic of the fruit of the Spirit, not an ebbing and flowing emotion. And
remember to choose joy!

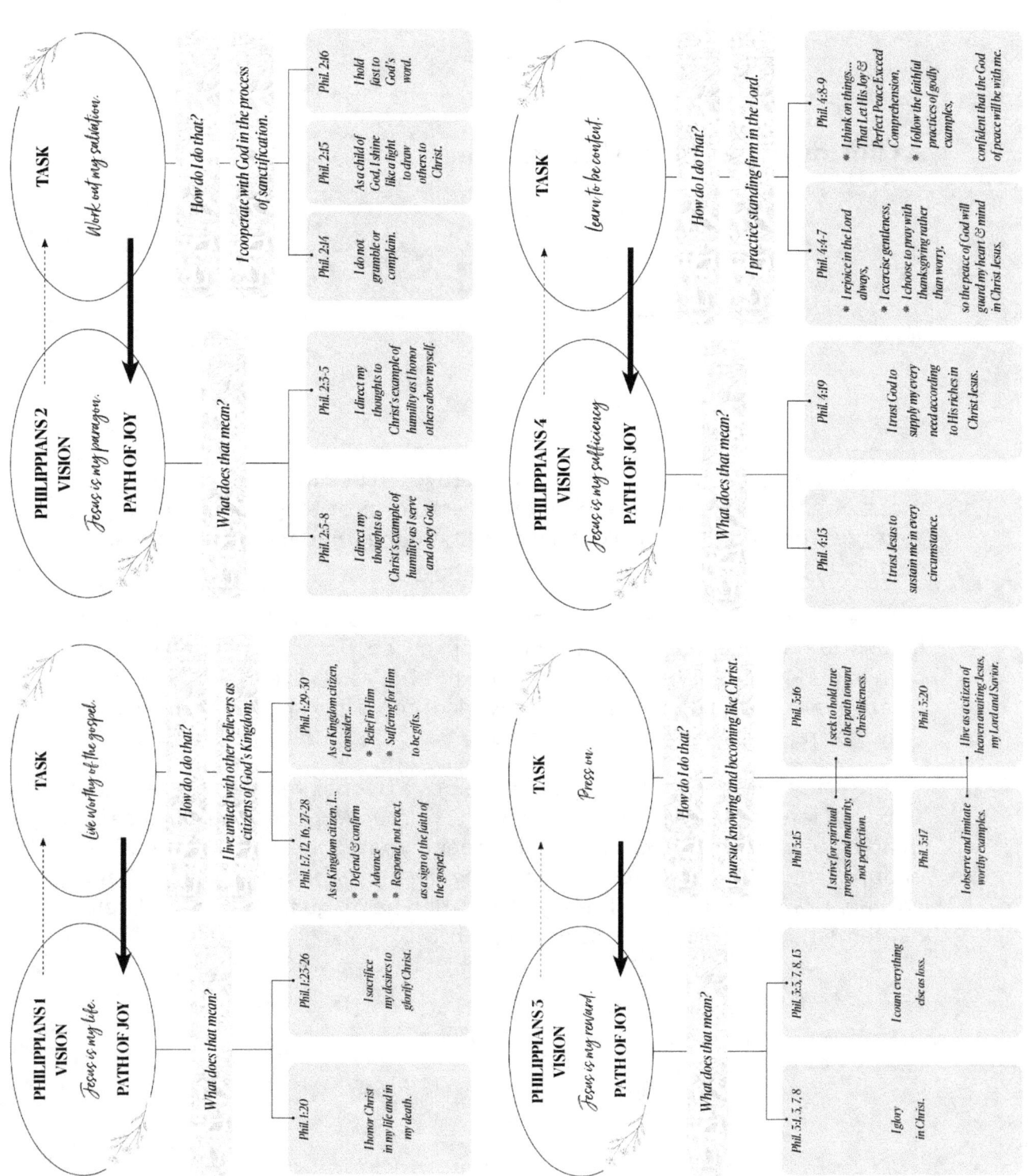

A Closing Prayer for Joyful Treading

Dear God, our Father,

We rejoice that You love us and have planted joy in us through Your Spirit. We praise You for showing us the path of life and for providing fullness of joy in Your presence (Ps. 16:11). Thank you for this time together and for the blessing of studying Your Word.

I come before You, Father, and lift all who finish this study today. I pray they recognize how blessed we are to serve You, a God who desires that His children experience joy in relationship with Him even as we live in a fallen world. Please, make these ladies aware of the work of Your Holy Spirit in their lives so they may rejoice in growing closer to You.

As each lady goes forward, I pray she develops a deeper, more joyful relationship with Jesus through the continued study of Your Word and the purposeful treading of paths of joy. May her joy be deeply rooted in the habit of finding enduring, deep delight in Jesus; in knowing the One who is her life, her paragon, her reward, and her sufficiency. Strengthen her to guard her joy and help her remember Your joy is her strength (Neh. 8:10).

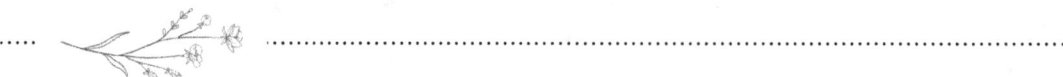

Finally, I ask that the well-worn paths of joy in the lives of these faithful treaders are a witness to others—an unmistakable two-track road testifying to steps of joy walked with the Savior.

"Now to [You] who [are] able to keep [them] from stumbling and to present [them] blameless before the presence of [Your] glory with great joy, to the only God, our Savior, through Jesus Christ our Lord, be glory, majesty, dominion, and authority, before all time and now and forever. Amen."

(Jude 24-25)

(Grab those boots and tread on, ladies!)

The Path Behind

Group Discussion of Week 7

SESSION 8

The Path Ahead

"As you keep treading, remember your Savior walks beside you. And together, you form a two-track road...well-worn paths that lead toward heaven on the horizon while producing a joyful, stronger, deeper relationship with Christ now."

Leader Guide

Please read the following. The structure of your group time for this study is different from other studies. The information below is critical for successful implementation.

Thank you for selecting this study and for your commitment to faithfully lead your group of ladies through it. I am praying for you as you prepare for the study as a whole and for the discussion sessions individually.

Study preparation: As the leader, you will need to determine how to best meet the needs of your group. I offer the following options for your consideration.

> ❋ *Option 1:* Although you are the study organizer and leader, you may want to cultivate leadership and share the responsibility for facilitating the discussions and/or activities. Be ready to "coach" each lady on how to pray and adequately prepare for the discussion or weekly activity.

> ❋ *Option 2:* Sometimes in my Bible study group when we know we will have a busy semester, we spread each week of study over a two-week period to give people time to complete all the lessons. You can still meet each week (for fifteen weeks), but you might try discussing days 1-3 one week, then completing 4-5 and the group activity the next. Consider what works best for your group.

> ❋ *Option 3:* Continue as you normally do. You were chosen to lead for a reason!

No matter which option you choose, be sure you email me at CatherineLHill@ CatherineLHillWrites.com to request the digital folder with all the details for the discussion and activities.

Discussion preparation: Intentional planning for each discussion session is a valuable use of your time and beneficial for the growth of the ladies in your group. This Bible study may differ from others you have done in that there are no videos. Therefore, I have designed some group activities to follow the discussion time each week. The activities require a small investment of time to become familiar with the activity and think about how it will work best with your group. Some activities require common resources such as sticky notes, printer or construction paper, and pens or markers. The activities are specifically designed to prepare ladies for the lessons in the upcoming week, and they are usually mentioned at some point in the lessons. These "Looking Ahead" activities should require about 20-30 minutes for the activity and discussion. As I mentioned above, please email me at CatherineLHill@CatherineLHillWrites.com to receive a digital folder with weekly discussion questions and instructions detailing each activity. I hope you enjoy them!

In addition to preparing, be sure to plan ways to **connect**. Emails, social media, Saturday morning walks, whatever you come up with to help people feel a part. Be creative!

Finally, but most importantly, **pray**. Don't go forward in the strength you have had in the past. The ladies you lead will be facing different challenges than previously...and so will you. Invoke fresh mercy, grace, strength, and wisdom so you can cooperate in what God desires to do now.

Endnotes

Week 1

1. O.S. Hawkins, *The Jesus Code: 52 Scripture Questions Every Believer Should Answer* (Nashville, TN: Thomas Nelson, 2014), 1-2.

2. *Merriam-Webster.com Dictionary*, s.v. "joy," accessed December 22, 2023, https://www.merriam-webster.com/dictionary/joy.

3. Pamela Ebstyne King and Frederic Defoy, "Joy as a Virtue: The Means and Ends of Joy," *Journal of Psychology and Theology* 48, no. 4 (2020): 309, https://doi.org/10.1177/0091647120907994.

4. Alisdair MacIntyre, *After Virtue: A Study in Moral Theory*, 3rd ed. (Notre Dame, IN: University of Notre Dame Press, 2007), 272-275.

5. Pamela Ebstyne King and Frederic Defoy, "Joy as a Virtue: The Means and Ends of Joy," *Journal of Psychology and Theology* 48, no. 4 (2020): 327, https://doi.org/10.1177/0091647120907994.

6. Pamela Ebstyne King, "What Is Joy and What Does It Say About Us?," interview by Dr. Jamie D. Aten, *Psychology Today*, July 28, 2020, https://www.psychologytoday.com/us/blog/hope-resilience/202007/what-is-joy-and-what-does-it-say-about-us.

7. John H. Sammis, "Trust and Obey," 1887, Timeless Truths Free Online Library, accessed December 22, 2023, https://library.timelesstruths.org/music/Trust_and_Obey/.

8. Ann Omley, "The Wise Man and The Foolish Man," 1948, Timeless Truths Free Online Library, accessed December 22, 2023, https://library.timelesstruths.org/music/The_Wise_Man_and_the_Foolish_Man/.

9. Guy Winch, *The Squeaky Wheel: Complaining the Right Way to Get Results, Improve Your Relationships, and Enhance Self-Esteem* (New York, NY: Walker Publishing Company, Inc., 2011), 11.

10. Shawn M. Talbott, *The Cortisol Connection: Why Stress Makes You Fat and Ruins Your Health—and What You Can Do About It* (Alameda, CA : Hunter House, 2002), 1-3.

11. Peggy M. Zoccola and Sally S. Dickerson, "Assessing the relationship between rumination and cortisol: A review," *Journal of Psychosomatic Research* 73, no. 1 (2012): 2, https://doi.org/10.1016/j.jpsychores.2012.03.007.

12. Shawn M. Talbott, *The Cortisol Connection: Why Stress Makes You Fat and Ruins Your Health—and What You Can Do About It* (Alameda, CA: Hunter House, 2002), 4.

13. Bruce S. McEwen, *The End of Stress as We Know It* (Washington, D.C.: Joseph Henry Press, 2002), 110.

14. Rick Hanson, "How to Trick Your Brain for Happiness," *Greater Good Magazine*, last modified September 26, 2011, https://greatergood.berkeley.edu/article/item/how_to_trick_your_brain_for_happiness.

15. Shawn M. Talbott, *The Cortisol Connection: Why Stress Makes You Fat and Ruins Your Health—and What You Can Do About It* (Alameda, CA: Hunter House, 2002), 69.

16. Eberhard Fuchs and Gabriele Flügge, "Adult Neuroplasticity: More Than 40 Years of Research," *Neural Plasticity*, vol. 2014, Article ID 541870, https://doi.org/10.1155/2014/541870.

17. Jeffrey M. Schwartz, "Neuroplasticity and Spiritual Formation," Biola's Center for Christian Thought, last modified April 18, 2019, https://cct.biola.edu/neuroplasticity-and-spiritual-formation/.

18. Guy Winch, *The Squeaky Wheel: Complaining the Right Way to Get Results, Improve Your Relationships, and Enhance Self-Esteem* (New York, NY: Walker Publishing Company, Inc., 2011), 93.

19. Jeffrey M. Schwartz, "Neuroplasticity and Spiritual Formation," Biola's Center for Christian Thought, last modified April 18, 2019, https://cct.biola.edu/neuroplasticity-and-spiritual-formation/.

Week 2

1. *The Early Spread of Christianity,* "Biblica Open Bible Maps," 2023, accessed and adapted November 1, 2024, https://open.bible/maps/, use permitted under CC BY-SA 4.0, https://creativecommons.org/licenses/by-sa/4.0/.

2. Joseph Jacobs and Samuel Krauss, "Tarsus," Jewish Encyclopedia, accessed on November 15, 2023, https://jewishencyclopedia.com/articles/14255-tarsus.

3. John Charles Pollock, *The Apostle: A Life of Paul* (Colorado Springs, CO: Chariot Victor Publishing, 1985), 14-17.

4. "Up," Directed by Pete Docter, Emeryville, California: Disney/Pixar Studio, 2009.

5. "The Preparation of Paul," Ligonier, last updated March 19, 1992, https://www.ligonier.org/learn/devotionals/the-preparation-of-paul .

6. *The Early Spread of Christianity,* "Biblica Open Bible Maps," 2023, accessed and adapted November 1, 2024, https://open.bible/maps/, use permitted under CC BY-SA 4.0, https://creativecommons.org/licenses/by-sa/4.0/.

7. Associates for Biblical Research, "Gods, Gold And The Glory Of Philippi," Biblical Archaeology, last modified Fall, 2004, https://biblearchaeology.org/research/new-testament-era/2343-gods-gold-and-the-glory-of-philippi.

8. Eduard Verhoef, *Philippi: How Christianity Began in Europe: The Epistle to the Philippians and the Excavations at Philippi* (London: Bloomsbury, 2013), 8, 13.

9. Mark Cartwright, "Philippi," *World History Encyclopedia,* last modified May 4, 2016, https://www.worldhistory.org/Philippi/.

10. *The Early Spread of Christianity,* "Biblica Open Bible Maps," 2023, accessed and adapted November 1, 2024, https://open.bible/maps/, use permitted under CC BY-SA 4.0, https://creativecommons.org/licenses/by-sa/4.0/.

11. A. T. Robertson, *Paul's Joy in Christ: Studies in Philippians* (New York, NY: Fleming H. Revell Company, 1917), 27.

12. Eduard Verhoef, *Philippi: How Christianity Began in Europe: The Epistle to the Philippians and the Excavations at Philippi* (London: Bloomsbury, 2013), 10-13.

13. Mark Cartwright, "Philippi," *World History Encyclopedia,* last modified May 4, 2016, https://www.worldhistory.org/Philippi/.

Group Session #3

1. "Inscription on a church wall in Sussex England c. 1730," Goodreads, accessed on February 3, 2024, https://www.goodreads.com/quotes/784358-a-vision-without-a-task-is-but-a-dream-.

Week 3

1. "Inscription on a church wall in Sussex England c. 1730," Goodreads, accessed on February 3, 2024, https://www.goodreads.com/quotes/784358-a-vision-without-a-task-is-but-a-dream-.

2. Corrie ten Boom and Jamie Buckingham, *Tramp for the Lord* (Fort Washington, PA: Christian Literature Crusade and Old Tappan, NJ: Fleming H. Revell Company, 1974), 18-21.

3. Corrie ten Boom and Jamie Buckingham, *Tramp for the Lord* (Fort Washington, PA: Christian Literature Crusade and Old Tappan, NJ: Fleming H. Revell Company, 1974), 9.

4. Corrie ten Boom and Jamie Buckingham, *Tramp for the Lord* (Fort Washington, PA: Christian Literature Crusade and Old Tappan, NJ: Fleming H. Revell Company, 1974), 23.

5. Christ Patton, "Do You React or Respond?," Christian Faith at Work, last modified on November 27, 2013, https://www.christianfaithatwork.com/do-you-react-or-respond/.

6. A. T. Robertson, *Paul's Joy in Christ: Studies in Philippians* (New York, NY: Fleming H. Revell Company, 1917), 90.

7. *Merriam-Webster.com Dictionary*, s.v. "just," accessed January 24, 2024, https://www.merriam-webster.com/dictionary/just.

8. "Justification," Ligonier, last modified September 21, 2021, https://www.ligonier.org/guides/justification.

9. Albert Martin, "Repentance That Leads to Life," Ligonier, last modified May 18, 2014, https://www.ligonier.org/learn/devotionals/repentance-leads-life.

10. Strong's G2962, Bible Hub, accessed January 6, 2024, https://biblehub.com/strongs/greek/2962.htm.

11. Strong's G4739, Bible Hub, accessed January 8, 2024, https://biblehub.com/strongs/greek/4739.htm.

12. Strong's G4866, Bible Hub, accessed January 8, 2024, https://biblehub.com/strongs/greek/4866.htm.

13. Alexander MacLaren, "Philippians," *Expositions of Holy Scriptures*, Bible Hub, accessed on January 25, 2024, https://biblehub.com/commentaries/maclaren/philippians/1.htm.

14. Strong's G4176, Bible Hub, accessed January 11, 2024, https://biblehub.com/strongs/greek/4176.htm.

15. A. T. Robertson, *Paul's Joy in Christ: Studies in Philippians* (New York, NY: Fleming H. Revell Company, 1917), 102-105.

16. A. T. Robertson, *Paul's Joy in Christ: Studies in Philippians* (New York, NY: Fleming H. Revell Company, 1917), 106.

Week 4

1. Willy Corswant, *A Dictionary of Life in Bible Times* (New York: Oxford University Press, 1960), 207.

2. H.A. Ironside, *Galatians* (New York: Loizeaux Brothers, 1941), 222-223.

3. *Vocabulary.com Dictionary*, s.v. "exhortation," accessed February 12, 2024, https://www.vocabulary.com/dictionary/exhortation.

4. *Betterwordsonline.com Dictionary*, s.v. "paragon," accessed January 15, 2024, https://www.betterwordsonline.com/dictionary/paragon.

5. Catherine B. Allen, *The New Lottie Moon Story* (Nashville, TN: Broadman Press, 1980), 21-23, 30-33.

6. Nancy Drummond, *Lottie Moon: Changing China for Christ* (Scotland, U.K.: Christian Focus Publications, 2014), 132-182 of 1437 Kindle.

7. Catherine B. Allen, *The New Lottie Moon Story* (Nashville, TN: Broadman Press, 1980), 35-62.

8. Catherine B. Allen, *The New Lottie Moon Story* (Nashville, TN: Broadman Press, 1980), 62-72.

9. International Mission Board, "Tell me about her mission," *Lottie Moon*, IMB, accessed January 16, 2024, https://www.imb.org/about/lottie-moon/.

10. Catherine B. Allen, *The New Lottie Moon Story* (Nashville, TN: Broadman Press, 1980), 237-238.

11. International Mission Board, "Tell me about her mission," *Lottie Moon*, IMB, accessed January 16, 2024, https://www.imb.org/about/lottie-moon/.

12. Charles R. Swindoll, *Swindoll's Living Insights New Testament Commentary: Philippians, Colossians, Philemon* (Carol Stream, IL: Tyndale House Publishers, Inc., 2017), 39.

13. *Thayer's Greek Lexicon*, Strong's G5426, Bible Hub, accessed February 3, 2024, https://biblehub.com/greek/5426.htm.

14. Jeffrey M. Schwartz, "Neuroplasticity and Spiritual Formation," Biola's Center for Christian Thought, last modified April 18, 2019, https://cct.biola.edu/neuroplasticity-and-spiritual-formation/.

15. Catherine B. Allen, *The New Lottie Moon Story* (Nashville, TN: Broadman Press, 1980), 287.

16. International Mission Board, "What are her letters home?" *Lottie Moon*, IMB, accessed January 16, 2024. https://www.imb.org/about/lottie-moon/.

17. Strong's G2758, Bible Hub, accessed February 19, 2024, https://biblehub.com/strongs/greek/2758.htm.

18. J.I. Packer, *Knowing God* (London: Hodder and Stoughton, 1975), 61, 63.

19. *HELPS Word-Studies*, Strong's G38, Bible Hub, accessed March 1, 2024, https://biblehub.com/greek/38.htm.

20. W.E. Vine, "Sanctification," *Vine's Concise Dictionary of Bible Words* (Nashville, TN: Thomas Nelson Publishers, 1999), 326.

21. "The Sanctification of a Believer," Biblical Resources, accessed March 3, 2024, https://www.biblicalresources.org/resources/sanctification/.

22. "The Sanctification of a Believer," Biblical Resources, accessed March 3, 2024, https://www.biblicalresources.org/resources/sanctification/.

23. "The Sanctification of a Believer," Biblical Resources, accessed March 3, 2024, https://www.biblicalresources.org/resources/sanctification/.

24. John F. Walvoord, "Philippians 2: At the Name of Jesus Every Knee Should Bow," Walvoord, accessed on March 3, 2024, https://walvoord.com/article/190.

25. W.E. Vine, "Sanctification," *Vine's Concise Dictionary of Bible Words* (Nashville, TN: Thomas Nelson Publishers, 1999), 326.

Week 5

1. Francesca Bologna, "Historical City Travel Guide: Rome, 1st century AD," The British Museum, last modified May 15, 2020, https://www.britishmuseum.org/blog/historical-city-travel-guide-rome-1st-century-ad.

2. Ellen Hunter, "What did the ancient Romans eat for breakfast?," Ancient Rome, last modified February 24, 2023, https://www.learnancientrome.com/what-did-the-ancient-romans-eat-for-breakfast/?expand_article=1.

3. "The Judaizer's True Motives," Ligonier, last modified April 24, 2009, https://www.ligonier.org/learn/devotionals/judaizers-true-motives.

4. Erich Bridges, *Lives Given, Not Taken: 21st Century Southern Baptist Martyrs* (Richmond, VA: International Mission Board, SBC, 2005), 193.

5. Erich Bridges, *Lives Given, Not Taken: 21st Century Southern Baptist Martyrs* (Richmond, VA: International Mission Board, SBC, 2005), 198.

6. Erich Bridges, *Lives Given, Not Taken: 21st Century Southern Baptist Martyrs* (Richmond, VA: International Mission Board, SBC, 2005), 206.

7. Erich Bridges, *Lives Given, Not Taken: 21st Century Southern Baptist Martyrs* (Richmond, VA: International Mission Board, SBC, 2005), 191-219.

8. Erich Bridges, *Lives Given, Not Taken: 21st Century Southern Baptist Martyrs* (Richmond, VA: International Mission Board, SBC, 2005), 191-192.

9. "You're in Love, Charlie Brown," created by Charles M. Schulz, directed by Bill Melendez, Lee Mendelson Film Productions and Bill Melendez Productions, 1967.

10. Pamela Ebstyne King and Frederic Defoy, "Joy as a Virtue: The Means and Ends of Joy," *Journal of Psychology and Theology* 48, no. 4 (2020): 313-314, https://doi.org/10.1177/0091647120907994.

11. Janice L. Templeton and Jacquelynne S. Eccles, "The Relation Between Spiritual Development and Identity Processes," in *The Handbook of Spiritual Development in Childhood and Adolescence,* ed. Eugene C. Roehlkepartain, Pamela Ebstyne King, Linda Wagener, Peter L. Benson (Thousand Oaks, CA: Sage Publications, 2006), 259.

12. Charles R. Swindoll, *Swindoll's Living Insights New Testament Commentary: Philippians, Colossians, Philemon* (Carol Stream, IL: Tyndale House Publishers, Inc., 2017), 65.

13. Erich Bridges, *Lives Given, Not Taken: 21st Century Southern Baptist Martyrs* (Richmond, VA: International Mission Board, SBC, 2005), 192.

14. Gordon Franz, "Going for the Gold: The Apostle Paul and the Isthmian Games," Bible Archaeology, last modified July 16, 2012, https://biblearchaeology.org/research/contemporary-issues/3009-going-for-the-gold-the-apostle-paul-and-the-isthmian-games.

15. Strong's G1377, Bible Hub, accessed April 12, 2024, https://biblehub.com/greek/1377.htm.

16. A. T. Robertson, *Paul's Joy in Christ: Studies in Philippians* (New York, NY: Fleming H. Revell Company, 1917), 202.

17. A. T. Robertson, *Paul's Joy in Christ: Studies in Philippians* (New York, NY: Fleming H. Revell Company, 1917), 201-202.

18. Nick Huggett, "Zeno's Paradoxes," in *The Standford Encyclopedia of Philosophy,* ed. Edward N. Zalta and Uri Nodelman, last modified March 6, 2024, https://plato.stanford.edu/archives/spr2024/entries/paradox-zeno/.

19. Charles R. Swindoll, *Swindoll's Living Insights New Testament Commentary: Philippians, Colossians, Philemon* (Carol Stream, IL: Tyndale House Publishers, Inc., 2017), 73-74.

20. Kelly Minter, *Encountering God* (Nashville, TN: Lifeway Press, 2021), 6.

21. A. T. Robertson, *Paul's Joy in Christ: Studies in Philippians* (New York, NY: Fleming H. Revell Company, 1917), 209.

22. C.S. Lewis, *Mere Christianity* (San Francisco: Harper San Francisco, Harper edition, 2001), 134.

Week 6

1. James A. Brooks, "Introduction to Philippians," *Southwestern Journal of Theology* 23, (Fall 1980), Preaching Source, accessed on April 8, 2024, https://preachingsource.com/journal/introduction-to-philippians/.

2. Kimberly D. Hill, "Maria Fearing," in *Alabama Women: Their Lives and Times*, ed. Lisa Lindquist Dorr and Susan Youngblood Ashmore (Athens, GA: University of Georgia Press, 2017), 98.

3. Karen Ellis, "Ancestors on Mission: Maria Fearing (1838-1937)," Karen Angela Ellis, last modified February 28, 2017, https://karenangelaellis.com/2017/02/28/ancestors-on-mission-maria-fearing-1838-1937/.

4. Kimberly D. Hill, "Maria Fearing," in *Alabama Women: Their Lives and Times*, ed. Lisa Lindquist Dorr and Susan Youngblood Ashmore (Athens, GA: University of Georgia Press, 2017), 92.

5. Karen Ellis, "Ancestors on Mission: Maria Fearing (1838-1937)," Karen Angela Ellis, last modified February 28, 2017, https://karenangelaellis.com/2017/02/28/ancestors-on-mission-maria-fearing-1838-1937/.

6. Kimberly D. Hill, "Maria Fearing," in *Alabama Women: Their Lives and Times*, ed. Lisa Lindquist Dorr and Susan Youngblood Ashmore (Athens, GA: University of Georgia Press, 2017), 92-93.

7. Karen Ellis, "Ancestors on Mission: Maria Fearing (1838-1937)," Karen Angela Ellis, last modified February 28, 2017, https://karenangelaellis.com/2017/02/28/ancestors-on-mission-maria-fearing-1838-1937/.

8. Kimberly D. Hill, "Maria Fearing," in *Alabama Women: Their Lives and Times*, ed. Lisa Lindquist Dorr and Susan Youngblood Ashmore (Athens, GA: University of Georgia Press, 2017), 93.

9. Karen Ellis, "Ancestors on Mission: Maria Fearing (1838-1937)," Karen Angela Ellis, last modified February 28, 2017, https://karenangelaellis.com/2017/02/28/ancestors-on-mission-maria-fearing-1838-1937/.

10. Kimberly D. Hill, "Maria Fearing," in *Alabama Women: Their Lives and Times*, ed. Lisa Lindquist Dorr and Susan Youngblood Ashmore (Athens, GA: University of Georgia Press, 2017), 94-95.

11. Kimberly D. Hill, "Maria Fearing," in *Alabama Women: Their Lives and Times*, ed. Lisa Lindquist Dorr and Susan Youngblood Ashmore (Athens, GA: University of Georgia Press, 2017), 95-99.

12. John MacArthur, "The Sufficiency of Christ," Grace To You, last modified February 22, 1987, https://www.gty.org/library/sermons-library/80-36/the-sufficiency-of-christ.

13. A. T. Robertson, *Paul's Joy in Christ: Studies in Philippians* (New York, NY: Fleming H. Revell Company, 1917), 247-248.

14. *Thayer's Greek Lexicon*, Strong's G842, Bible Hub, accessed May 15, 2024, https://biblehub.com/thayers/842.htm.

15. Theodore Roosevelt, "Theodore Roosevelt, Quotes," Goodreads, accessed May 21, 2024, https://www.goodreads.com/quotes/6471614-comparison-is-the-thief-of-joy.

16. Robin Kramer, "Don't Let Emotions Drive the Bus," Robin Kramer Writes, last modified March 16, 2019, https://www.robinkramerwrites.com/2019/03/dont-let-emotions-drive-bus.html#:~:text=Emotions%20are%20like%20toddlers.,throwing%20them%20in%20the%20trunk.

17. Charles R. Swindoll, *Swindoll's Living Insights New Testament Commentary: Philippians, Colossians, Philemon* (Carol Stream, IL: Tyndale House Publishers, Inc., 2017), 84-85.

18. *Englishman's Concordance*, Strong's G5426, Bible Hub, accessed May 21, 2024, https://biblehub.com/greek/strongs_5426.htm.

19. Alex Korb, "The Grateful Brain: The Neuroscience of Giving Thanks," Psychology Today, last modified November 20, 2012, https://www.psychologytoday.com/us/blog/prefrontal-nudity/201211/the-grateful-brain.

20. Charles Stanley, "Satan's Strategy to Defeat Us," Sermons.love, accessed on June 6, 2024. https://sermons.love/charles-stanley/5338-charles-stanley-satans-strategy-to-defeat-us.html.

Week 7

1. Apostle Paul Life, Teaching & Theology, "Philippi: A loyal church, A long tradition," Christian Pilgrimage Journeys, accessed on April 14, 2024. https://www.christian-pilgrimage-journeys.com/biblical-sources/apostle-paul-life-teaching-theology/philippi-a-loyal-church-a-long-tradition/

2. Bas Verplanken and Jie Sui, "Habit and Identity: Behavioral, Cognitive, Affective, and Motivational Facets of an Integrated Self," *Frontier in Psychology* 10, no. 1504 (2019), 9, https://doi.org/10.3389/fpsyg.2019.01504.

About the Author

Dr. Catherine L Hill has always been an avid student of the Bible with a sincere love of God's Word. Although she and her husband have moved often, she has still led Bible studies, spoken at women's retreats, and taught Bible Fellowship Groups on Sunday mornings. Catherine's earnest desire is that those who hear move beyond an information-based knowledge about Jesus to a personal relationship with their Savior that overflows with love.

Well-Worn Paths: Treading Paths of Joy Through a Study of Philippians is Catherine's debut endeavor as an author. And yet, she can see God's fingerprints throughout her life preparing her for this role. From her passion for students and learning as a teacher to her knowledge of lesson development and professional learning as a curriculum designer to the cultivation of research and writing skills as a doctoral student–not to mention the tenacity required to finish that doctorate during the onset of Covid–all contributed knowledge and experiences that God used to equip Catherine for this purpose. Although the calling to write is unexpected, the call to bear fruit that will remain (John 15:16) is not, so Catherine is grateful for this opportunity.

Catherine and her husband, Johnny, currently live just outside of Dallas. They have a daughter, Rachel, and a son and daughter-in-law, Joshua and Amanda. More importantly (wink!), they have two grandsons who are dearly loved by their "Pops" and "Nana."

Catherine will be writing more about God's unexpected callings at CatherineLHillWrites.com.